CONTENTS

Neal Benezra

In the fall of 2007, visitors to the San Francisco Museum of Modern Art will discover our fifth-floor galleries transformed nearly beyond recognition by the immersive environments of Olafur Eliasson. Indeed, from the moment they walk into the exhibition, our viewers will have embarked upon an itinerary deliberately conceived to engage all of the senses. This is a body of work that offers a feast for the eyes but also appeals to hearing, touch, and smell, introducing a diversity of materials—from light and mirrors to wood, water, and live moss—into SFMOMA's spaces. Looking beyond the sheer sensual delight of Eliasson's work, however, we come to appreciate the artist's larger mission: to prompt an unusual level of engagement between artwork and viewer, and in so doing to set in motion perceptions, interactions, and experiences that are typically considered improbable—if not unfeasible—in the museum context.

Though only forty years old, Eliasson has emerged as a singularly influential artist on the international stage, and SFMOMA is proud to present *Take your time: Olafur Eliasson*, his first survey on American soil. The presentation is a journey through significant works past and present, from the 1993 installation *Beauty*, which brings a veritable rainbow into the galleries, to an array of 2007 projects conceived in response to the Museum's architecture, most notably a vertiginous, kaleidoscopic tunnel enveloping the catwalk bridge that spans the atrium.

Take your time is the result of an extraordinary collaboration between the artist and Madeleine Grynsztejn, SFMOMA's Elise S. Haas Senior Curator of Painting and Sculpture and a foremost authority on Eliasson's oeuvre. As Madeleine points out in her insightful essay in this volume, to present this artist's work is to grapple with a provocative set of challenges to the status quo of museum practice—to our very understanding of what art is and can do, and to the role of the museum in society at large. It is a testament to her dedication and tenacity, and to the professionalism of the entire SFMOMA staff, that this momentous exhibition and catalogue have come to fruition in such successful fashion.

A project of this magnitude is simply not possible without the significant financial assistance of numerous benefactors. Madeleine joins me in thanking the members of SFMOMA's Board of Trustees for their unstinting commitment to Eliasson's work. We are exceedingly grateful to Helen and Charles Schwab and the Mimi and Peter Haas Fund for coming on board as the exhibition's lead sponsors. Generous support is provided by the Bernard Osher Foundation, the Barbro Osher Pro Suecia Foundation, and Collectors Forum, with additional support from Patricia and William Wilson III, the Andy Warhol Foundation for the Visual Arts, the National Endowment for the Arts, and the American-Scandinavian Foundation. Support for education programs has been provided by Helen Hilton Raiser in honor of Madeleine Grynsztejn.

In our efforts to bring together the very best of Eliasson's oeuvre, we have enjoyed the cooperation of some of the artist's most devoted collectors and patrons. For their generous loans we are indebted to the Collection Fonds National d'Art Contemporain, Ministère de la Culture, Paris; Arthur and Carol Goldberg; Michael and Jeanne Klein and the Menil Collection, Houston; John and Phyllis Kleinberg; Martin Z. Margulies; the Museum Boijmans Van Beuningen, Rotterdam, the Netherlands; the Museum of Contemporary Art, Los Angeles; Eileen Harris Norton; Peter Norton; Ruth and Carl Pite; a private collection; James and Dana Tananbaum; the Tate; and the artist and his representatives at Tanya Bonakdar Gallery, New York, and neugerriemschneider, Berlin.

A number of distinguished museums will be hosting this exhibition as it tours internationally in the coming years, and we extend our warmest wishes to our valued partners and colleagues Glenn D. Lowry, Alanna Heiss, Klaus Biesenbach, and Roxana Marcoci of the Museum of Modern Art and P.S.1 Contemporary Art Center, New York, and John R. Lane, Bonnie Pitman, and Charles Wylie of the Dallas Museum of Art.

Finally, these acknowledgments would not be complete without an expression of deepest thanks to Olafur Eliasson. Olafur has been a tirelessly thoughtful, generous, and creative collaborator over the several years that this exhibition has been in the making, and we are honored to have had this opportunity to work so closely with him and his talented studio staff. His exceptional vision transfigures the museum into a site of wonder, offering a heightened experience of art to active, aware, and self-critical audiences everywhere.

ACKNOWLEDGMENTS

Madeleine Grynsztejn

This exhibition has benefited immeasurably from an international corps of staunch and generous Eliasson supporters. Lenders, both public and private, have parted with cherished works for the sake of this undertaking, and we are deeply in their debt. For their support of the exhibition we thank Pamela Clapp and Joel Wachs. Of great help in facilitating loans were Catherine Clement, Stephane Doré, Sjarel Ex, Emi Fontana, Josef Hefelstein, Hou Hanru, Jessica Morgan, Paul Schimmel, Nicholas Serota, Jeremy Strick, and Philippe Vergne. Volunteering astute scholarly insights and offering important research materials were James Meyer, Hans Ulrich Obrist, James Rondeau, Andreas Ruby, Philip Ursprung, Olga Viso, and John Welchman. For their hospitality I would like to thank Kathy Fuld, Lars Grambye, Alfredo Pernin, Tjibbe Spruit, and Elena Tzotzi.

Throughout this project I have turned for assistance to the artist's primary gallery representatives, who have given graciously of their time, thoughts, and information. From the outset, Tanya Bonakdar and her staff at Tanya Bonakdar Gallery have been unfailingly gracious, dedicated, and insightful. I am grateful to her, Ethan Sklar, Jules Gaffney, James Lavender, Claudine Nuetzel, and Claire Pauley for their unparalleled assistance in locating important works and documentation, facilitating loans, and providing much-needed materials. Tim Neuger and Burkhard Riemschneider of the Berlin gallery neugerriemschneider were invaluable allies throughout the project, and they have my gratitude for their generous and diligent attention to our many inquiries.

A project of this type requires far more than the standard institutional approach to exhibition making. I am grateful to a superb team of colleagues here at SFMOMA for their close cooperation, enthusiastic support, and significant share in realizing an intricate and complicated project. There is, frankly, no more knowledgeable, dedicated, and spirited museum staff anywhere. Essential to an ambitious undertaking of this kind is the encouragement and wise counsel of our director, Neal Benezra, to whom I owe a special debt for allowing the project to develop to its fullest potential. J Mullineaux and his staff—especially Elizabeth Epley, Jennifer Mewha, Andrea Morgan, and Blair Winn—graciously rose to the challenge of funding this exhibition. Thanks to the enlightened oversight of Ruth Berson and Jessica Woznak, with Emily Lewis, Jillian Slane, and Mia Patterson in attendance, the exhibition and its tour have remained on excellent organizational and fiscal footing. Olga Charyshyn demonstrated logistical ingenuity in transporting artworks to and from the Museum and tour venues. Under Jill Sterrett's direction, conservators Michelle Barger, Marie-Chantale Poisson, and Theresa Andrews presided over Eliasson's works with their usual care, judiciousness, and creativity. Also working tirelessly on behalf of the project have been Barbara Rominski and the staff of the SFMOMA library as well as Layna White, Susan Backman, Don Ross, and Jeanne Friscia in the Department of Collections Information and Access. The exhibition's exemplary installation was overseen by Kent Roberts and Rico Solinas, who, aided by Steve Dye, Jeff Phairas, and a hard-working team of installers, brought to the task their gifted organizational abilities and professional dedication. I am also grateful to Ikuko Satoda and to Joe Brennan and Rick Peterson for their expertise.

In the Department of Painting and Sculpture, assistant curator Apsara DiQuinzio has my deep respect and heartfelt thanks for her extraordinary contribution to this project. Her coordination of every aspect of this show, and the creative thinking and writing she brought to the project, played an inestimable role in the exhibition and this book. I salute her professionalism, talent, tenaciousness, and humor. I am also indebted to Kate Mendillo for her graceful, steady, and calming influence and for her excellent research and administrative assistance. My departmental colleagues Janet Bishop, Alison Gass, and former curatorial associate Joshua Shirkey have lent support in countless ways, offering advice and encouragement and relieving me of myriad tasks by taking on additional burdens themselves. The project stayed on track thanks to numerous interns and volunteers who provided able and enthusiastic help: we thank Eveline L. Kanes for providing German translations, and Megan Campbell, Nicola Cicchetti, Sonya Derman, Anna Gritz, Andrea Nitsche, and Kate Sutton for their research and assistance.

I am deeply appreciative of those who, under the direction of Chad Coerver, crafted this beautiful and thought-provoking catalogue. My greatest thanks go to Karen Levine for bringing her unerring editorial finesse, heroic management skills, and tireless determination to the project. Karen added sharpness and clarity to every stage of the editorial, design, and production process. Jennifer Sonderby created a design that is as elegant and inventive as it is respectful of the artist's exacting standards for his books. If this volume does visual justice to Eliasson's work, it is thanks to her sensitive touch. We are grateful to Jody Hanson for stepping in to handle design production, and to James Williams, who supervised the printing of the book as well as the graphics and printed materials for the San Francisco presentation. The catalogue's rich array of plates testify to the image-gathering skills of Lindsey Westbrook, who also worked in tandem with Joshua Shirkey to compile the artist's most exhaustive and accurate chronology to date. Amanda Glesmann and Suzanne Stein made helpful contributions during the final stages of research and editing, and Susan DeRenne Coerr created a refined and comprehensive index under challenging time constraints. We are pleased to have Thames & Hudson as our copublishing partner, and we salute Jamie Camplin, Susan Dwyer, and their colleagues in New York and London for their early and ongoing support of the project.

The Publications Department joins me in thanking the authors who have enhanced this catalogue with their fresh and thoughtful essays: Mieke Bal, Klaus Biesenbach and Roxana Marcoci, Daniel Birnbaum, Pamela M. Lee, and Henry Urbach. We are exceedingly grateful to Robert Irwin for bringing his prodigious intelligence to bear on the dialogue with Eliasson that appears in this book. Special thanks also go to Hugh M. Davies and his staff at the Museum of Contemporary Art San Diego for hosting this conversation, with additional thanks to Adele Irwin for her warm welcome.

SFMOMA's Department of Education, especially Dominic Willsdon, Frank Smigiel, Julie Charles, Annie Lawson, Tana Johnson, Peter Samis, and Gregory Sandoval, created a rich and innovative schedule of interpretive programming to accompany this exhibition, with additional input from Anne-Marie Conde. I thank Nancy Price, Simon Blint, Shannon Dean, Libby Garrison, and Robyn Wise for bringing this exhibition to the attention of the public through media relations, marketing efforts, and audience outreach.

This project in its every detail has been brought to successful fruition thanks to the contributions of the extraordinary people staffing Olafur Eliasson's studio. Without their keen eyes, detailed attention, care, and intelligence this project would not have been possible. Foremost among them are Sebastian Behmann and Felix Tristan Hallwachs for their sophisticated address of the countless complexities inherent in the show's architectural and technical design, as well as its exemplary installation at every venue. Caroline Eggel, Anna Engberg-Pedersen, and archivist Biljana Joksimović were invaluable allies in the production of this publication, demonstrating unparalleled knowledge, creativity, and dedication in every daunting phase of the book's evolution. Petra Rickhof likewise contributed her expert organizational skills. In addition we thank Ben Allen, Robert Banović, Robert Biedrzycki, Matti Blind, Jan Bünnig, Heide Deigert, Sophie Erlund, Søren Fischer, Thilo Frank, Anja Gerstmann, Ricardo Gomes, Gonca Gücsav, Anna Sofie Hartmann, Frank Haugwitz, Michael Heimann, Anders Hellsten Nissen, Sandrina Hoffmann, Erik Huber, Jöran Imholze, Asako Iwama, Sharron Ping Jen Lee, Holger Jenal, Gianluca Malgeri, Lauren Maurer, Jan Mennicke, Felix Meyer, Kirsten Palz, Norbert Palz, Néstor Pérez Batista, Sven Pfeiffer, Malene Ratcliffe, Bettina Röder, Martin Roßmann, Kerstin Schmidt, Mila Seder Infante, Arndt Sellentin, Fredrik Skåtar, Myriam Thomas, Einar Thorsteinn, Christian Uchtmann, Derek Wang, and Matt Willard.

I have been sustained by the intelligence and warm support of a number of individuals who lent an ear, shared ideas, and gave suggestions and encouragement.

Each of the following has made an immeasurable difference in my thinking and greatly increased the pleasure of this project: Richard Armstrong, Ann Goldstein, Helen Molesworth, Philip Nowlen, Rochelle Steiner, Ann Temkin, and Sylvia Wolf. My writing has, as always, benefited from David Frankel's sage intellectual contributions and elegant editorial skills. No one was a greater supporter of this project than my favorite member of the general public, Tom Shapiro, whose constancy, encouragement, and perceptive comments have helped me every step of the way. I also wish to thank art historian Marianne Krogh Jensen, Olafur Eliasson's wife and critical intellectual partner, and their children, Zakarias Krogh Eliasson and Alma-Rose Krogh Eliasson, for their generous understanding and forbearance throughout the organization of this project.

I can't begin to adequately convey my respect, admiration, and gratitude to Olafur Eliasson. This marks the tenth year of our friendship, and I thank him for the sheer joy and intellectual excitement of his work and for the fact that he has entrusted me with this project. Olafur has up to now controlled much of the treatment of his own work in exhibition and in publications, which is why I thank him all the more for his generosity in working with SFMOMA on this more traditional survey. During the multiyear process of assembling this exhibition, he has contributed in innumerable ways—by creating new works; enduring countless conversations, inquiries, and demands; and giving unstintingly and graciously of his time. His remarkable artworks and ideas have already had a seismic impact on the cultural dialogue, and I have no doubt he will continue to engage and inspire artists and cultural thinkers for years to come. For his extraordinary efforts, and for the opportunity to be enriched by him and his rigorous and deeply felt art in the process, I am profoundly grateful.

(Y)OUR ENTANGLEMENTS: OLAFUR ELIASSON, THE MUSEUM, AND CONSUMER CULTURE

Madeleine Grynsztejn

I see potential in the spectator—in the receiver, the reader, the participator, the viewer, the user.

I . . . regard museums . . . as spaces where one steps even deeper into society, from where one can scrutinize society.

—Olafur Eliasson[1]

In the winter season of 2003, a "blockbusting two million visitors"[2] went to the Tate Modern, London, to see Olafur Eliasson's *Weather project* (pls. 1–2, 15, 196–97) in the museum's massive Turbine Hall. Entering that giant space, they saw that its architectural contours had been obscured—or made fluid and seemingly boundless—by a hazy atmosphere resembling light London fog, actually an artificial mist pumped in from sixteen visible nozzles attached to humming motors set throughout. Ahead of the visitor, at the far end of the hall's five hundred-foot-long expanse and at a height of about ninety feet, hung a giant yellow orb like a dark winter sun. Above, some three hundred mirrored ceiling panels spanned the entire chamber, covering a total area of just over thirty-two thousand square feet. The hall's already gargantuan proportions were reversed and doubled by the reflections in these panels, which were suspended from the nearly hundred-foot-high roof so that their trussing was visible to visitors on the museum's uppermost floor. The construction of the sun shape was also easily revealed as visitors neared it: this was simply a semicircular steel frame, fifty feet in diameter, fitted with approximately

1–2
Olafur Eliasson
The weather project, 2003
Installation views at the Tate Modern, London,
2003. Monofrequency lights, projection foil, haze
machine, mirror foil, aluminum, and scaffolding.
Courtesy the artist; Tanya Bonakdar Gallery,
New York; and neugerriemschneider, Berlin

A note about the captions: Artwork dimensions
are variable unless otherwise indicated. "EXH."
denotes works in the SFMOMA presentation.

two hundred yellow sodium lamps of the kind used for streetlights (see pl. 1). Reflected
in the ceiling panels, this frame appeared round. In front of it a second semicircular
frame stretched with projection-screen material diffused the lamplight into a yellow
aureole, turning everything and everyone in its vicinity into a duotone milieu of yellow
and shades of black. The staggered alignment of the ceiling panels reflecting the top half
of the orb created the effect of a sun cut through with jagged lines—half illusory, like a
desert mirage. Basking in Eliasson's artificial, heatless sunlight, scores of captivated
visitors lay on the cold floor, seeking out their tiny reflections in the ceiling high above.
They occasionally assembled themselves into human patterns of abstract shapes, sym-
bols, or spelled-out words (pl. 2). The work became "a spectacle and tabloid news, its
popularity almost transcending logic."[3]

The extraordinary popularity of *The weather project* prompts reflections
on the ambivalent relationship between progressive contemporary art practice and a
range of forces—the museum, "the spectacle," and consumer culture—with which, now
more than ever, it is in inevitable and unsettled discourse.[4] The analysis and address of
the connections, overlaps, adaptations, and misidentifications among these spheres are
an essential part of the lives of artists such as Eliasson as well as many museum professionals. Simply put, we have arrived at a point when art, the museum, and cutting-edge

commerce increasingly share visual modes of organizing meaning and express related ambitions to provide the individual with what have been described as "models of experience, opportunities for self-recognition, and the ingredients of identity."[5]

An abiding purpose of the museum has been to disseminate knowledge and ways of thinking that open avenues for understanding ourselves and the world around us. The museum is one of the prime ideological institutions in which we can wrangle with an array of existing or proposed views and belief systems that we can then choose to admire and emulate or contest and eschew. It is a space for fundamental thinking about the ways in which we can and do construct selves and negotiate ways of being in the world, and the raw materials that it employs to catalyze this human capacity are images, objects, and ideas.[6] At the same time, in the economic sphere, we find ourselves today in the midst of a new stage of advanced capitalism involving a shift from industrial to cultural production. What commerce is now selling is images and ideas—precisely the purview of the museum. The industries producing culture and experience (as opposed to the traditional industries producing goods and services) "are the fastest growing sector of the global economy"[7] and are increasingly the dominant ideological instruments in Western society. Film, television, tourism, shopping malls, destination entertainment centers, theme towns, amusement parks, fashion, the music industry, and the simulated worlds of online space "are the front line commercial fields"[8] that permeate every aspect of daily life, conscripting the private and social to commercial ends. And activities that in the past were sought in the cultural realm—those possibly transformative experiences through which one could intimately compose a life—are fast becoming purchasable in the marketplace as distinct economic offerings, in the form of intense and pleasurable lived experiences.[9]

The contest between the cultural and commercial spheres over thinking and doing is one of the defining tensions in contemporary Western society. And the museum is the knife-edge location where this contest is being played out, for here the conditions that determine or influence our sense of self are scrutinized in a conscious and concentrated way. What roles are art and the museum to play in an arena in which culture and the marketplace are moving ever closer? What kinds of practices are required to address this condition? What do those practices look like in the face of advanced capitalism's aesthetic saturation? And what larger philosophy of being might those practices suppose? In response to these open and pressing questions, tasks for both the artist and the museum must include the preservation of criticality and self-reflexivity and the creation of an oppositional space, however partial and provisional, for analysis, discussion, disturbance, transgression, and potential dissent from the prevailing logic and rote habits of the media/communications/entertainment spectacle.[10] At their best, the artist and the museum propose possibilities outside of the identities, forms, and functions given to us elsewhere in the culture. In that project they may collude and collaborate with the commercial sphere—and indeed to some extent they probably must—but they mitigate their complicity by working toward a strengthened experience of self that, while it cannot be entirely autonomous or external to the imperatives of capital, touches back on whatever touches that individual.

Enter the work of Eliasson, which at its core makes a case for the proactive subject, for the individual's return to a heightened sense of him- or herself in the act of perceiving and acting, and by extension for the conscious ownership of all manner of processes of cognition that tend to be standardized, automated, and otherwise impoverished by a mediating world. If both the commercial and the cultural spheres are "intimately, structurally involved in the construction of the subject,"[11] Eliasson's work is equally intimately involved in underlining the potential of that subject's ability—perceptual and ideological—to recognize those systems as constructions and to respond to them by producing constructions of his or her own devising. With his many titles using the possessive pronoun *your* (as in *Your sun machine* [1997], *Your natural denudation inverted* [1999], and *Your egoless door* [2005]), Eliasson openly calls for an actively engaged spectator, casting the viewer in a principal role in the aesthetic production of the artwork. This is the central tactic in his arsenal of strategies for encouraging individual awareness, reflection, and ultimately a greater consciousness of the workings of large economic and political frameworks. Other moves, such as those of *The weather project,* include exposing the materials and mechanics that produce a work's effects; delivering singular and unique impressions that defy the preference of the marketplace for the prefabricated and reproducible; and creating the context for a social dimension—a space for plural human activities, encounters, and communicative pleasures—that counters the formatted and unitary collective encouraged by commodification.

These are among the methods by which Eliasson extracts the "little difference"[12] that makes his work an uncovering rather than a celebration of the commodity system, even as it also carefully registers the penetration of spectacle-oriented culture—the mass immersive viewing environment of *The weather project* being a prime example. Today's advanced art and modes of institutional analysis often consciously internalize aspects of the commodity system, including spectacle, precisely in order to demystify them, provoking experiences that cause a fundamental rift in the viewer's usually smooth process of absorption.[13] The double bind inherent in this practice of critical intervention is underlined—and the practice itself potentially undermined—when, paradoxically, the work itself becomes a popular success, as *The weather project* did. This is the challenge, then, for both Eliasson and the museum: to wrest meaning from popularity by accomplishing the work of deciphering and unmasking, pushing the commercial sphere to act accountably and catalyzing approaches that deflect its less responsible logics and machinations.

Much has been written on Eliasson's biography: born in Denmark, he is of Icelandic extraction and was partly raised in Iceland's dramatic and ancient landscape. That landscape, it is often pointed out, informs his artistic use of elemental materials such as light, wind, and heat; arctic moss and solidified lava; and especially water, in all its various stages from liquid to solid—steam, fog, mist, moisture, ice.[14] Less has been written on the relationship of Eliasson's work to the museum and on their mutual ideological aspirations. If the museum is, in today's culture, a preeminent instrument for seeing—both physically and ideologically—it is also the perfect container for Eliasson's object lessons in seeing *differently*, in a productive apperception operating in constant tandem with the environment.

To underline the productive operation of our perceptual capacities, Eliasson often opens his exhibitions with *Room for one colour* (1997; pl. 178), a space empty of objects but filled with a yellow light that seems almost solid in its chromatic density. Emanating from a ceiling bank of monofrequency bulbs, the thick hue drenches the otherwise empty space and its inhabitants in a yellow-tinted field. At the same time that we are experiencing the color yellow, we are also neurologically compensating for the lack of other colors in the room. As a result, when we look through the space to the next gallery, it seems in the glow of retinal excitement to be bathed in deep purple (yellow's opposite and afterimage)—though the walls are actually white. Eliasson thus makes the spectator's visual processing part of the aesthetic equation, opening the space of his work to the generative workings of human vision and in turn interweaving body and room, "external" events and "internal" sensations. Meanwhile, the work of art itself becomes the interface between site and subject and an emergent property of both. As Maurice Merleau-Ponty wrote of perception generally, "The properties of the object and the intentions of the subject . . . are not only intermingled; they also constitute a new whole. . . . It is impossible to say 'which started first' in the exchange of stimuli and responses."[15] *Room for one colour* invites us to see that the substance of experience is not prescribed but rather corporeally *enacted* from moment to moment, a realization that is subsequently available for transposition to the world at large. This demonstration of a "perceiver-dependent world"[16]—proof positive of our capacity to influence what influences us—makes us aware that even if reality may be in part a given, we can continually negotiate and widen the field of possible experience.

Eliasson's emphasis on active corporeal vision is but one of the means by which he upends ingrained visual habits and models of perception that may limit sight and insight. His works often take on the enduring illusionistic tools that art and art history have refined since the Renaissance to structure and codify the variety and appearance of the visible world: such classic principles as Albertian one-point perspective, Euclidian geometry, and Cartesian coordinate systems, all of which formalize an essentially optic (as opposed to haptic) relationship between viewer and viewed. These constructions presuppose and reflect a belief in an external world of stationary and objective truth, and also in an equally static and autonomous observing subject, imagined as a disembodied eye free from the physiological idiosyncrasies of its retinal apparatus. Eliasson's work enlists, then counteracts, all of these archetypal devices.

The idea of a detached observer relating on an exclusively scenic level to an independent world fully exterior to him- or herself is radically contravened, for example, by *Sunset kaleidoscope* (2005; pls. 220–21), a six-foot-long rectangular box open at both ends to show a mirror-lined interior with a motorized, slowly rotating

3
Olafur Eliasson
Window projection, 1990
Installation view at Studio Olafur Eliasson,
Copenhagen, 1990. Spotlight, gobo, and tripod.
Courtesy the artist; Tanya Bonakdar Gallery,
New York; and neugerriemschneider, Berlin

yellow disc at its center. Made to fit through an open window, the box melds reflections of disc, observer, and outside view into a kaleidoscopic explosion of mirrors mirroring mirrored images, subject also to the continual flux of the urban environment's variable sky, light, sound, and weather. This vertiginous, ambiguous, and constantly changing image world is a long way from the clear, stable, rational centrality projected by Albertian perspective and from the idea of the self implicit in Cartesian principles. The Renaissance polymath Leon Battista Alberti likened painting in perspective to opening a window on the world; *Sunset kaleidoscope* both literalizes that metaphor and invalidates it. (In this respect, it advances a concept first proposed by Eliasson in 1990, when he projected the shape of a window onto a windowless wall [see pl. 3].) Within this restless plane, the self cannot come to rest except as a continually and actively constructed contingent observer, whose visual dispersal effectively shatters the classic supposition of a stable and unified position from which one thinks, perceives, and acts. This collapse of traditional visual coordinates is also a condition for bringing other visual sensations into being, and this is where Eliasson's work shows its philosophical implications. For if, as is commonly understood, visual cognition is a means to understand the places available to the subject at present, then the more open and multiple the given visual phenomena, the greater the range of possible observer positions, and the less circumscribed and possibly debased our experience of the world.[17]

In *Remagine* (2002; pls. 160–62) Eliasson explores the geometry of perspective, which is basic to conventional pictorial composition, in such a way as to remind the viewer of its artificial underpinnings. Installed at eye level on one side of the gallery is a clearly exposed bank of theater lamps that project various square, rectangular, and trapezoidal shapes onto the wall opposite. A computer program connected to the lamps choreographs these shapes in white light as a slow sequence of planar forms cyclically appearing, disappearing, and increasing and decreasing in intensity. Within this richly nuanced and continuously varied orchestration, shapes float freely or are variously linked—here by abutment, there by superimposition—in a playful exploitation of the spatio-visual distortions inherent in the laws of perspective and in the perceptions they inculcate. Yoked angled forms produce a tease of visual foreshortening and horizon effects; an attenuated trapezoid, joined along one edge to the short side of a rectangle, conveys the illusion of half a room. As shapes overlap, a new, brighter form carrying greater optical weight will advance visually in space. Instead of providing a single, statically ordered perspectival arrangement, geometry here loosens its hold, unfolding decentered, dispersed, heterogeneous configurations almost cinematically over the wall.

In promoting this kind of awareness of conventions of seeing, Eliasson's work encourages a critical attitude toward normative processes of perception while at the same time offering viewers opportunities to expand their ability to envision. He likewise understands their kinetic involvement in his work as yet another, embodied and maximally individuated, way of seeing. *Notion motion* (2005; pls. 4, 137, 226–33) is a case in point: walking into a darkened gallery, the visitor steps onto a floor of wooden planks, like an esplanade. What looks like a blank wall to one side is in fact a gray

4
Olafur Eliasson
Notion motion, 2005 (EXH.)
Installation view at the Museum Boijmans Van Beuningen, Rotterdam, Netherlands, 2005. HMI spotlights, tripods, water, foil, projection foil, wood, nylon, and sponge. Museum Boijmans Van Beuningen, on loan from the H+F Mecenaat

floor-to-ceiling scrim that divides the room roughly in half. Behind the scrim, and as yet invisible to the viewer, is a large, shallow basin filled with water, on which is trained a spotlight. A number of the floor's planks are slightly raised, as if loosened from their grid, and one feels impelled to step on them. This activates a mechanical device under the floor, which sends a pole and crossbar skimming across the surface of the water in the adjoining space, creating ripple effects that the angled spotlight projects onto the screenlike scrim. The result is a dramatic, constantly changing composition of white skeins and shadows—a large, living abstract painting.

As the ripples subside, the composition's initially sharp contours become more diffuse and faint until one or more of the spectators figures forth more imagery by stepping on the raised boards. In encouraging performative action in this way, *Notion motion* connects object to subject. Located fully in neither the object nor the actions of the subject, the piece is situated instead in an elastic unfolding "between the spectator and the machine"[18]—in experience. Ultimately *Notion motion* proposes an evocative cancellation of the line along which each body understands itself as apart from its surroundings, a reduction of our estrangement from a now more fully enveloping universe. Eliasson describes his works as "devices for the experience of reality,"[19] and that reality is not to be found either inside or outside the body. It lies at the living edge between a haptic self and a heterogeneous and constantly changing universe, in an encounter somewhere between a concrete event and its luminous apperception. What the works compel, then, rather than any settled endpoint, is a process of negotiation. The philosophy posited by *Notion motion* stands at the heart of Eliasson's entire enterprise, which at its core coheres clearly and powerfully as a serious argument for an embedded and exhilarating being-in-the-world.[20]

Eliasson's affirmation of a "self-choosing, world-creating subject"[21] informs not only his artworks but also the ways in which they are physically deployed. Since his first opportunity to exhibit his work in depth, in *The curious garden* at the Kunsthalle Basel, Switzerland, in 1997 (pls. 51–54), Eliasson has conceived of the exhibition space as a site soliciting a peripatetic observer and an itinerant vision. In his one-person shows he choreographs diverse works into suites of consecutive and related encounters designed with circumnavigation in mind: exhibitions such as *The mediated motion* (Kunsthaus Bregenz, Austria, 2001; pls. 110–21), *The blind pavilion* (Venice Biennale, 2003; pls. 176–94), and this SFMOMA survey (p. 255) make use of paths, ramps, staircases, and bridges to insist on a body and gaze in motion. An Eliasson exhibition invites visitors to be enveloped by, circulate in, and act upon an installation that is continually responsive to their own unique and manifold approaches, itineraries, and velocities. Multiple sensory impressions—a blast of air from a fan swinging wildly from a ceiling at the end of a long cord (*Ventilator* [1997; pl. 71]), the smell and texture of arctic moss (*Moss wall* [1994; pl. 30]), the touch of humidity on skin (*Beauty* [1993; pls. 5, 31]), the sound of lava rocks crunching underfoot (*Lava floor* [2002; pls. 163–64])—further heighten the level of a somatic participation that is as much felt as seen.

This kind of participation calls us out of and beyond ourselves, an effect reinforced when witnessed and shared by others. Along with the personal, subjective quality of each visitor's responses to Eliasson's works, a central aspect of his oeuvre is its social dimension. The work is fundamentally activated by the perception and participation of oneself *and* others, by "the very apprehension of other people and their movements . . . [amid] the optical [and physical] texture of the work."[22] Sharing our singular impressions in this way, we come into a "being-in-common" or "being-with," as opposed to a "being-in-solitude"[23]—into a community of sorts, a loose and differentiated collectivity of individuals defined not by a common interest or essential feature but simply by a copresence in a "constructed situation"[24] designed (in part) to generate provisional but compelling social bonds. In this way Eliasson's art, and the museum as its site of operation, together perform a crucial social function: they embody a notion of the public sphere at a time when it is a receding ideal. The traditional conception of the public sphere as a cohesive and homogenous collective body or location is now understood as outdated, for it in no way corresponds to our present-day reality, in which countless differences (ideological, sexual, class, or otherwise) polarize and fragment us into multiple publics with radically divergent means and quality of access to any collective arena. Indeed, at present we seem to be utterly incapable of a common discourse or forum. Under these circumstances, the idea of a communal condition has taken on a utopian sense of urgency in artistic practice.[25] If "the public sphere has to be 'made,' it is not 'there' anymore,"[26] then the museum and Eliasson advance a way of imagining sociability and shared identification that is unregulated, open-ended, and plural, turning the museum into a model for civic space. In this sense Eliasson's work seems a direct response to Miwon Kwon's call for "a public sphere, where one might bracket, temporarily, one's private, personal interests to imagine a collective identification. . . . Such an effort to imagine a democratic public sphere anew is necessarily an exercise in abstraction, and the (art) work to be done seems to be located in the space of coming together of this different sort of intimacy *and* publicity."[27]

Given the means and ends of Eliasson's practice—the unfolding nature of his art and installations, the central role of the spectator/participant—it does not surprise that he

5
Olafur Eliasson
Beauty, 1993 (EXH.)
Installation view at the Hara Museum of Contemporary Art, Tokyo, 2005. Fresnel lamp, water, nozzles, hose, wood, and pump. Museum of Contemporary Art, Los Angeles, purchased with funds provided by Paul Frankel

has in recent years become deeply interested in the institution of the museum, and that the museum has engaged in turn with him. After all, the museum's fundamental mode of communication is the exhibition display—a diachronic unfurling of sequentially presented objects whose juxtapositions, analogies, and associations are designed to build toward an intensity of experience, meaning, and aesthetic charge. Presenting its narratives along a physical trajectory that is coordinated but not enforced, and that leaves room for the spectator to compose his or her own image world, the museum is "among the few remaining oases where the pleasure of heterogeneous and self-selected 'flow experience' can still be enjoyed."[28] It has historically operated along a continuum embracing on the one hand the object of display (from which devolve activities such as collecting, classifying, preserving, and displaying, and an address of the spectator as primarily passive and introspective while pursuing aesthetic enjoyment and learning) and on the other the perceiver (leading to the functions of education and other more socially interactive activities assuming a less docile viewer/participant). Today, however, the museum has moved to one extreme of this continuum, where it puts an unprecedented focus on visitor experience.[29] At the forefront of this trend are projects such as that of the Hirshhorn Museum and Sculpture Garden in Washington, D.C., where Eliasson has contributed to a comprehensive master plan that reexamines and potentially reconfigures the museum's physical facilities with a view to producing the strongest possible sense of engagement on the part of the visitor.[30] The collaboration—less a building plan than a philosophical analysis of museum space—starts from the desire to increase visitors' sense of ownership of and responsibility for their various trajectories, encounters, and connections at the Hirshhorn. This involves an address of their circulation through the space of the museum, be it on the museum's Web site or inside the building itself, but their active psychic and physical responses are the primary focus.

Eliasson's collaboration with the Hirshhorn points to a fundamental ambition shared by both the artist and the museum establishment in general: to create a space in which a person can consciously participate in his or her own life and time. Eliasson's artworks, like the offerings of the museum, propose and foster acts of the imagination as well as narratives that return to the viewer the ability to associate creatively with the world, and in this way they undertake the movement toward meaning that is at the core of subjective experience. Herein lies the ideological dimension of both his work and the museum's: they call the viewer to agency. In offering instances of intellectual freedom and experiential plenitude, this art and this cultural institution provoke modes of self-awareness and action that counter the diminishment of self in our advanced technological age.

Both Eliasson and the museum envision perception as an action: purposeful, voluntary, and expressive of an individual's autonomy. To the degree that the self undertakes a willful and creative apperception of the world, she or he is potentially resistant to the regulatory imperatives of a modernizing society. Furthermore, to invite the individual to intervene mentally or physically, as Eliasson does, is to open the work to multiple avenues of interpretation that necessarily, if provisionally, transgress a prescribed order. This strategy points to a more expansive model for being in the world, one that will return viewers to themselves as less docile members of society.

And yet . . . the very kind of participatory, sensorial, individualized engagement that Eliasson and the museum advance is also the engine driving today's cutting-edge consumer culture. The new "experience economy" calls on businesses to "experientialize their goods" as a way to increase their economic potential.[31] In an extremely efficient marketplace now capable of mass customization, individuals are invited to fashion their self-expression, indeed their selves, through their choice of clothes, leisure activities, and consumer goods. The constantly evolving technoculture of the online world, with its participatory platforms (Wikipedia, YouTube) and rhetoric of "user-generated content," acclimatizes audiences to ever higher levels of active participation, circulation, and coproduction. At the same time, in the physical world, shopping malls and entertainment centers enlist the observer's body in intense, immersive environments. Given that the activation of the viewer has long been thought to have an emancipatory dimension—sparking an awareness that can be applied to life and politics—what happens to that potential when it is also the locus of the operations of mass-media culture? It has been noted that "in the seventies and eighties, we lived in a society of spectacle, in the nineties in the society of participants, and we are now developing a 'society of interactors.'"[32] If so, how can the promise of individual human agency offered by both Eliasson and the museum remain a critical or oppositional stance?

These are among the most important questions facing contemporary museum and artistic practices, and the directions taken in response to them will reflect critically on the integrity, credibility, relevance, effectiveness, and import of the role of visual arts in society well into the future. While the answers are being grappled with right now, it is clear that they necessitate neither railing against consumer culture nor attempting to break clean from it (an impossible and in any case undesirable notion, for it is too important to be left alone). Rather, they center on the quality of engagement that the museum and art can offer. Beyond their visual and pedagogical pleasures and their social dimensions, what both the museum and Eliasson volunteer are visual models for thinking about and discussing the nature and direction of the society in which we live. The success of the museum and of the artwork lies in presenting aesthetic experiences of intellectual strength and beauty that are also (and centrally) vehicles for heightened consciousness, cultivating our capacity to reflect on the everyday conditions with which we are engaged. To pose questions rather than (or in addition to) delivering on consumer desires—to produce interference patterns that disrupt the mass media's smooth transmission—these are acts that return the museum and the artwork to their potential, however partial or limited, for public criticality.[33] In this way, art and the museum open a space for opinion, debate, and agency, creating a kind of spatial politics in the process. And perhaps, in occupying that space, the individual may come to see that the kind of engagement offered by consumer culture is by comparison less one of heightened activity than simply a "more developed form of sedentarization,"[34] less interactive than "interpassive,"[35] a field on which we do not truly act so much as receive a limited opportunity to manipulate its givenness (however refined and multifarious).[36]

This is a gradualist argument, given the adjacency of art and commerce.[37] It is also, however, a necessary means of operating in the world. "As against the grandiose claims that are made for the historical avant-gardes, here is . . . an art of the little deal"[38]—an art of incremental resistances that seeks not to change the world but to sharpen our perception of it. In dedicating themselves to this goal, the artist and the museum cultivate the antinomy, thin-edged yet irrefutable, that separates art and commerce. This is how, while maintaining an awareness of our position as necessarily adulterated, artist and museum nevertheless remain deeply committed to the emancipatory potential ultimately manifested in the subject, who represents "both the location of operations of power *and* the potential for resistance."[39]

For Eliasson, the trigger to a sharpened speculative impulse centers on the notion of legibility, apparent in his work's conspicuous exposure of its own fabrication and in the literalism of its materials. Nearly all of his art deflects its own imaginative power by divulging the functional machinations that drive its effects. In *Notion motion,* for example, a second entrance gives access to the water basin and spotlight behind the screen that carries the work's painterly reflections, calculatedly disclosing the system that constructs its appearances. The smooth surface of illusion and its technical construction thus form two equal poles between which the visitor can move. Full disclosure is also exercised in *Remagine,* where the viewer simultaneously experiences affect and equipment, the image and its generating apparatus (the overt, noisy, heat-producing lighting gear), and in *Double sunset* (pls. 6, 78), where Eliasson made no attempt to camouflage the scaffolding of the enormous corrugated-steel disc that loomed over the Utrecht skyline in 1999. The spectacular sun shape of *The weather project* was similarly demystified when closer approach revealed its facture out of yellow sodium lights, interrupting the spectator's full absorption and complicity in an all-embracing experience. In each case we are attuned to a certain reflexiveness, a resistance to all-out illusionism. The work never disappears into transparency; the illusion is never complete. This dual move, generating an emotional response while unveiling its material basis, is central to the art's content, for it disables our impression not just of the work but also of the world as a naturalized, uninterrupted continuum. In the process of this appraisal, the mind becomes

6

Double sunset, 1999
Installation view in Utrecht, Netherlands, 1999.
Xenon lamps, steel, and scaffolding. Courtesy
the artist; Tanya Bonakdar Gallery, New York;
and neugerriemschneider, Berlin

conscious of its own cognition. "Seeing yourself seeing" is Eliasson's term for this condition of awareness, and it is key to all of his work: "[It] is crucial . . . that experience is presented undisguised to the spectator," he says. "Otherwise, our most generous ability to see ourselves seeing, to evaluate and criticize ourselves and our relation to space, has failed, and thus so has the museum's socializing potential."[40]

Eliasson's insistence on a criticality rooted in legibility logically extends to a concern with disassembling the situation in which the viewer often experiences his work—that is, the museum. This sets him within the tradition of artistic practice known as institutional critique, a tradition on which he expands. In the latter half of the 1960s—a period in which all kinds of authority, cultural and otherwise, were profoundly challenged—the museum became an object of artistic analysis, investigation, and unveiling, preeminently in the work of artists such as Michael Asher, Marcel Broodthaers, Daniel Buren, and Hans Haacke. Using methods ranging from strategic intervention in museum protocols to parodic subversion of exhibition displays, these artists exposed the previously unobserved or hidden support structures sustaining these institutions as well as the ideological underpinnings informing their modes of presentation. In the forty years since, this politically progressive artistic practice (whose most compelling current exponents include Andrea Fraser, Louise Lawler, and Fred Wilson) has gradually shifted "away from grand *oppositions* to subtle *displacements*"[41]—away from explicit criticism of the museum and toward more subtle but no less powerful or radical conceptual tactics that own up to the relationship between artist and museum as foil and sponsor.[42] Without in any way giving up on the self-questioning central to institutional critique, such artists, Eliasson included, ultimately set out less to deconstruct the museum antagonistically than to embolden it as a place from which to articulate a speculative and critical approach.

Hence Eliasson's interest in, for example, the museum's information systems. For *The weather project,* in addition to constructing the display in the Turbine Hall, the artist appropriated the agendas of promotion and interpretation affiliated with his piece by the Tate. Recognizing that the viewer's experience of art is influenced by the museum's mediation—in the form of advertising campaigns, press releases, wall texts, and educational programs—Eliasson worked with the Tate's staff to develop his own outreach plan, devising alternative methods of communication that revealed their elements of stage management as such to the viewer. Advertising posters, for instance, featured simple statements on the weather, making no direct comment on the work (see pls. 7–8). At least in terms of the museum's actions, the viewer retained the possibility of an unmediated

7–8
Practise / Tate Modern
Advertisements for *The weather project,*
London, 2003

experience of the installation. In this way Eliasson enjoined the museum to partner with him in protecting the reception of his art.[43]

With *The light setup* (2005; pls. 214–17) and *Omgivelser* (Surroundings, 2006), Eliasson delivered subtle blows to the "white cube," the gallery space that for most of the twentieth century constituted the international standard for the presentation of art and has been a central target of institutional critique. As defined in Brian O'Doherty's classic series of articles from 1976, the white cube is a hermetic, clean, white-walled, evenly lit room designed to eliminate awareness of the wider world and its contingencies of time and change. Here the visitor may apply an undistracted focus to the art object on display, which in this impartial environment is also posited as free from outside forces, whether natural, economic, or political. O'Doherty and other writers and artists of the period subjected this principle to forceful critique, arguing that, far from supplying a neutral context, the white cube impinged on the viewing experience in indisputable if subtle ways—most of all by neutralizing the historical circumstances touching the work on view, while itself remaining near invisible and therefore inculpable.[44]

The light setup put the light of the white cube itself on display in hair-trigger focus. Working in the Malmö Konsthall in Sweden, the artist illuminated a large, empty hall with fifteen hundred fluorescent lights placed behind giant screens on the walls and ceiling, programming them to deliver different shades of white—ivory, chalky, creamy, milky, pearlescent. Clearly there is no such thing as a normative, pure color white, and Eliasson's demonstration of this attuned the viewer to the way light actively affects perception—it is never neutral or impartial. For *Omgivelser* the artist equipped the hermetic white cube of a commercial gallery in Copenhagen with windows and doors opening onto a narrow corridor that wrapped around the immediate exterior of the gallery walls. Mirrors installed on the corridor's floor, ceiling, and side walls visually recapitulated the space, turning it into an endlessly receding and ever-changing environment that was real and virtual in equal measure: a physical, three-dimensional volume and a two-dimensional reflection combined to create an impossibly rich, infinite field of vision. Exceeding the fixed, bounded, and orderly plan of the traditional gallery, this space "freely complicates itself . . . opens itself up to question," loosening so as to allow for something new—"other affects, other precepts."[45] We enter into an experience of the work in which neither subject nor object can claim authority or dominance. As we look at the work's mirrored surfaces "the work looks back,"[46] and we visually fuse with the topic of our attention. Undoing any dualism between artwork and perceiver, Eliasson's intervention enables us to come into a new whole: a richly emotional and corporeal experience unfolding in direct relation to a dynamic exterior world.[47]

This interweaving of viewer and field of vision recalls the continuity between environment and retinal response in *Room for one colour* and also in *360° room for all colours* (2002; pls. 167–72), a roofless, circular enclosure that does away with the

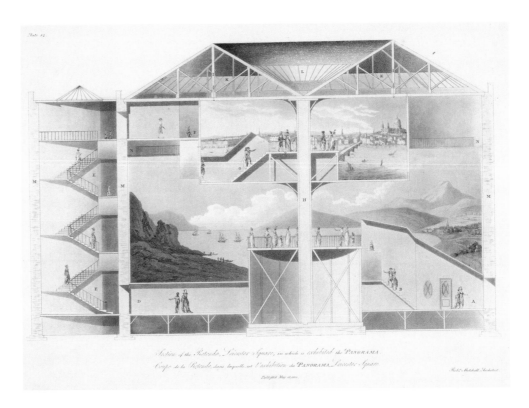

9
After Robert Mitchell
Section of the Rotunda, Leicester Square,
in which is exhibited the Panorama, 1801
Etching and aquatint. 12⅝ x 18⅜ in.
(32.1 x 46.7 cm). British Museum, London,
Department of Prints and Drawings

standard gallery's right angles. Instead we are enveloped by a seamless, curved projection panel, behind which a matrix of tinted lights is programmed to saturate the wall with a single color at a time, gradually building in intensity until it engulfs the room and the people inside in a wide, glowing band. The hue then slowly fades as the next in the sequence begins to emerge and eventually to overtake it in fluid and sumptuous chromatic succession. As this surface of pure color undergoes modulations in hue, its palette is compounded by the eye's release of complementary color afterimages, which, projected back into the space of the work, overlap with the colors emitted by the wall, and so on in a living, pulsating, lambent reciprocity. In both structure and effect, *360°* *room for all colours* calls up an immersive device of times past, the panorama, an archetypal nineteenth-century display mechanism in which the viewer stood in the center of a 360-degree cylindrical painting and was treated to absorbing screen entertainments of urban, pastoral, or historical scenes (see pl. 9). Playing with an architectural form belonging to an early genre of spectacular display, Eliasson engages with a formative museum paradigm.

    Model room (2003; pls. 10–11, 173) similarly evokes the subjects and display methods of earlier museum collections and presentations, merging studio, workshop, and gallery space. A prodigious number of models, prototypes, molds, and materials, in various stages of development, are hung from the ceiling and walls and cluttered along specially designed shelves.[48] Like a number of Eliasson's completed sculptures, these models derive their forms from structures used by scientists to visualize abstract data; hence the Möbius strips made of copper, quasi-crystals made of foamcore and foil, small mirrored geodesic domes, and kaleidoscopes of all kinds. The room exposes and demystifies

10–11
Olafur Eliasson
Model room, 2003 (EXH.)
Installation views at the Lunds Konsthall,
Lund, Sweden, 2005 (left), and the Reykjavík
Art Museum—Hafnarhús, 2004 (right).
Chipboard display cabinets and mixed-media
models, maquettes, and prototypes. Courtesy
the artist; Tanya Bonakdar Gallery, New York;
and neugerriemschneider, Berlin

Eliasson's artistic process, which is shown to be one of constant exploration and experimentation. A touchstone work in his oeuvre, *Model room* is crucial in pointing to a mode of thinking that opens out into risky and inconclusive territory—a field of trial and error, false starts, ongoing puzzlings, and delightful discoveries. In the passage from reverie to resolution, Eliasson emphasizes the former. His fundamental approach to art making is not declarative but speculative; rather than striking a stance, he follows his curiosity in a process of attentive inquiry that lets intellectual and emotional sparks fly.

It is a kind of deeply pleasurable, alert, open-ended thinking that we may imagine to have been elicited, at an earlier period, by the *Wunderkammer*, or "curiosity cabinet," that meeting place of aesthetics and exploration, dating from the sixteenth and seventeenth centuries, that is the museum's indirect ancestor—a miscellany of "Pictures, Books, Rings, Animals, Plants, Fruits, Metals, monstrous or Extravagant Productions, and Works of all Fashions; and, in a Word, all that can be imagin'd curious, or worth enquiry, whether for Antiquity or Rarity, or for the Delicacy and Excellency of the Workmanship."[49] Like Eliasson's *Model room*, the *Wunderkammer* was an overloaded, plural sensory environment that exuberantly juxtaposed wildly different categories of materials and objects solely on the basis of their capacity to arouse wonder through their beauty, rarity, novelty, or strangeness (see pl. 12). By the late eighteenth century, the age of the Enlightenment, such repositories of the marvelous had added instructive purpose to the experience of delight, showing mechanical inventions and scientific instruments whose principles (such as electricity or perpetual motion) were revealed and explained to the audience or observer.[50] Much in the same spirit as Eliasson's demystifying approach, such object lessons and "scenes of instruction"[51] first seduced their viewers with dazzling displays, then invited them to marvel equally at the methods used to fabricate the effects. Vividly savored experiences like these drew no strict line between subjective experience and objective analysis, wonder and comprehension, mind and body. A powerful appeal to the senses was thus married to an equally pleasurable address of the intellect, and the result was a kind of "embodied" or "sensationalized knowledge"[52]—a form of intelligence that did not (yet) divorce rational competence from the force of an aesthetic experience that was not merely sensate but meaningful.

At the very borderline between sensation and thought is wonder, a sensory and cognitive mode that Eliasson gently insists his work and the museum (again) take up as an epistemology for the present day.[53] This "re-enchantment of wisdom"[54] offers a covert rebuke to a systematic, unquestioning, and unquestioned consumer culture and its notions of spectacle. Wondering, writes Stephen Greenblatt, "is at least partly independent of the structures of politics and the marketplace."[55] It is also the outgrowth of a deeply personal mode of being in the world. The feeling of wonder, where and when it surprises us, alerts us to a highly personal boundary of intelligibility that is unique to each person: "the place where at this moment in our own history and development we are able to see a question."[56] It is a line that moves with us as we gain in understanding, and to follow its course is to welcome the sting and stimulation of a voluntary life. For Eliasson, wonder is an ethical imperative; it is the quality of experience that prompts us toward an intensive engagement with the world, that continually reawakens us to a fresh consideration of the everyday and the lives we choose to live in it. As "philosophy begins in wonder,"[57] so Eliasson's works, and the museum at its best, urge us to stay close to the root condition of all inquiry and knowledge—to start the important work of constructing meaning at a ground level from which independent thinking and action are possible, even necessary.

Since the beginning of recorded time, the rainbow has stood as the archetypal symbol of

12
Giralomo Viscardi after Giovanni Battista Bertoni
The Calzolari Museum, 1622
Engraving. 11 x 13¹⁄₂ in. (27.9 x 34.3 cm). Getty Research Institute, Los Angeles

wonder.[58] It should therefore come as no surprise that the rainbow should be the subject of Eliasson's first fully mature work, *Beauty*. First produced in 1993, the installation consists of a perforated hose placed high against a darkened interior wall. The hose releases tiny drops of water, producing a curtain of mist upon which is trained a spotlight. The economical means of creating this work—water tap, hose, electrical socket, spotlight— are all clearly exposed. The visitor, her bodily sensations piqued by the sound of barely condensed liquid hitting the floor and the touch of humidity on skin, visually receives the refractive effects of light passing through water, and this interface between eye and phenomenon produces the vision of an astonishingly beautiful rainbow. The work is radically subjective, for it is absolutely dependent on and unique to each viewer's position: certain colors in the rainbow are emphasized, or the arc may disappear altogether, depending on the angle between observer, light source, and raindrop, such that the piece cannot be seen identically even by two people standing side by side. That this celestial phenomenon has found its way indoors, that the mechanisms by which it is brought into being are overt, and that the image itself could not be more familiar or clichéd—none of this detracts from a magical enjoyment and even exhilaration in the face of the piece, an overwhelmingly affective experience. Surmounting distances between our being and the world, this pleasure of wonder aided by nature and artifice is the gift that Eliasson's work consistently makes to us.

NOTES

1. Olafur Eliasson, in Doug Aitken, *Broken Screen: 26 Conversations with Doug Aitken; Expanding the Image, Breaking the Narrative*, ed. Noel Daniel (New York: D.A.P., 2006), 114; Eliasson, "Vibrations," in *Olafur Eliasson: Your Engagement Has Consequences; On the Relativity of Your Reality*, by Olafur Eliasson et al. (Baden, Switzerland: Lars Müller Publishers, 2006), 72.

2. Bruce Millar, "The Sun King," *Times Magazine* (London), March 20, 2004.

3. Michael Kimmelman, "Putting the Spectator at the Center," *International Herald Tribune*, March 16, 2004.

4. When I use the term *museum* I mean here and henceforth the kinds of progressive institutional practices that are particularly evident at contemporary art museums. I use the word *spectacle*—whose meaning has evolved since it was first popularized by Guy Debord's seminal book *The Society of the Spectacle* (1967; repr., New York: Zone Press, 1994)—to refer to a specific effect of advanced capitalism, in which an excess of scale and dramatic effect (often conveyed through commercial images) infuses social experience, at times at the expense of independent values and personal determination.

5. A 1977 memo from Warner Communications, quoted in Greil Marcus, *Lipstick Traces: A Secret History of the Twentieth Century* (Cambridge, MA: Harvard University Press, 1989), 44.

6. My description of the museum's work here is of course limited to characteristics relevant to the present discussion. The museum is also many other things, not least of which a vehicle for aesthetic enjoyment and instruction.

7. Jeremy Rifkin, *The Age of Access: The New Culture of Hypercapitalism, Where All of Life Is a Paid-For Experience* (New York: Jeremy P. Tarcher, 2000), 140.

8. Ibid.

9. Conversely, and to complicate matters further, the museum is now being drawn into the commercial realm as never before, as is apparent in the architectural keying of new museum buildings to recreation, retail, and tourism. These buildings are becoming increasingly important in cities' urban and economic planning, a phenomenon nicknamed the "Bilbao effect" for the impact that the Guggenheim Museum's Frank Gehry–designed building has had on that Spanish city since the structure opened to the public in 1997.

10. See Frazer Ward, "The Haunted Museum: Institutional Critique and Publicity," *October* 73 (Summer 1995): 71–89.

11. Ibid., 73.

12. Gilles Deleuze writes, "The more our daily life appears standardized, stereotyped and subject to an accelerated reproduction of objects of consumption, the more art must be injected into it in order to extract from it that little difference which plays simultaneously between other levels of repetition." Quoted in Hal Foster, *The Return of the Real: The Avant-Garde at the End of the Century* (Cambridge, MA: MIT Press, 1996), 68.

13. For an astute discussion of the post-avant-garde tactic of using aspects of capital against itself rather than positing a violent break with the status quo, see Rosalind Krauss, "The Cultural Logic of the Late Capitalist Museum," *October* 54 (Autumn 1990): 11.

14. For a more general survey of Eliasson's career see my "Attention Universe: The Work of Olafur Eliasson," in *Olafur Eliasson*, by Madeleine Grynsztejn et al. (London: Phaidon, 2002).

15. Maurice Merleau-Ponty, quoted in Francisco J. Varela, "The Reenchantment of the Concrete," in *Incorporations*, ed. Jonathan Crary and Sanford Kwinter (New York: Zone Books, 1992), 331. *Room for one colour* demonstrates Eliasson's debt to the insights of phenomenologists such as Merleau-Ponty and Varela as well as Henri Bergson and Edmund Husserl, with whom he shares the conviction that human experience, including perception, is embedded in a corporeal self, that the world is accordingly understood from within a physiological being, and that reality is conditioned by a perceiver who is him- or herself always responsive to unfolding circumstance.

16. Ibid., 330.

17. See Scott Bukatman, "The Artificial Infinite: On Special Effects and the Sublime," in *Visual Display: Culture Beyond Appearances*, Discussions in Contemporary Culture 10, ed. Lynne Cooke and Peter Wollen (New York: Dia Art Foundation, 1995), 258.

18. Olafur Eliasson, "Conversation between Olafur Eliasson and Hans Ulrich Obrist—Berlin, October 2001," in *Chaque matin je me sens different, chaque soir je me sens le même* (Paris: Musée d'Art moderne de la Ville de Paris, 2002), n.p.

19. Olafur Eliasson, quoted in Markus Wailand, review of *Surroundings surrounded* at the Neue Galerie am Landesmuseum Joanneum, Graz, Austria, *Frieze*, no. 5 (September–October 2000): 127.

20. For a more extensive reading of the sources and effects of *Notion motion*, see Mieke Bal's essay in the present volume.

21. Jonathan Crary on the work of Robert Irwin, in "Robert Irwin and the Condition of Twilight," in *Robert Lehman Lectures on Contemporary Art*, vol. 3, ed. Lynne Cooke and Karen Kelly with Bettina Funcke (New York: Dia Art Foundation, 2004), 83.

22. Ibid., 80.

23. These terms belong to the philosopher Jean-Luc Nancy, whose writings on community have influenced current artistic practices centered on social collaboration. See in particular chapter 1 of *The Inoperative Community*, ed. Peter Connor (Minneapolis: University of Minnesota Press, 1991), and "Of Being-in-Common," in *Community at Loose Ends* (Minneapolis: University of Minnesota Press, 1991), 1–12. Nancy does not see the experience of community as secondary or extrinsic to a way of being in the world; to the contrary, "We are saying that community is the decisive mode" ("Of Being-in-Common," 2). He starts not from the solitary subject or individual but from the relation of being "in common, with one another" (ibid., 6). In this respect, "the Cartesian subject would form the inverse figure of the experience of community" (*The Inoperative Community*, 31).

24. Guy Debord, in *On the Passage of a Few People through a Rather Brief Moment in Time: The Situationist International, 1957–1972*, ed. Elisabeth Sussman (Boston: Institute of Contemporary Art / MIT Press, 1989), 198.

25. It is important to note here the difference (as I see it) between Eliasson's practice and the socially collaborative art that is sometimes described under the rubric of relational aesthetics, a term coined by Nicolas Bourriaud in his 1998 book *Relational Aesthetics*, trans. Simon Pleasance and Fronza Woods with Mathieu Copeland (Dijon, France: Les presses du réel, 2002). Proliferating in the 1990s, this kind of art making typically appropriates extant social structures and proffers situations wherein the public is central as both material and audience. While Eliasson's work creates a social dimension, it does not employ normative social forms as media. Perhaps, having grown up in Denmark, considered an exemplary model of a social welfare state, Eliasson is slightly skeptical of enterprises committed to social good, lest they teeter too easily into dogma. Not surprisingly, the Scandinavian contemporary-art community is at the forefront of socially engaged artistic practices and their theoretical articulation. See essays by Claire Bishop and Lars Bang Larsen in *Participation*, ed. Bishop (London: Whitechapel Ventures Limited; Cambridge, MA: MIT Press, 2006), 10–17 and 172–83, respectively.

26. Jürgen Habermas, *The Structural Transformation of the Public Sphere: An Inquiry into a Category of Bourgeois Society*, trans. Thomas Burger with Frederick Lawrence (Cambridge, MA: MIT Press, 1991), 201.

27. Miwon Kwon, "Public Art as Publicity," *republicart*, http://www.republicart.net/disc/publicum/kwon01_en.htm (accessed April 18, 2007; my italics).

28. Hilde S. Hein, *The Museum in Transition: A Philosophical Perspective* (Washington, DC: Smithsonian Institution Press, 2000), 150.

29. The reasons for this shift are many. For one, the American museum establishment has increased efforts to reach out to segments of the public not previously considered to be among its primary audiences. This move comes in part in the wake of 1980s multiculturalism, but greater attendance has also been urged by economic pressures—fed by museum expansions in the 1980s and 1990s combined with decreased public funding—that make it more crucial to offset expenses with admission revenues. Further incentive comes from sources of funding—government agencies, private corporations, and other public sectors—that measure the success of their contributions by attendance figures.

30. The Hirshhorn's undertaking is in progress at the time of this writing, and I give my heartfelt thanks to Olga Viso, the museum's director, for sharing the gist of it with me in a conversation on August 24, 2006.

31. B. Joseph Pine II and James H. Gilmore, *The Experience Economy: Work Is Theater and Every Business a Stage* (Boston: Harvard Business School Press, 1999), 16.

32. Alicia Framis, quoted in Nicolas de Oliveira, Nicola Oxley, and Michael Petry, *Installation Art in the New Millennium: The Empire of the Senses* (London: Thames & Hudson, 2003), 106.

33. See Ward, "The Haunted Museum," 72.

34. Jonathan Crary, "Eclipse of the Spectacle," in *Art After Modernism: Rethinking Representation*, ed. Brian Wallis (New York: New Museum of Contemporary Art, 1984), 293.

35. Hal Foster, *Design and Crime: And Other Diatribes* (London: Verso, 2003), 162.

36. Contemporary museums and installations like Eliasson's are not altogether free spaces, of course, for they are necessarily conditioned and constrained by the parameters of site and artwork. "I create semi-totalitarian structures, if you like," says Eliasson—structures that generate an inherently guided, if purposeful, action. See Joachim Bessing's interview, "Experiencing Space: Olafur Eliasson," in *The light setup*, exhibition brochure (Lund, Sweden: Lunds Konsthall; Malmö, Sweden: Malmö Konsthall, 2005), n.p.

37. Lest we think that the museum has overnight succumbed to audience-broadening (i.e., market) forces, it is worth noting that the museum's use of media associated with entertainment goes back to the first such institution founded in the United States, in Philadelphia in 1786, by the painter Charles Willson Peale, who coined the term *rational amusement* to describe his crowd-pleasing enterprise. Conversely, should we wonder about the roots of present-day popular entertainment, we might note that Peale's collection was eventually taken over by P. T. Barnum. The museum's current period of populism dates back to 1976 and the Metropolitan Museum of Art's blockbuster traveling exhibition *Treasures of Tutankhamun*, and it was further advanced in the 1980s with the development of "event-space" museum architecture. More recently, and especially since the mid-1990s, contemporary artists have increasingly flirted with fashion, celebrity, and popular culture, appropriating their forms of representation in ways that sometimes risk being more collusive than critical. Eliasson's own involvement with projects affiliated with BMW (he is presently designing the company's sixteenth "art car" using the frame of a hydrogen-powered BMW) and Louis Vuitton (in 2005 he contributed an elevator/environment to its Paris flagship store) keeps him on constant alert to the art/entertainment divide.

38. Ward, "The Haunted Museum," 89.

39. Jonathan Crary, *Suspension of Perception: Attention, Spectacle, and Modern Culture* (Cambridge, MA: MIT Press, 1999), 3 (my italics).

40. Olafur Eliasson, in *Projects 73: Olafur Eliasson; Seeing yourself sensing*, exhibition brochure (New York: Museum of Modern Art, 2001), n.p.

41. Hal Foster, "What's Neo about the Neo-Avant-Garde?," *October* 70 (Fall 1994): 26.

42. Andrea Fraser, one of today's most eloquent practitioners of and writers on institutional critique, remarks, "It's not a question of being against the institution: We are the institution. It's a question of what kind of institution we are, what kind of values we institutionalize." Fraser, "From the Critique of Institutions to an Institution of Critique," *Artforum* 44, no. 1 (September 2005): 283.

43. It needs to be said that the museum profession is no stranger to self-reflection and self-analysis: it has voluntarily examined its own inner workings for decades. Particularly since the 1960s period of social activism, a revisionist "New Museology" has rigorously questioned the museum's approaches to issues of value, meaning, access, control, interpretation, and authenticity in relation to representational practices, particularly as to how one culture may represent another. This literature is large, important, and ongoing.

44. Brian O'Doherty's articles, originally printed in *Artforum*, are collected in his book *Inside the White Cube: The Ideology of the Gallery Space* (Santa Monica, CA, and San Francisco: Lapis Press, 1976).

45. John Rajchman, *Constructions* (Cambridge, MA: MIT Press, 1998), 18, 8.

46. Dan Graham describing his own work, in *Two-Way Mirror Power: Selected Writings by Dan Graham on His Art*, ed. Alexander Alberro (Cambridge, MA: MIT Press, 1999), 158. I quote Graham here to underline his work's obviously important precedent for Eliasson's explorations. Not coincidentally, the mirror is a master trope in the history of art—like perspective and geometric optics, it is among the classic devices that Eliasson employs only to subvert.

47. For the San Francisco Museum of Modern Art's survey exhibition, it should be noted, Eliasson is developing a new piece, titled *Space reversal* (2007), that draws on *Omgivelser*'s visual vocabulary.

48. These objects are drawn from the basement of Eliasson's Berlin studio, a space he shares with his sometime collaborator, the Icelandic artist and architect Einar Thorsteinn, a specialist in the study of complex geometric forms.

49. So Maximillian Misson, a seventeenth-century tourist and *Wunderkammer* connoisseur, described the cabinet of Count Mascardo in Verona in an account published in 1699. See Lorraine Daston, "Curiosity in Early Modern Science," *Word & Image* (October–December 1995): 396. While the museum did not grow directly out of *Wunderkammern*, it was informed by them as well as by nineteenth-century world's fairs and international expositions. It is these latter models that most directly correlate to present-day institutional display.

50. This was the case with Peale's collection. In paintings made by Peale and his sons, the collection is shown with "portraits high on the wall . . . while lower forms of life . . . filled the cases and the floor below." In addition to "displaying insects, minerals, and fossils . . . additional rooms [held] tables for exhibiting experiments" as well as a mastodon skeleton and live and taxidermied animals. In one of the more extreme examples of curatorial multitasking, "When a live grizzly on display escaped and ran through the hall, Peale was forced to shoot him." See Susan Stewart, "Death and Life, in That Order, in the Works of Charles Willson Peale," in Cooke and Wollen, *Visual Display*, 32–33.

51. Stephen Bann, "The Return to Curiosity: Shifting Paradigms in Contemporary Museum Display," in *Art and Its Publics: Museum Studies at the Millennium*, ed. Andrew McClellan (Malden, MA: Blackwell Publishing, 2003), 122.

52. Barbara Maria Stafford, *Artful Science: Enlightenment Entertainment and the Eclipse of Visual Education* (Cambridge, MA: MIT Press, 1994), 51.

53. I say "again" because, as Bann has pointed out, wonder makes a cyclical appearance in museum culture and has in fact been revalorized in present-day practices, as museum professionals recognize once more that "being delighted and amazed is an important part of learning. . . . We are now experiencing a kind of historical *ricorso* to curiosity whose effects are often perceptible just where we might least expect them: that is, in the conception and display of immediately contemporary works of art." Bann, "The Return to Curiosity," 118.

54. Francisco J. Varela, *Ethical Know-How: Action, Wisdom, and Cognition* (Stanford, CA: Stanford University Press, 1999), 75.

55. Stephen Greenblatt, "Resonance and Wonder," in *Exhibiting Cultures: The Poetics and Politics of Museum Display*, ed. Ivan Karp and Steven D. Lavine (Washington, DC: Smithsonian Institution Press, 1991), 53.

56. Philip Fisher, *Wonder, the Rainbow, and the Aesthetics of Rare Experiences* (Cambridge, MA: Harvard University Press, 1998), 81.

57. Socrates, in Plato, *Theaetetus*, trans. Benjamin Jowett (Indianapolis, IN: Bobbs-Merrill Educational Publishing, 1949), 17.

58. See Fisher, *Wonder, the Rainbow, and the Aesthetics of Rare Experiences*, 33.

YOUR LIGHT AND SPACE

Pamela M. Lee

History is not external and objectified in a situation but is inside the spectator.
—Olafur Eliasson[1]

Your only real thing is time. You've paid a visit to a contemporary art institute, the hallowed white cube of curatorial lore, to find your expectations checked by a confounding situation. Usually when you go to such places your attention is drawn to a discrete object—a painting, a sculpture, a video installation—and said object tends to follow proper white-cube decorum, whether hanging quietly on a wall, sitting obediently on the floor, or confined to the dim recesses of a media theater. Here, though, your experience is less contemplative than restive, less pitched to aesthetic reflection than geared to tracking the multitude of effects produced by the peculiar array of materials set before you. In a dark room, Olafur Eliasson has constructed a visibly elevated platform on top of the floor; on it rests a pool of black water, edge to edge. A neon light mounted above, creating an orbit of concentric circles, flashes its reflection across the water's mirrorlike surface, a techno-simulation of a ripple effect (see pl. 13). With your vision barely adjusting to the space, you intuit—and then consciously acknowledge—the operational logic of the work. This peculiar chiasmus between light and space is ultimately continuous with your time as you move through the gallery: your time as it is interwoven with the constituent elements of the work. In the catalogue for this exhibition, which was staged at the Institute of Contemporary Art in Boston in 2001, Eliasson confirms this point by placing rhetorical stress on the ineluctable "now": "The sense of time that I work with is the idea of a 'now.' . . . There is only a 'now' . . . our belief in time is just such a construct."[2]

Your strange certainty still kept. Or consider this situation, first installed by the artist in 1996, in which a cinematic logic shapes your experience of viewing. There's water cascading from the ceiling, and strobe lights shine over the relieflike space (see pls. 14, 42). The plash of heavy drops—the concentrated sound of falling water— is matched in kind by the freeze-frame staging of the scene as the lights flash across the water's surface. As if a reel of film were momentarily stilled, sound and vision seem condensed to the level of a frame, each bead of water both articulate and articulated. You are allowed to observe closely what typically rushes by in an uninterrupted sequence. And you chart—if with the strange certainty afforded by the exposure of the work's technical apparatus—the manifold ways in which you process this sensuous datum, whether rain falling or lights flashing, your senses of hearing and seeing working perpetually in concert with each other.

The rhetorical device that introduces this essay—the use of the possessive pronoun *your* to situate the reader relative to the work—is consonant with the practices to which the text is devoted. Since the early 1990s, Eliasson has produced a body of work that variously engages questions of subject-object relations, exploring the ways in which the subject's encounter with his or her surroundings prompts larger revelations about the nature of perception itself. He takes recourse to a diverse array of media to dramatize these claims, often through seemingly meteorological investigations and their phenomena: rain, ice, sun, wind. Though Eliasson uses advanced media and collaborates freely with engineers and architects, he also mobilizes elemental but no less complex materials such

13
Olafur Eliasson
Your only real thing is time, 2001
Installation view at the Institute of Contemporary Art, Boston, 2001. Neon, water, scaffolding, and wood. The Dakis Joannou Collection, Athens

as light, water, moss, and mist to solicit the range of the human sensorium. What am I seeing here, the work seems to demand, and how am I made to see it? How does my body's trajectory shape the course of vision itself? In what ways does representation become reality, and, more pointedly, in what ways is my relation to nature predetermined by what one might call the technics of naturalization? Critics often invoke the traditions of the Romantic landscape and the sublime to describe Eliasson's work, but something even more fundamental is at play. As theoretical ballast for these investigations, Eliasson and those who write about him frequently call upon the discourses of phenomenology—especially the philosophy of Maurice Merleau-Ponty—to articulate the necessarily embodied and thus contingent act of perception in confronting his work.[3] Seeking an art-historical touchstone, the artist and his critics reach for a more immediate point of reference: the Light and Space movement associated with figures such as Robert Irwin and James Turrell in Southern California during the 1960s and 1970s. Eliasson's use of the possessive pronoun in his titles tallies perfectly with phemenological interpretations of his work as well as its references to the Light and Space movement.[4] Like Irwin and Turrell before him, Eliasson implicates his observer in a feedback loop of self-perception. "Seeing oneself seeing" is the oft-recited mantra articulating Eliasson's ambition for the viewer, and it is a phrase that goes far to explain one's immediate encounter with his work. But in this essay I want to push the implications of this conceit further, so as to historicize, if provisionally, its more recent perceptual logic. One has to

14
Olafur Eliasson
Your strange certainty still kept, 1996
Installation view at Tanya Bonakdar Gallery, New York, 1996. Water, strobe lights, acrylic, foil, pump, hose, and wood. The Dakis Joannou Collection, Athens

wonder, after all, what particular "you" occupies this privileged, because possessive, position. What imagined viewer is held in thrall to an imaginary conversation with the work of art, and can make claims for *owning* the experience by extension? In taking Eliasson at his word—in thinking not only about the "now" of the observer but also about time as "inside the spectator"—we need to ask what *your* light and space might mean for the current moment.

Indeed, critiques of phenomenology hold that its putative subject is timeless and universal, unmarked by any number of influences that shape one's experience of the world, whether economic, sociocultural, ethnic, national, or gendered. Eliasson himself has voiced suspicion of the ways in which phenomenology has been deployed in the service of normalizing spatial experience: in the art criticism of the 1990s, he opined, "phenomenology became a tool to justify a new kind of essentialism."[5] But light and space, as Eliasson's works amply demonstrate, are no mere abstractions. They are deeply material things. And, like all material things, they are equally subject to the pressures of history that frame the terms of their larger representation.

In the following, then, I stress the historical dimensions of light and space in Eliasson's art in part to address a question about reception. A critical debate on this artist's work turns on the ways in which he deliberately exposes the mechanisms producing his ambient effects, and on whether his work complies with the twinned logics of advanced capital and spectacular culture.[6] "At his most successful," one critic put it, "Eliasson creates situations that defy immediate comprehension while using very evident means."[7] The writer is referring to the fact that while Eliasson often makes work that compels or even awes the spectator with the theatrical, multisensory experience it provides, he never conceals the apparatus behind his illusions. The dazzling effects conjured by Eliasson's work, which typically takes natural phenomena as its point of departure, are simultaneously derealized for the spectator by the matter-of-factness of his props. Daniel Birnbaum puts it as such in writing on *Your sun machine* (pls. 47–50), staged at Marc Foxx Gallery in Los Angeles in 1997: "The overtness of the technical setup is typical of Eliasson's art . . . there is no concealment of how the effects are produced. . . . There are no secrets, just a fascinating optical phenomenon to behold."[8]

Nowhere was this notion better put to the test than in Eliasson's most famous piece, the monumental *Weather project* (2003; pls. 1–2, 15, 196–97) installed at the Tate Modern, London, as part of its Unilever Series. The Tate's enormous Turbine Hall set the stage for a virtual horizon, a crepuscular scenario dwarfing the more than two million viewers who flocked to see it during the course of the exhibition. At the back end of the hall, something like a gargantuan sun emitted an intense orange light, veiled occasionally by a cloudlike mist that appeared and dissipated throughout the day. It was as though a microclimate had invaded the Tate, causing meteorological phenomena to drift in and out of its cavernous space. Of course, this was a manifestly engineered landscape. Radiant nature had been domesticated by a complex media apparatus. The sun was, in fact, a half disc composed of hundreds of monofrequency lamps; the ceiling of the Turbine Hall had been covered in mirrors, which, by reflecting the half disc on the back wall, produced the illusion of a giant sphere.

The effects of this techno-horizon were such that the audience for *The weather project* engaged in a variety of behaviors out of character for the hushed spaces of a classical museum. As James Meyer colorfully describes it, visitors sprawled out on the floor of the Turbine Hall as if catching rays on an industrial beachhead.[9] In clusters they lay prone, gazing up into the vault and basking in their collective mirrored reflection, revealing the Tate itself to be "a narcissistic museum."[10] It was precisely this kind of behavior that led some, including Meyer, to assert that Eliasson's technics were captive to the workings of media spectacle and mass entertainment.[11] As an earlier citation suggested, arguments in this vein criticized the artist for producing "situations that defy immediate comprehension while using very evident means." They seemed to ask why this was a necessarily acceptable or even celebrated condition for the viewing of contemporary art. At what point had the museum, with its high Enlightenment pedigree, crossed over into the realm of sideshow or amusement park?

15
Olafur Eliasson
The weather project, 2003
Installation view at the Tate Modern, London,
2003. Monofrequency lights, projection foil,
haze machine, mirror foil, aluminum, and scaf-
folding. Courtesy the artist; Tanya Bonakdar
Gallery, New York; and neugerriemschneider,
Berlin

In later returning to *The weather project* I will discuss the ways in
which it renovates the terms of *your* light and space and, in the process, complicates
the reception of Eliasson's work from the position of both its detractors and its supporters.
For the terms through which this critical debate is expressed, I would argue, risk
distracting us altogether from another question of perception. The remainder of this
essay traces a path from one aspect of the Light and Space movement to Eliasson's

present activities. It does so through recourse to phenomena that inform a recent historiography of perception and the environment: the notions of habitability, on the one hand, and immersion, on the other. We shall see that the issues raised by both concepts are not only a function of the technology deployed, but also, far more importantly, of the expectations—and ideologies—each spectator brings to his or her encounter with the work of art.

Addressing Eliasson's work in relation to these ideas demands a genealogy of sorts, one that treats questions of art and the range of its media as keyed to the diverse workings of the sensorium. That the artist himself describes a strong affinity with Robert Irwin, as evidenced by the conversation in the very catalogue you now hold, suggests an art-historical kinship more pressing than the Romantic landscape painting to which Eliasson's environments are frequently compared. Of course, the connection between perception and art itself has a far longer history. It is a history of media. Since the eighteenth century, when G. E. Lessing elaborated the distinction between the spatial and temporal arts in his treatise *Laocoon*, we have been captive to a theory of the arts that classifies them into discrete media, each correlating to a specific sense, whether optic, haptic, or aural. This is one of the central tenets of modernism, and it finds its most (in)famous expression in the writings of Clement Greenberg.

Yet almost as long as this narrative has circulated, so too has a counternarrative that insists upon the interrelation of the various arts and, by extension, the interworkings of the senses. For the purpose of discussing Eliasson's reception, it is not incidental that these relations (or interrelations) were all but a given in the popular entertainments that emerged in the nineteenth century; Jonathan Crary has authoritatively addressed the ways in which the panorama, for example, dramatized the shifting character of the sensorium using the technics of industrialization.[12] There is a repressed account of intermedia in the arts as well, and it is one that Eliasson's work tacitly courts, particularly in its references to the Light and Space movement. By the 1960s, whether as an inadvertent or explicit challenge to Greenberg's modernism, theories of intermedia found diverse articulation, ranging from manifestos by the various members of Fluxus, to Donald Judd's "Specific Objects," to Marshall McLuhan's discussions of media as prosthetic subjectivity, to the multiple definitions of expanded cinema.[13] Given the overarching stress on perception in general accounts of Light and Space, its practices are surprisingly rarely discussed through the terms of intermedia. Yet it is this tradition in which we must locate the concerns raised by Eliasson's work today.

To be sure, the loose grouping of figures identified as Light and Space, "space-light," or "phenomenological" artists is associated with neither the brooding climes of the Nordic landscape nor Berlin's new urbanism (both signal points of reference in Eliasson's biography), but rather with Los Angeles in the 1960s. No programmatic statement guided the making of this work, and no collective exchanges on the part of the artists solidified a single critical or social position. Yet some forty years before Eliasson

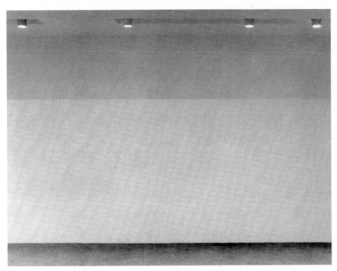

16
Robert Irwin
Eye Level Wall Division, 1973
Installation view at Pace Gallery, New York, 1973.
Wood and Sheetrock. Courtesy the artist

fashioned a construction out of mist, a curtain of water shot through with a strobe light, and installations incorporating moss and ice, the Light and Space movement was building toward a highly attuned exploration of human perception through hybrid forms of media. Artists as diverse as James Turrell, Maria Nordman, Eric Orr, Robert Irwin, and Michael Asher were producing work from materials that could only be described as ambient: light and shadow, fog and water, dampened noise (see pl. 16). The gestures employed in making this art were largely minimal, if not minimalist.[14] Whether through steady manipulations of the optical field or the scantest interventions into the mundane surfaces of architecture, these artists, critics repeatedly claimed, were mining the ever-rich terrain of the sensorium. They did so through the slightest calibration of color or noise or atmosphere, as if to recruit their respective audiences to a theater of cognitive reckoning.

Both period and contemporary surveys of the work have sought to find an overarching rationale to justify the movement's name. Too often they make use of the language of essences, whether natural or mystical, to describe the art's ambient sensibilities. As Jan Butterfield put it, making a taut comparison to minimalist sculpture, these works were "statements reduced to an essence."[15] This school of thought saw the work as belonging to a historical tradition that could at once claim Suprematism and Luminism as its heirs, as if invocation of the terms *light* and *space* as media was enough to explain what was specific to its respective practices.[16] By the same token, a certain state pride animated considerations of the work's myriad effects. "The effect of California itself on Light and Space art must not be ignored," Butterfield wrote with hindsight.

> The sunny skies, sparkling water, and soft sand are as much a part of the feeling of the place as subways, skyscrapers, and gridded streets are of Manhattan. To live in Southern California is to be conscious of curiously softened color and vast space. The quality of the light is striking.[17]

Considerations of the environment were formative to the Light and Space artists, but we need to question just what kind of environment this might be. The above statement, for one, is an argument for site-specificity of the picture-postcard variety. What the postcard metaphor itself calls forth is the photographic construction of nature. What goes missing in the assessment is any acknowledgment of mediation, as if the figures associated with Light and Space were exercising little more than a type of aesthetic nativism.

Opposing this reading of Light and Space art as merely illustrating California's natural light, other observers sought to describe the work through the language of spirituality: references abound to Zen Buddhism, tantric space, and the third eye. Hal Glicksman offered a more interesting, because seemingly contradictory, spin on this account; he vehemently rejected the idea of light as the movement's impetus, or at least the natural light of the canyons and beaches. "The interest in light phenomena," he noted, "relates, rather, to the interest in oriental mysticism . . . and to the presence in the area of the aerospace industry."[18]

For the contemporary reader, the merging of "oriental mysticism" and the aerospace industry may seem entirely perverse: Glicksman's take on the quasimeditative aspects of much of this work seems at odds with an offhanded reference to technology. And yet Southern California's peculiar confluence of the aerospace and entertainment industries—not to mention a very particular history of "oriental mysticism"—surely had as much to do at that time with the question of light and space as with any unmediated relation to the environment.[19] In fact, the terms *aerospace* and *entertainment* would give rise to one of the most infamous art and technology collaborations of the decade, the Art and Technology Program sponsored by the Los Angeles County Museum of Art. From 1967 to 1971 the program sought to forge ties between corporate industry—a Lockheed International or an IBM, for example—and a startling range of contemporary artists, including such unlikely cohorts as Jean Dubuffet, Öyvind Fahlström, and Tony Smith. More than seventy collaborations were established during the course of the program.[20] As Maurice Tuchman, the curator of the eventual exhibition, wrote:

> A newcomer to this region is particularly sensitive to the futuristic character of Los Angeles, especially as it is manifested in advanced technology. I thought of the typical Coastal industries as chiefly aerospace oriented (Jet Propulsion Laboratory, Lockheed Aircraft); or geared toward scientific research (The Rand Corporation, TRW Systems); or connected with the vast cinema and TV industry in Southern California (Universal Film Studios).[21]

To certain sensibilities, the contemporary landscape Tuchman paints is drear, sharing nothing with images of glorious sunsets in Malibu, the impossibly golden dream of Southern California ideology. Instead he frames (though without a critic's prejudice) a peculiar topography of the environment in which the culture industry finds its logical ally in the military-industrial complex. The meshing of these conditions is critical for a number of artists associated with Light and Space—especially Irwin and Turrell. It is their contributions to the Art and Technology Program that prove most meaningful in relation to Eliasson's practice. Indeed, Eliasson has consistently partnered with engineers and designers in the production of his work (a frequent collaborator is the artist and architect Einar Thorsteinn), and in 2006 his studio hosted a symposium related to his concept for a hydrogen-powered car for BMW (see pl. 130). As we shall see, this kind of event resonates strongly with the scientific ambitions of the Light and Space movement.

Irwin and Turrell were ultimately to collaborate with the Garrett Corporation, one of the "patron sponsors" of the Art and Technology Program. Founded by Cliff Garrett in the 1940s, the company became a critical player in Los Angeles's aerospace (especially military) industry in the 1960s. Its investigations into the possibility of manned spacecraft led to new forms of scientific research. According to a promotional notice in the back pages of the museum's publication, "Its Life Sciences Department developed environmental control systems (temperature, pressure, air purity) for all NASA space vehicles. Its simulation of weightlessness helps research into long-life space missions."[22] This is of interest not just because so much art of this period tapped into a generalized space-age aesthetic (think of the work of Larry Bell—a participant in the Art and Technology Program and, it turns out, one of Irwin's collaborators), but also because questions of controlling the environment through advanced technology were bedrock to many of the explorations of the Light and Space movement.

Irwin had drawn up a list of "techniques and experimental phenomena" he wished to study through the program, "including Space craft cabin/support environment: investigations necessary to determine what perceptual awarenesses are necessary for basic orientation and stability."[23] It was the Garrett Corporation—and, in particular, the research of Dr. Edward Wortz—that would solidify Irwin and Turrell's research plans. Head of the organization's Life Sciences Department, Wortz was trained as an experimental psychologist focusing on "human perceptual responses in special conditions" (namely manned lunar flights and outer space); his knowledge of new perceptual technologies would prove critical for the Light and Space artists. Irwin, Turrell, and Wortz engaged in a number of intensive experiments for the Art and Technology Program, including research on sensory deprivation involving meditation and biofeedback, anechoic chambers (environments insulated from noise and external stimuli), and so-called Ganzfelds. The Ganzfeld would enjoy a certain acclaim in the Light and Space movement. As Wortz explained, it is

> a visual field in which there are no objects you can take hold
> of with your eye. It's a complete 360 degree field, or at least
> has to include total peripheral vision, and it's entirely homog-
> enous in color, white in our case. . . . Its unique feature is that
> it appears to be light filled. That is, light appears to have sub-
> stance in the *Ganzfeld.*[24]

This idea was particularly influential for Turrell, a former student of psychology; the manipulation of these fields became the basis for his artistic practice long after his collaboration with Irwin and Wortz ended.[25]

17–18
Robert Irwin, Larry Bell, and Frank Gehry
Design for conference room, First National
Symposium on Habitability, Venice, California, 1970

Such experiments with anechoic chambers and Ganzfelds point ultimately to the significance of habitability for Irwin, Turrell, and others in the Art and Technology Program, for both devices prompt questions about technological stimuli and the perception of the environment. Habitability is a concept of marked importance for space-age astrophysicists, engineers, biologists, therapists, and sociologists. Concerned with the sustainability of life systems within a given environment, it can be linked more broadly to the interest in systems that emerged in the postwar moment. In the late 1960s the exploration of such issues was undertaken by scientists working with NASA and the aerospace industry. For their part, Irwin and Wortz convened the First National Symposium on Habitability, which took place May 11–14, 1970, in the artist's studio in Venice, California (see pls. 17–18). In a novel conference setting designed by Irwin, Bell, and Frank Gehry (and in discussion rooms devised by Bell, Duane Valentine, Ed Moses, and Irwin), participants from both academia and private industry addressed the concept of habitability from a variety of disciplinary perspectives, including the humanistic concerns with which the artists more actively engaged.[26] Wortz's invitation to conference participants defined the terms of the symposium:

> [It] will be concerned with "habitability" as a general phenomenon influencing the planning of undersea vehicles and stations, lunar bases, space stations, space craft, terrestrial vehicles and structures, and urban settlements. The symposium will probe our current understanding of the concept of habitability; the factors which influence the quality of life associated with various environments; the need for and characteristics of habitability criteria; the planning and design of a "habitable" environment; and will further seek to develop testable hypotheses relevant to this subject.[27]

In short, habitability was code for understanding humanity's relation to a changing (because futuristic) environment. And yet, for all the talk of cohabitation, the four-volume documentation of the proceedings reveals more than a little tension between the scientists and humanists. How one communicated the terms of these new environments—how one measured or represented *responses* to them—polarized the symposium's respective audiences. For Wortz, one of the objectives of the conference was "to bring together people who deal with factual knowledge and people who deal with intuitive knowledge. The two live in very distinct . . . realities. Unfortunately in our society their realities are seldom integrated."[28] The artists' contributions to the discussion suggest a fundamental split between the language of scientific communication and that of humanist discourse. In listening to three scientists struggle to speak about the humanistic dimensions of habitability, Irwin detected a pronounced hostility to the more intuitively minded speakers: "I somehow link the problem of verbal expression and the topic of our symposium together. I feel in some sense that the idea of verbal communication—putting forth ideas abstractly—is somehow the seat of the problem in making progress in habitability."[29]

Wortz and Irwin's observations distill the challenges of the symposium to the matter of communicating intuitive information (undoubtedly related to the work of the artists and humanists) and factual information (the domain of the hard sciences). The terms through which the perception of the environment is articulated, and the stress placed on the divide between personal experience and scientific knowledge, are narrated as a disciplinary struggle: sensory intuition cannot logically be reduced to scientific or technical data. Another way to frame the conflict is to view it as that which is considered real (the actuality of one's experience) butting up against the forms of cultural representation that encode it.

Though the relative failures of the symposium recall the frisson or even divisive character of many art-and-technology collaborations of the 1960s, a more contemporary theory of habitability might see a far happier rapprochement, a point critical for Eliasson's reception. Indeed, the rhetoric through which Eliasson's art is commonly described suggests a different set of conditions motivating our relation to the environment. The notion of immersion, for one, might nuance accounts of Eliasson's work and its implications for the contemporary viewer.

When critics address Eliasson's media, they first tend to describe those elemental materials—water, ice, air—that recommend him as heir apparent to an erroneous reading of the Light and Space artists. Something about these media appeals to romantic or primitivizing sensibilities, insofar as their use is understood as a kind of artistic "statement reduced to an essence." As my interpretation of Irwin's habitability investigations shows, the art of Light and Space was not native, naive, or essentializing; it participated in a highly mediated and thoroughly technical approach to problems of human perception specific to its era's technological desideratum. It should go without saying that the same is true for Eliasson's work today, whether his art addresses media issues tacitly or specifically relative to questions of perception. In referring to his works as machines (as in the title *Your sun machine*), Eliasson himself renders this notion explicit. The tacit side of the equation, however, underscores what we might call an ethos of immersion, both in the general sense of the word (the feeling that one does not stand apart from the environment but is actively implicated within it as a participant) and in its technological multivalence (the simulacral worlds generated by the computer and digital technology). One would be more than hard-pressed to call Eliasson a computer artist, but this should not prevent us from considering how the effects his work generates and the critical reception it produces have internalized a model of immersion associated precisely with those worlds.

To this end, I need return to *The weather project* to detail how the critical reception of Eliasson's work dovetails with an ethos of immersion. I have described how the literature on his art speaks to an apparent contradiction: how the frequently seductive character of his environments—the illusionism—is matched in kind by his frank exposure of the apparatus. It is this tension that animates debates on his practice, particularly the extent to which it might traffic between intuitive and factual information (to borrow the language of habitability) and the ways in which his ambient effects jostle against the mechanisms of their representation. This has led to readings that either support or critique his work but are largely unable to theorize the coexistence of these seemingly contradictory positions as necessarily entwined perceptual *and* historical phenomena—as the material, in other words, of *your* light and space. As one writer reflected on *The weather project* and the unusual behavior it engendered on the part of its audience, "How does one dazzle without deceiving?" Her answer is largely affirmative, speaking to the installation's popular appeal: "Eliasson's work both seduces visitors and helps them lose their inhibitions. It forms a theatrical space where they can talk and react. Accessible and interpretable on every level, apolitical and ultimately a generator of collective emotional experiences, this is art for all."[30]

In contrast to the view that sees the work as democratic (the author inevitably refers to Eliasson as one of the most popular contemporary artists), James Meyer sees something problematic in the reception of *The weather project.* Deliberating on the question of scale in contemporary art, Meyer singles out Eliasson's work as effectively abusing the terms of scale wrought by the discourses associated with minimalist sculpture in the 1960s. Meyer is no mere art-world pundit; as an authority on Minimalism, he has written exacting texts on the uses of phenomenology within that movement's critical reception. Writing on the trend to fill the spaces of the contemporary museum with ever more gargantuan and spectacular installations, Meyer sees

The weather project as dwarfing its viewers so that no active—that is, critical—mode of spectatorship is possible. Leaving aside the question of how the term *spectacle* is theorized in contemporary art criticism, he posits that *The weather project* is emblematic of "an instrumentalization of the phenomenological tendency itself, within a scenario of unrelenting global museological competition."[31]

Whether in support or critique of Eliasson's art, both forms of reception take an all-or-nothing approach to his practice. And this approach, I think, presents a stumbling block with respect to elaborating a genealogy of his work that addresses his media's historical relation to the sensorium. Speaking to the coexistence of the work's spectacular effects alongside the revelation of the technologies that produce them, one critic wrote:

> The two tendencies in Eliasson's ambient works can't really be reconciled. But then again there is no reason why they should be. In the art practices of the last decade there has been a proliferation of strategies that all, in different ways, pit the ambient and the visualist against one another on each side of a divide that separates (bad) specularity from (good) forms of subversion or escape. But this groping for the imagined outside to the spectacular might also be symptomatic of a form of naiveté (or a disposition for moralizing) to which Eliasson's works, for all their evident niceness, are not necessarily prone.[32]

I agree that there is nothing remotely naive about Eliasson's practice (his grasp of his work's relationship to the museum as institution is nothing if not insightful). Yet I would also argue that the two positions are not so much irreconcilable—which suggests that they stand in dialectical relation to each other—as they are *coextensive.* Within the context of the First National Symposium on Habitability, where hard-nosed scientists clashed with intuitive artists and humanists, no such claim could be made: disciplinary languages were such that Irwin noted a profound disconnect between abstraction and verbal communication. Yet the historical terms that inform Eliasson's practice provide a different model for reflecting on what might appear a perceptual aporia.

Indeed, the epiphenomena associated with immersion might explain some of the knotty contradictions accorded Eliasson's work. It bears saying that immersive technologies stem from the same military-industrial impetus at the root of the 1970 symposium. By the 1980s, the notion of immersion had gained widespread currency with the rise of virtual reality, computer games, and the attendant cybercultural literature: the experience of walking on the moon, trawling the depths of the ocean, or voyaging the cosmos was, to follow many contemporary accounts, elaborated as a virtual theater of the sensorium.[33] By no means was this a passive theater, however. Immersion's not-so-subtle paradox is that the illusionistic worlds into which the user plunges—weightless, disembodied worlds where time, light, and space are effectively suspended as so much techno-artifice—are de facto conjoined to the awkward mechanisms that produce their perceptual effects, whether VR helmets, gloves, motion simulators, or joysticks. Any phenomenology of this media would have to reject the euphoric claims made about the seamless and dematerialized interface between hard and soft worlds. It would need to consider the movement between eye and body—the crux of Merleau-Ponty's chiasmatic intertwining—as mediated by the terms of very contemporary technical protocols.[34]

Though I would want to retain the historical specificity of this notion for an understanding of Eliasson's work, and will return to the implications of this history for the digital culture it implicitly courts, a phenomenology of the virtual undoubtedly inherits something from much earlier forms of media. The effects of an immersive sensibility are not solely the terrain of computer technology: the notion of a viewer seduced by media while wholly cognizant of its illusionistic mechanisms is at the root of popular narratives of the nineteenth century.[35] In his work on "the cinema of attractions," Tom Gunning has demonstrated that common anecdotes about early film audiences have remained largely unquestioned.[36] The myth holds that the first screenings of the Lumière brothers' *actualités* in 1895 produced a collective panic, with viewers actually believing a train was roaring toward them out of the depths of cinematic space. What this suggests is an acritical or naive relation to the medium on the part of its spectators. Gunning goes far to debunk the notion that viewers ran terrified from theaters as if incapable of separating representation from reality. Instead, his critical history of the period describes a form of reception based on the simultaneity of both viewing positions—of being immersed in the world represented *and* utterly aware of its technologies. In the process, they reject the sense that viewers were mere dupes to the spectacular effects of new media.

In line with such readings of early film, a theory of the cinematic apparatus—a form of media critique that foregrounds techniques of representation—could likewise inform Eliasson's immersive sensibilities. Elaborated under the influence of psychoanalysis in the 1970s, apparatus theory details the ways in which cinema produces what Jean-Louis Baudry calls "an impression of reality" more real than real—as if in a dream or Plato's cave.[37] This otherworldly impression, however, is predetermined by the material conditions and technics of cinema, whether the projection of the film or the physical situation of the viewer in a dark theater. For many writers on the topic, then, the relation between the dreamlike quality of the spectator's experience and the unimpeachable physicality of the apparatus expresses the ideological effect of cinema at its very foundation. What gives an impression of reality in a film scene is like ideology itself: its truths might appear self-evident, transparent, or real, but they are necessarily continuous with the material and social conditions of its construction and projection.

We might ascribe a comparable logic to Eliasson's immersive sensibilities.

19
Lars von Trier
Still from *Dogville*, 2003
35mm film, 178 min. Courtesy Lions Gate
Entertainment / Photofest

In fact, the artist himself consistently acknowledges certain movies as thematically and structurally consonant with the perceptual logic his environments stage. He has, for instance, spoken frequently about *The Truman Show* (1998), a movie in which the Jim Carrey protagonist discovers his life has been put on display for a mass television audience—a kind of mise-en-abyme media nightmare. Likewise, Eliasson has also made explicit reference to the films of the Dogma group as analogous to the exposure of his staging techniques. Lars von Trier's *Dogville* (2003), for instance, was entirely filmed on a soundstage; the devices usually conscripted to produce the illusion of the mise-en-scène were wholly denaturalized by the staginess of the town's representation (see pl. 19).

These references from the intermedia domain suggest that the terms of *your* light and space for Eliasson are far more expansive than his reception typically affords. On the one hand, this may be a question of art-historical and critical method and how it applies to contemporary material: How, in other words, are historical influences rationalized in discussions of very recent work? But the break—and continuity—between Light and Space in the 1960s and 1970s and *your* light and space today also underscores an issue of transparency at the heart of these respective practices, however historically removed they may be from each other. Indeed, this illusion of transparency is even more pervasive in the contemporary environment, where digital technologies enact progressively more seductive impressions of reality, from video games to the virtual world of Second Life to the dazzling special effects of blockbuster films. What, then, is at stake for Eliasson's audiences, who collectively embrace the illusions of his "natural" environments while remaining utterly aware of their mechanisms? Perhaps the technics of ideology—as much as the phenomenology of the subject—are what Eliasson's perception machines are staging. Perhaps his work illustrates the terms by which we perceive and accept everyday reality—whether nature or the museum or the amusement park—as so much techno-mediation.

NOTES

1. Jessica Morgan, interview with Olafur Eliasson, in *Olafur Eliasson: Your Only Real Thing Is Time* (Boston: Institute of Contemporary Art; Ostfildern-Ruit, Germany: Hatje Cantz, 2001), 16.

2. Olafur Eliasson, quoted in Jane Ingram Allen, "Putting the Viewer First: Olafur Eliasson," *Sculpture* 20, no. 8 (October 2001): 30.

3. Among many examples, see Madeleine Grynsztejn et al., *Olafur Eliasson* (London: Phaidon, 2002).

4. I am hardly the first writer to highlight this aspect of Eliasson's work. Among many examples of criticism that speak to this conceit, see Ina Blom, "Beyond the Ambient / Jenseits des Atmosphärischen," trans. Bram Opstelten, *Parkett*, no. 64 (May 2002): 20–31.

5. Olafur Eliasson, in Tim Griffin, "In Conversation: Daniel Buren and Olafur Eliasson," *Artforum* 43, no. 9 (May 2005): 213.

6. By "spectacular culture" I refer to the considerable art-historical literature that takes Guy Debord's notion of the spectacle as its critical touchstone for theorizing the aestheticization of everyday life and the penetration of both the public and the private sphere by relations of advanced capital. See Debord, *The Society of the Spectacle* (1967; repr., New York: Zone Books, 1994). The very use of the term *spectacle* has been subject to debate; some suggest that Debord's very specific formulation of the term has been conflated with more generalizing notions of "media spectacle."

7. Carol Diehl, "Northern Lights," *Art in America* 92, no. 9 (October 2004): 113.

8. Daniel Birnbaum, review, *Artforum* 36, no. 8 (April 1998): 106–7.

9. James Meyer, "No More Scale: The Experience of Size in Contemporary Sculpture," *Artforum* 42, no. 10 (Summer 2004): 220–28.

10. I borrow this provocative phrase from Miwon Kwon. In an informal conversation, Kwon used this expression to describe *The Eye of the Storm*, Daniel Buren's 2005 exhibition at the Solomon R. Guggenheim Museum, New York. At the center of Frank Lloyd Wright's famous building, Buren placed a structure covered with mirrors that reflected the museum's interior architecture and

its viewers. Interestingly, *Artforum* has published a conversation between Buren and Eliasson that variously addresses both artists' relation to the museum as institution and the uses of phenomenology in art criticism (see note 5).

11. See Meyer, "No More Scale."

12. See Jonathan Crary, *Suspensions of Perception: Attention, Spectacle, and Modern Culture* (Cambridge, MA: MIT Press, 1999). Crary has written on behalf of Eliasson's work from the perspective of nineteenth-century questions of aesthetics and perception (see his "Visionary Abstraction," in *Olafur Eliasson: Your Lighthouse; Works with Light 1991–2004* [Wolfsburg, Germany: Kunstmuseum Wolfsburg; Ostfildern-Ruit, Germany: Hatje Cantz, 2004], 20–32).

13. See Donald Judd, "Specific Objects" (1965), reprinted in *Complete Writings, 1959–1975* (Halifax: Press of the Nova Scotia College of Art and Design; New York: New York University Press, 2005), 181–90; Marshall McLuhan, *Understanding Media: The Extensions of Man* (London: Routledge, 2001); and Gene Youngblood, *Expanded Cinema* (New York: Dutton, 1970).

14. On Minimalism versus Light and Space, see Rosalind Krauss, "Overcoming the Limits of Matter: On Revising Minimalism," in *American Art of the 1960s*, ed. John Elderfield (New York: Museum of Modern Art, 1991), 123–41.

15. Jan Butterfield, *The Art of Light and Space* (New York: Abbeville, 1993), 14.

16. Ibid., 15.

17. Ibid.

18. Hal Glicksman, interview with Marge Goldwater, in *Los Angeles in the Seventies* (Fort Worth: Fort Worth Art Museum, 1977), 5.

19. In point of fact, the convergence of certain practices associated with "oriental mysticism"—namely, sitting meditation—was understood by many practitioners at the time to be consonant with the operations associated with cybernetics, systems theory, and their technological and therapeutic applications, such as biofeedback. Certain schools of Buddhism in particular were seen as compatible with theories of deep ecology, itself informed by systems

theory. On this relation, see Joanna Macy, *Mutual Causality in Buddhism and General Systems Theory* (Albany: State University of New York Press, 1991).

    As an interesting historical addendum to this phenomenon of the 1960s, I need mention that Dr. Edward Wortz, who would play a critical role in Robert Irwin's technological investigations, was, until his death in 2005, a highly regarded therapist within the Buddhist community of Southern California and wrote widely on meditation. See Michael Anderson, "Interview with Ed Wortz," prod.aps. roadhouse.com.au/units/interest_groups/ buddhism/publications.asp (accessed January 16, 2007).

20. The program's final results were notoriously uneven and the resulting criticism ferocious. For an introduction to the controversies surrounding these types of collaborations in the 1960s, see my "Eros and Technics and Civilization," in *Chronophobia: On Time in the Art of the 1960s* (Cambridge, MA: MIT Press, 2004).

21. Maurice Tuchman, *A Report on the Art and Technology Program of the Los Angeles County Museum of Art, 1967–1971* (Los Angeles: Los Angeles County Museum of Art, 1971), 9.

22. Ibid., 366.

23. Ibid., 127.

24. Edward Wortz, quoted in Craig Adcock, "Perceptual Edges: The Psychology of James Turrell's Light and Space," *Arts Magazine* 59, no. 6 (February 1985): 124.

25. Turrell was invited to participate in the program on Irwin's recommendation; he eventually dropped out after disagreements with Irwin and Wortz.

26. Andrew Perchuk has addressed the particular staging of the conference room—and the symposium more generally—in his research on Irwin's role in the Los Angeles art world from the 1950s through the 1970s: "Robert Irwin: Against the Gestalt" (lecture, Getty Research Institute, Los Angeles, May 1, 2004). See also the section on habitability in his *From Otis to Ferus: Robert Irwin, Ed Ruscha, and Peter Voulkos in Los Angeles, 1954–1975* (PhD diss,

Yale University, 2006), 149–52.

27. Edward Wortz, quoted in Tuchman, *Report*, 141.

28. Edward Wortz, in *First National Symposium on Habitability*, vol. 4 (Los Angeles: AiResearch Manufacturing Co., 1971), 150.

29. Robert Irwin, in *First National Symposium*, 63.

30. Ann Colin, "Olafur Eliasson: Vers une nouvelle réalité / The Nature of Nature as Artifice," trans. C. Penwarden, *Art Press*, no. 304 (September 2004): 39.

31. For an essay that challenges the use of Guy Debord's theory of the spectacle in recent art criticism, see Dan Smith, "Size Matters," *Art Monthly*, no. 282 (December 2004–January 2005): 1–4. Smith's piece is a pointed rebuttal to Meyer's account of *The weather project* in "No More Scale." For Meyer's discussion of Eliasson's work as global spectacle, see page 226 of that text.

32. Blom, "Beyond the Ambient," 23.

33. Two well-known accounts of immersion and virtuality are Howard Rheingold, *Virtual Reality* (New York: Simon & Schuster, 1991), and Brenda Laurel, *Computers as Theater* (Menlo Park, CA: Addison Wesley, 1991).

34. For a brilliant reading that takes seriously the phenomenological dimensions of new media, see Marc Hansen, *New Philosophy for New Media* (Cambridge, MA: MIT Press, 2004).

35. On predigital histories of immersion, see Erkki Huhtamo, "Encapsulated Bodies in Motion: Simulators and the Quest for Total Immersion," in *Critical Issues in Electronic Media*, ed. Simon Penny (Albany: State University of New York Press, 1995), 159–86.

36. Tom Gunning provides a more historically nuanced reading of the credulous spectator in "An Aesthetic of Astonishment: Early Film and the (In)credulous Spectator," in *Viewing Positions: Ways of Seeing Film*, ed. Linda Williams (New Brunswick, NJ: Rutgers University Press, 1994), 114–33.

37. One of the classic texts of apparatus theory is Jean-Louis Baudry, "The Apparatus: Metapsychological Approaches to the Impression of Reality in Cinema" (1975), reprinted in *Film Theory and Criticism*, ed. Leo Braudy and Marsha Cohen (Oxford: Oxford University Press, 1999), 760–77.

TAKE YOUR TIME: A CONVERSATION

Olafur Eliasson and Robert Irwin

Olafur Eliasson: I've really looked forward to talking with you, because we seem to share certain interests—in temporality, for instance. Temporality is one of the few elements of my artistic practice that keeps growing in both meaning and implication, and what I particularly value in your work is the way in which you try to do justice to temporality by ascribing greater value to relativity. I believe that devoting attention to time has far-reaching consequences for the idea of objecthood and the dematerialization of the object. Artworks are not closed or static, and they do not embody some kind of truth that may be revealed to the spectator. Rather, artworks have an affinity with time—they are embedded in time, they are of time. This is why I sometimes call my works experimental setups; they are structures with which visitors can engage.

The value we ascribe to these unstable and unpredictable structures is much more relative than what we encounter in the experience industry as we know it today. A focus on temporality can become a threat to this industry, I think. Your work and mine are being disseminated by a type of experience industry called museums, which have more or less consciously taken it upon themselves to create a sense of timelessness in the objects they display. And they do this on our behalf.

Robert Irwin: But if they do, and we do let them do it, we're making a big mistake.

OE: Exactly. That is why I have decided to call the exhibition *Take your time*. Taking one's time means to engage actively in a spatial and temporal situation, either within the museum or in the outside world. It requires attention to the changeability of our surroundings. You could say that it heightens awareness of the fact that our actions have a specific speed, depending on the situation. The question is whether such temporal engagement is supported by society as well as by museums. Often the answer is no. So I think it is our responsibility as artists to challenge the shape of the museum, since museums claim to communicate the values of society.

RI: The museum is an old, old model that was set up essentially to deal with objects. You and I are not object makers; we're dealing with experiential processes. The museum structure is geared toward a particular kind of art making, which represents a particular set of values. What we're proposing is another set of values. Museums have to respond to that in kind. Right now there is no methodology to deal with the phenomenal in art.

OE: I first became interested in phenomenology when I was an art student, as it seemed to offer a means for understanding subjectivity and the ways in which one could engage with one's surroundings. But I have sensed a danger in phenomenology's being presented

20
Olafur Eliasson and Robert Irwin, San Diego, California, March 2006

as a kind of truth; there's a tendency to detach experience from social context by justifying it as a phenomenological situation. And it is a more dynamic conception of phenomenology, of course, that has been a source of inspiration in my work. To me the greatest potential of phenomenology lies in the idea that subjectivity is always susceptible to change. I like to think that my work can return criticality to the viewer as a tool for negotiating and reevaluating the environment—and that this can pave the way for a more causal relationship with our surroundings. Whereas earlier decades looked to phenomenology as a sort of formula that constitutes our surroundings, I think the 1990s showed that it can instead be a tool for negotiating these surroundings. It offers an inquisitive, explorative approach to the world that allows for multiple perspectives on artworks, subjectivity, and experience.

RI: When I was starting out I had a similar problem. In the sixties, when my paintings were acting out their own demise, I had the idea that nonobjective was going to translate as nonobject—i.e., purely phenomenal—but that was a red herring. While the same reasoning that had moved us away from a pictorial reality—from pictorial to phenomenal—applied equally to the realm of objects, it had nothing to do with object/nonobject; it had to do with how we see the object in context. Once you realize this, you've put yourself in a place in which everything is understood in sets of conditions. There may be such a thing as a universal or "high" art—it's certainly a pretty idea—but it's not the reality of our everyday world. In fact, everything is subject to fluctuating sets of conditions that in themselves are not static, and this dynamic of a world of qualities is the stuff of real-time perception.

OE: I agree.

RI: I try to deal with all those conditions. I'm also wrestling with the history of modern art. The big move is when we eliminate abstract references to art history, and the person walking through the work doesn't have to know anything about you or art. That puts it on the most immediate social level, because the observer's referencing the same cues you are. It's no longer an abstract referencing, it's an experiential one. Which is what I mean by phenomenological: it's made in real time.

We're in this funny spot right now—we've got one foot in museums, but philosophically we also have one foot over here. The game we're playing is riddled with contradictions—the world isn't going to change just because you and I feel this way. Basically, we're making things that may have implications for change. But we have to deal with the idea of the museum as a forum. The museum is a representation of a moment in time, and it eventually becomes a historical model. That's the natural evolution of museums. When a collection grows, the museum may end up showing incredible art—there's nothing wrong with that—but it doesn't maintain its position as an open forum.

What we're asking the museum to be is a forum for dialogue in which we can exercise just what we're doing right now. A museum can do that, generally, for only a very short period of time. We participate anyway, because that's how we interface as artists and work out the issues of being artists. But at the same time, in doing so, we actually compromise the critical point.

OE: I don't think a museum must be either a collection or a forum. If you take the ideas we've just discussed and apply them to the museum, its collection can become a forum—that is, a platform for discussion. I do think there's a way, and I have great faith in the spectator and in the self-reflective experience.

RI: Well, you and I are both optimists of the first order! But I have not seen any museum maintain its focus or commitment to acting as a forum. Twice I tested the parameters of the museum. The first time I was ever asked to do an installation, it was in 1970 and strangely enough at the Museum of Modern Art, New York. Jenny Licht, a very special woman, called me out of the blue and said she had an empty room I could play with. Unfortunately, she said, because the museum hasn't programmed it, there is no money and nobody can assist you, but would you be interested? I, of course, said yes, and then she told me I would have to do most of my work at night when the museum was closed. To say the least, it was a difficult task . . . pug-ugly little room next to a gallery filled with Brancusi sculptures. So now I am in there at night and I don't know how or what I'm

21
Robert Irwin
Untitled, 1970
Installation view at the Museum of Modern Art,
New York, 1970. Scrim, fluorescent tubes, and
stainless-steel wire. Courtesy the artist

going to do, and I have to walk in and out looking at these Brancusis, which are absolutely brilliant. What I finally did [pl. 21] was very simple—so simple as to be on the verge of nonexistent. The one feature of the room was a deep-set, slotted skylight the length of the space, with five corresponding lines of fluorescent lights set well up in the slot and an old-fashioned egg-crate light filter (two inches deep) flush with the surface. First I cleaned the skylight of years of scum. Then I changed out every other line of fluorescents so they alternated warm and cool, and the egg-crate filter fractured the light into very subtle bands of light-dark-warm-cool rainbows throughout the room. I then added a partial, translucent scrim ceiling to reproportion the room and float the rainbows of light in space. Add a disembodied stainless-steel line that suspended the eye in space, and you got a wonderful sense of color and space, seemingly without a source.

Now mind you, MoMA did not acknowledge, announce, or write about it. And yet in the end they insisted on institutionalizing it by putting a label on it. Of course, the minute you do this you automatically qualify it as "art," and in turn this usurps the role I have created for the observer: Is it there? Is it finished? How do I feel about it? Is it art? So I hired a kid to remove the label each day. In the short term this work resulted in a series of small installations lasting only as long as Jenny Licht did . . . but in the end the Modern hasn't been the Modern in years.

Later, in 1977, I was asked to do a retrospective by Marcia Tucker at the Whitney Museum of American Art. Instead I took the opportunity to ask (and act out) a proposition. If you ask the question "If perception is the pure subject of art, can we hold the dialogue for art to be the equal of making?" the answer is no. To make a long story short, to exercise this proposition I did a series of works—and a series of observations outside the museum—that in effect dissolved the walls of the museum as context and posited making as nonessential. But in the end the institution simply acted as if that part never existed. They don't even know that they own the whole thing, figuratively speaking. You know, it's like veils. I tell you something, and then I tell you something else; the more I do that, the less you're able to see.

OE: Only the veil metaphor is problematic, because it seems to suggest that art lies *behind* the veils. What is special in the case of conditional experience is, I think, what I sometimes call the introspective quality of seeing: you see whatever you're looking at, but you also see the way you're seeing. You can find pleasure or fear in what you're experiencing, but your experience of the thing is integrated as a part of the thing itself.

RI: "Perceiving yourself perceiving" is the phrase I use.

OE: Or "seeing yourself seeing"—I probably took that from you! Anyway, the potential lies in its deconstructive nature. I guess *deconstructive* is not quite the right word here, but it works: we can consider the surroundings as constructions, not truths.

RI: They're just conditions.

OE: Right. This implies that the museum has to make its ideology accessible to visitors, but many museums lack the self-criticality to make this happen. And it is not just the art world that is focusing on the quality, nature, and construction of experience—these issues have turned out to be big business in our experience economy. I think these examples are generally much less sophisticated, however, as the experience economy tends to patronize and commodify our feelings and perceptions. Therefore, it's as important as ever to focus on the self-evaluative quality of experience. This may sound naive, but I think you can apply introspective and self-evaluative tools to any situation—and this ultimately gives you the opportunity to reposition yourself in society.

RI: I share your naivete there. One of the things about being alone in the studio, which a lot of artists are most of the time, is that you sometimes think you have no contact. That you're not actually doing something in the world, that art is isolated. And that's a tough illusion to live with.

I actually like to think of art and philosophy as being very close together. This explanation is a little simplistic, but it makes the point clearly: I open my eyes in the morning, and the world appears totally formed. I don't sit there and think about that. I swing my legs around the edge of the bed, and I take the whole world with me— which is an incredibly complex thing to do. Everything appears given—not only given but actually accounted for. I don't ask myself, "How did I do that?" I just get up and go take a shower. But if I were to lie there for even an instant, two amazing things would be revealed: I would perceive that *I* actually put it together, and that it is *not* a given.

But if the mind actually had to think about what the body is telling it at every instant, it couldn't function. Now that just blows my mind. We've developed all these canons of philosophy and meaning having to do with the idea of consciousness, awareness, or cognition. But there's always this conceit that the mind somehow operates in a vacuum. In my view, the history of phenomenology—and, I think, modern art—is about the introduction of the opposite as an equal player. No hierarchy about the mind being more important than the body. I like to use the term *co-arising*, which doesn't make either perception or cognition sound more real or important. They're equally dependent and mutually exclusive. And yet, so that we can function, they operate as if they are one. The role of artists is, in a sense, to continually examine what's going on there. Not to be corny, but they step on the other side of that veil.

OE: This is also where feelings come into it. We've always been told that feelings are introverted states. It's curious that so little work has been done on the nature of feelings until recently; cognitive scientists, for example, have begun to focus on them. Our culture promotes a split between the mind and the body, which doesn't allow for an understanding of feeling as an extroverted activity.

RI: Right. A feeling is not just a response, it's an action.

OE: A feeling is a relationship between a mental and a physical state—it implicates both mind and body.

RI: That's what I mean by co-arising.

OE: And the idea that you as perceiver become a producer is the key issue here. You project your feelings onto your surroundings—this is how you relate to them.

RI: That's because values are essentially invested by your feelings. I see something, and by seeing it—attending to it, spending time with it, acting on it—I give it value. And so value is not neutral; once negotiated, it ultimately becomes a piece of you. It can reconstruct how you practice, or how you move in the world. In time, that has the implication of changing the structures around you. But it's a long-term project. The real change that comes from feelings and values has to be seeded, in a sense, and then it begins to act on things—on you, and then on how you make decisions and judgments, and therefore on how you construct the world.

OE: That is really a crucial concept. I have been doing some research on the relativity of white light used in museum spaces, the point being to emphasize the fact that the white cube is a construction. In my Berlin laboratory we have a white room for experiments with different kinds of light based on real-life observations in Reykjavík, Venice, and other cities. You can work in a really detailed way with the color spectrum of white light. Even though I still find the white cube a fairly attractive model to engage with, I think we owe it to the spectators to tell them that this kind of space is embedded in a long history, that it is culturally coded. There are so many things involved in viewing art—that's what makes it such a rich and complex field. How can we consider representation in a productive light? How may we deal with our memories of previous artworks when looking at a new one? All along there has been a hierarchy of the senses that influences the way we experience.

RI: The work I made in the next room here at the Museum of Contemporary Art San Diego [pl. 22] raises a lot of the questions you've just posed. It's very interesting—the room exists because somebody decided not to wall it up. Why did they leave it? It's a particularly arresting view. I've seen people walk into that gallery and say, "Well now, *this* is art. This is beautiful." And I've heard other people argue that it should've been walled up. I had no idea what to do at first. I mean, nobody had ever used that room, because it's not very usable—not many walls, and a little too much light, and it's got to compete with this view. So I got the idea of cutting a window. Not bad, but not enough. When I cut the window in the angle of the corners, that really resolved it. Then some interesting things happened that I had not anticipated. One is that the glass being tinted makes the cutout appear to be more in focus . . . add all the sounds and the air and so forth and it becomes, on a visceral level, more real. Suddenly all these issues about reality and meaning as "real" are all jumbled up. Because the minute you introduce the frame, you've introduced the old context of representation. To have the real thing instead of the representation within the frame, you suddenly have to wrestle with the idea of why this is *not* art.

OE: True, but I would like to suggest that the experience of something representational is not, qualitatively speaking, a less important kind of experience. To me there is nothing nonrepresentational. In art history there seems to be a tendency to insist that the real is better than the representational. I've often thought about you when I've said that looking at something representational is not about the quality of the experience; it's about whether the author of that representational image has the guts to acknowledge it's representational.

RI: Well, here's something that maybe we should kick around a little bit: the use of the term *real*. I'm of the opinion that most discussions about reality are not about reality at all—they're about meaning. I say to you, "The reality of the situation is . . . " and then I give you my point of view. I try to take reality and put it on my side. But there is nothing that's not real on one level or another. And so it's never really about reality per se—it's about this game of meaning. When you have a frame and a representation, that assumes a whole structure of meaning. And when you flatten that out, you're really having an argument about which of these meaning structures is most significant. The key here—

22
Robert Irwin
1° 2° 3° 4°, 1997
Installation view at the Museum of Contemporary Art San Diego, 1997. Apertures cut into existing windows. Museum of Contemporary Art San Diego, museum purchase in honor of Ruth Gribin with funds from Ruth and Murray Gribin and Ansley I. Graham Trust, Los Angeles

and I think it's really important—is that it's not an either/or situation. Modern art, basically, is both/and.

Piet Mondrian, for example, lays out a kind of whole new way of seeing. He starts with a subject like a tree and slowly takes it all the way down to the plus/minus paintings—to pure energy. He gives you different ways of seeing the tree. Neither is more real or important than the other, but they give you different realities.

OE: And they say something about each other as well.

RI: Yes. They are, as they say, perfectly complementary. I love the idea of two truths existing simultaneously—or three or four or five. That throws a wrench in the whole works, in a way. It suggests an entirely different idea of social organization.

Have you ever heard of a little book by Edwin Abbott called *Flatland*?

OE: Yes, I know it.

RI: The interesting thing about the book is that having described the rules of Flatland, Abbott introduces the third dimension. The beauty of it is that no matter what happens in the third dimension, there is a two-dimensional explanation for why it is not, in fact, true. Actually, I think that right now we're wrestling with how to go from a three-dimensional model to a four-dimensional one. How do you actually do that? How do you deal with a four-dimensional way of seeing? And what kind of social practice or order will result?

OE: Exactly. I have worked with that as well, and I have several names for it. The most obvious one that comes to mind is the fifth dimension—the fourth being time. It might also be called the dimension of engagement, because it allows for a greater relativity in our understanding of the other three or four dimensions. To emphasize the importance of engagement, I have tried to connect it with temporality by introducing the idea of *Your Engagement Sequence,* or YES. Any situation or object can be made relative and negotiable if you insist that YES is a necessary component of the perceptual process. We could say that YES destabilizes truth, turning it into an individual experience.

RI: So, adding the observer.

OE: Yes. The key issue is the role of the engaged spectator or user. The question is whether the activities or actions of that user in fact constitute the artwork. Let's say that without the participation of the user there is nothing. This is not a new idea, but we need to take it to the point of saying that the user is the source of the artwork. And the psychology—the memories, expectations, moods, and emotions—that a person brings to the work is an important part of it. The word *user,* by the way, might seem utilitarian, but I find it rather lovely and demystifying. I don't mind considering art in a slightly

23
Robert Irwin
Part I: Prologue: x18³, 1998
Installation view at Dia Center for the Arts, New
York, 1998. Scrim, theatrical gel, and fluorescent
tubes. Courtesy the artist

utilitarian perspective, since we need, I think, to engage more directly with society.

At the end of the 1980s the Light and Space artists were highly inspirational to me, as they really worked with the subject as a projector or producer of the context—as a highly sophisticated and resourceful agent of dematerialization. I first encountered your work, and that of Maria Nordman, through books. I found it really complex and exciting. I was, to be honest, completely shocked, because it seemed so relevant to me. When I saw your 1998 work *Prologue: x18³* [pl. 23] at Dia Center for the Arts, what struck me was that it was about society and identity and subjectivity. The installation was really a part of the city; it was about the spatial questions that one has to resolve every day.

RI: The subject/object thing was something that I stumbled upon, in a way, in the 1960s. Frank Stella was doing his octagonal paintings at that time, with the holes in the center, and I was doing the dot paintings. And he said to me, "Why do you go to all that trouble to fold the canvas under and clean up the edges?" I said, "Because it's there and needs attending. Why don't you?" And he said, "Because it's not important." Wow, that just blew my mind. Somebody presents you with this absolutely clear distinction, and you realize you're talking about two different kinds of seeing.

In other words, I look around at the world, and it's loaded with these kinds of frames. But, actually, there are no frames in our perception. It's a continuous envelope in which we move. You realize that framing is a device. If I want to get from here to there, certain pieces of information are critical. So there are things that become focused—framed, in a way—and things that become invisible. I call these structures highly stylized learned logics—which is not to say that they're not real or functional. This is not an either/or proposition—it's both/and. And that's a big difference. Once you allow for the possibility of two kinds of "reality," it changes all the rules of the game.

If you break the frame of the painting/object you lose something very critical—the existing cultural agreement. Every mark made on a canvas, for someone conversant with the history of painting, can be weighed with and against the whole history of marks, underwriting a sophisticated and nuanced understanding. Initially when you break the frame you only have the crude question of in/out, since this in/out is a clear issue raised by the radical history of modern thought. The question for the modern artist is not just what would be the extended "frame of reference," but also how would it work.

OE: At least for the time being, the breaking of the frame *is* the new frame. It might be perpendicular to the old idea of the frame, but it is also a frame.

RI: Well, I suppose it could be structured into one. But for the artist making the initial inquiries, the immediate issue modern art presented to our generation is what would a nonhierarchical structure look like and how would it work. The piece I did at Dia— when I finished it I had a great uneasiness about it; there was something I couldn't put my finger on. I kept going back there, and I finally realized I had something that was a pretty good example of a nonhierarchical structure. I hadn't set out to do that, even though I'd been talking about it for a long time. You could enter the piece from any point; there was no beginning, middle, or end. At every point you had a minimum of eight choices to make, but there was no hierarchy in those choices. And when you left, you found the necessity to go back to it again, because it didn't have handles on it.

OE: It was also nonhierarchical in terms of time. One of the reasons I went back was that not one moment seemed more important than another, which for an artistically organized experience is very unusual.

RI: I very much like the idea that you aren't led through something or told where to go, but instead are given a continuous set of qualitative choices. The choices are not dictatorial in any way. You're the one who has to make them. You're put in this position of actually constructing the aesthetics of the experience as you go, because each time you make a choice you change the nature of the experience.

OE: Yes—this is particularly evident in ephemeral situations. It's very hard for us to classify the ephemeral, but there are interesting ways of probing our individual responses to these situations. For example, I've done a couple of afterimage works using a screen that completely surrounds you. One is called *360° room for all colours* [pls. 167–72]. If two people enter at different times, the mixture of the afterimage and the projected light will give each person a different impression of color. If you enter while the screen is blue, your eye will produce an orange afterimage; if I come in while it's green, my eye starts to produce red. But your afterimage is going to fade from orange to red and mine will not. So it's like a little house of individuality. After ten minutes, we may start seeing the same thing, physiologically speaking, but we may still think something different.

RI: You've obviously thought a great deal about interfacing with the observer. I think the thing that's crucial is not having an ambition for them on their behalf—some idea of correctness or meaningfulness.

OE: Yes, I completely agree.

RI: Most of our histories are in fact homogeneous—that is, once our most basic concepts are in place. On the basis of their seeming permanence we can progress in an orderly manner. And like rungs on a ladder we seem to progress upward, replacing or refining one idea with another to gain those wonderful structures we call civilizations. Over time, based on their success, these structures can take on the character of beliefs. The structures that we live in and through permutate into structures that live in and through us. In effect, even though we invented them, at some point we become captives of them. This makes questioning them one of the hardest things a human being can do.

Having said that, the history of modern thought is a radical history. To know this you only need to witness the radical reductions in art through the nineteenth century—attempts to find a place to begin again. The philosopher Edmund Husserl best characterized this process as the need for a phenomenological reduction . . . a going back to the beginning to ask the critical question "How might it be otherwise?" So all the things we're talking about are ways of rethinking this. The shift from object to subject, and from being to circumstance, is right at the heart of the matter.

For thirty years, everything I did didn't exist. I love that as a question. I mean, "What do you mean, it doesn't exist?" Let's assume, for a second, that it's art. It challenges the whole idea of how art is dealt with or presented, how it's accumulated, how histories are made. And so you realize that these things have structural, social, critical implications. They ask questions that need to be sorted out by society. It's going to take a long time before we see whether or not it actually works, and how it works, and what kind of social structure it makes, because we're changing all the rules of the game. At this point we can only speculate about what the results might be.

This text is an abridged version of a conversation recorded at the Museum of Contemporary Art San Diego on March 27–28, 2006. The artists and the San Francisco Museum of Modern Art thank Hugh M. Davies, Stephanie Hanor, Rachel Teagle, and Jenna Rowe for their hospitality and assistance, and Karen Levine and Anna Engberg-Pedersen for their work on the transcript.

PROJECTS 1991–2001

Project descriptions by Apsara DiQuinzio.

Artwork dimensions are variable unless otherwise indicated. "EXH." denotes works in the SFMOMA presentation.

24
Mental, 1993
Installation view at Charlottenborg
Udstillingsbygning, Copenhagen, 1993.
Mirror with sound. Courtesy the artist; Tanya
Bonakdar Gallery, New York; and neugerriem-
schneider, Berlin

A mirror covers the wall on the short side of a
gallery, matching the exact height and width
of the space and visually doubling the length
of the room. Entering the gallery, the viewer
hears the soft, rhythmic pulse of the artist's
heartbeat.

25
Wannabe, 1991
Installation view at Café Krasnapolsky,
Copenhagen, 1991. Spotlight. Courtesy
neugerriemschneider, Berlin

A single spotlight is mounted on the ceiling
and directed onto the floor. The cone of white
light beckons visitors to stand illuminated in a
public space.

26–27
I believe, 1992
Installation views in Copenhagen, 1992.
Billboards mounted on aluminum. Each
110 1/4 x 149 2/3 in. (280 x 380 cm). Courtesy
the artist; Tanya Bonakdar Gallery, New York;
and neugerriemschneider, Berlin

Approximately fifty billboards placed throughout
the city display the same digitally manipulated
photograph: a mirror image of light radiating
through cloud formations in the sky.

28
Infinity, 1991
Installation view at Overgaden—Institut for
Samtidskunst, Copenhagen, 1992. Projector
and color filter foil. Kunstmuseum Basel,
Switzerland

A projector with a blue filter, suspended from
the ceiling, throws a luminous horizontal line
onto the long wall of a darkened gallery at
the artist's eye level. The blurred contour of
the line mimics that of the horizon.

29
Expectations, 1992
Installation view in Copenhagen, 1992. HMI
lamp, color filter foil, tripod, and lens. Courtesy
the artist; Tanya Bonakdar Gallery, New York;
and neugerriemschneider, Berlin

An unannounced weeklong intervention in
which a lamp in the courtyard of a building
cast a lambent red line across the brick facade,
evoking the natural horizon.

30
Moss wall, 1994 (EXH.)
Installation view at the Neue Galerie am
Landesmuseum Joanneum, Graz, Austria, 2000.
Wood, moss, and wire. Courtesy the artist;
Tanya Bonakdar Gallery, New York; and
neugerriemschneider, Berlin

A hidden wood-and-wire structure anchors
reindeer moss to a gallery wall. Throughout
the duration of the installation, the expanse
of soft moss changes shape and color, giving
off natural odors in the process.

31
Beauty, 1993 (EXH.)
Installation view at the Hara Museum of
Contemporary Art, Tokyo, 2005. Fresnel lamp,
water, nozzles, hose, wood, and pump.
Museum of Contemporary Art, Los Angeles,
purchased with funds provided by Paul Frankel

In a dark room, a curtain of fine mist sprays
from a perforated hose mounted on the ceiling. A spotlight shines obliquely through the
mist, producing a rainbow that is only visible
to viewers from certain perspectives.

32–33
No nights in summer, no days in winter, 1994
Installation views at Forumgalleriet, Malmö,
Sweden, 1994. Steel, gas, and flame. 29 2/3 x
29 2/3 in. (65 x 65 cm). Courtesy the artist;
Tanya Bonakdar Gallery, New York; and
neugerriemschneider, Berlin

A blue ring of burning gas hangs from the ceiling near one wall of an empty gallery, generating
a loud hissing noise that fills the space. As viewers
approach, the sensation of heat intensifies and
they notice the flickering flames.

34–35
Suney, 1995
Installation views at the Künstlerhaus
Stuttgart, Germany, 1995. Mylar. Courtesy the
artist; Tanya Bonakdar Gallery, New York; and
neugerriemschneider, Berlin

A yellow Mylar sheet bisects a gallery into two
unequal spaces, each with a separate entrance.
When viewers standing on either side look
through the transparent plastic, the opposite
space appears to be a yellow room.

36–39
*Eine Beschreibung einer Reflexion,
oder aber eine angenehme Übung zu deren
Eigenschaften* (A description of a reflection,
or a pleasant exercise on its qualities), 1995
Installation views at neugerriemschneider,
Berlin, 1995. Projector, projection foil, mirrors,
motor, and tripod. Collection of Christian
Boros, Berlin

A round reflective panel, resting at an angle,
divides a darkened gallery from floor to ceiling.
A projector suspended from the ceiling directs
a beam imitating daylight onto a small concave
mirror in a corner of the gallery. The mirror
bounces the light onto a motorized, bent mirror affixed to a tripod behind the reflective
panel. This rotating mirror reflects a moving
pattern of light onto the stretched surface,
where visitors see its dynamic magnification.

40
Crystal stone wall series, 1996 (EXH.)
Thirteen framed gelatin silver prints. Each
10 5/8 x 13 in. (27 x 33 cm); 49 5/8 x 59 1/8 in.
(126 x 150.2 cm) overall. San Francisco Museum
of Modern Art, fractional and promised gift of
James and Dana Tananbaum

This irregularly shaped grid of black-and-white
pictures hones in on changing patterns of
basalt in the Icelandic landscape. The close
distance at which they were taken turns the
jagged natural rock formations into photographic abstractions.

41
Thoka, 1995
Installation view at the Kunstverein in Hamburg, Germany, 1995. Floodlights, fog machine, fans, color filter foil, and control unit. Courtesy the artist; Tanya Bonakdar Gallery, New York; and neugerriemschneider, Berlin

This site-specific work for the Kunstverein's front facade remained illuminated from dusk until midnight, when an automated controller turned it off. A fog machine, floodlights, and fans affixed to the facade behind translucent panels of glass generated an effulgent, yellow cloud of light that blurred the contours of the building. During daylight viewers could see the structural components comprising the work.

42
Your strange certainty still kept, 1996
Installation view at Tanya Bonakdar Gallery, New York, 1996. Water, strobe lights, acrylic, foil, pump, hose, and wood. The Dakis Joannou Collection, Athens

In a dark gallery, water circulates through a low-tech plumbing system consisting of a per-forated hose, a basin, and connective piping. Droplets of water noisily rain down from the hose fixed to the ceiling; the basin collects the water and redirects it through a pump. Strobe lights attached to the ceiling capture droplets as they descend, making them seem frozen in time.

43–44
By means of a sudden intuitive realisation, 1996
Installation views at the Inhotim Centro de Arte Contemporânea, Minas Gerais, Brazil, 2006. Fiberglass, plastic sheets, water, pump, and strobe light. 198 x 198 x 120 in. (502.9 x 502.9 x 304.8 cm). Inhotim Centro de Arte Contemporânea

For the original version of this work, conceived for *Manifesta 1* in Rotterdam, the Netherlands, the artist placed a white, geodesic dome over an existing fountain in a garden. A strobe light inside seemingly suspended the droplets of water during their descent. The work has since been re-created for a private collection in Brazil; here the artist constructed a fountain inside the readymade dome.

45
The waterfall series, 1996 (EXH.)
Fifty framed chromogenic prints. Each 15 x 10 1/4 in. (38 x 26 cm); 81 3/4 x 114 in. (207.6 x 289.6 cm) overall. Collection of Arthur and Carol Goldberg

The images comprising this series have been altered using colored photographic filters to emphasize the unique attributes of each Icelandic waterfall depicted.

46
Die organische und kristalline Beschreibung (The organic and crystalline description), 1996
Installation view at the Neue Galerie am Landesmuseum Joanneum, Graz, Austria, 1996. Projector, wave machine, convex mirror, and color filter foil. Thyssen-Bornemisza Art Contemporary (T-B A21), Vienna

Light generated by a powerful, freestanding projector passes through a wave machine con-taining layers of colored foil and bounces off a large convex mirror into a darkened space. As viewers walk through the room, the luminous yellow projection produces undulating effects on the surrounding walls while natural light passes through blue filters lining the windows. The combined effect renders the illusion of sun-light refracting through water.

47–50
Your sun machine, 1997
Installation views at Marc Foxx Gallery, Los Angeles, 1997. Aperture cut into existing roof. Courtesy the artist and Tanya Bonakdar

For this site-specific piece, the artist cut a circular hole in the ceiling, permitting a beam of sunlight to enter the gallery. Throughout the course of each day, as the earth rotated around the sun, the gleaming circle traveled through the room, moving across the walls and floor before disappearing at nightfall.

26

27

28

29

30

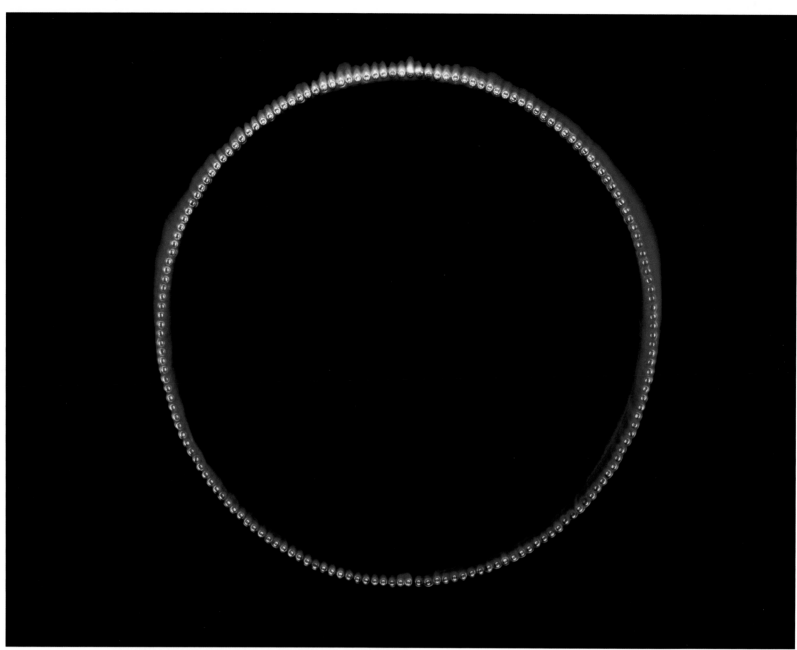

32

33

34

35

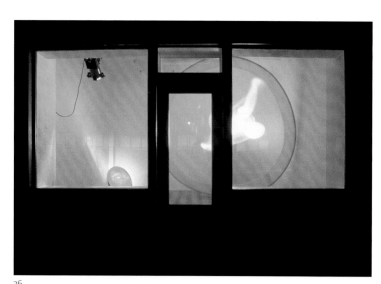

36

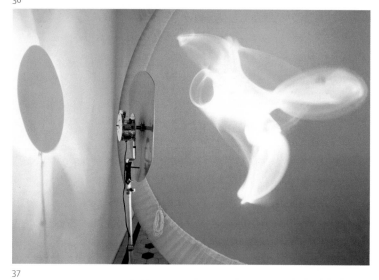

37

38

39

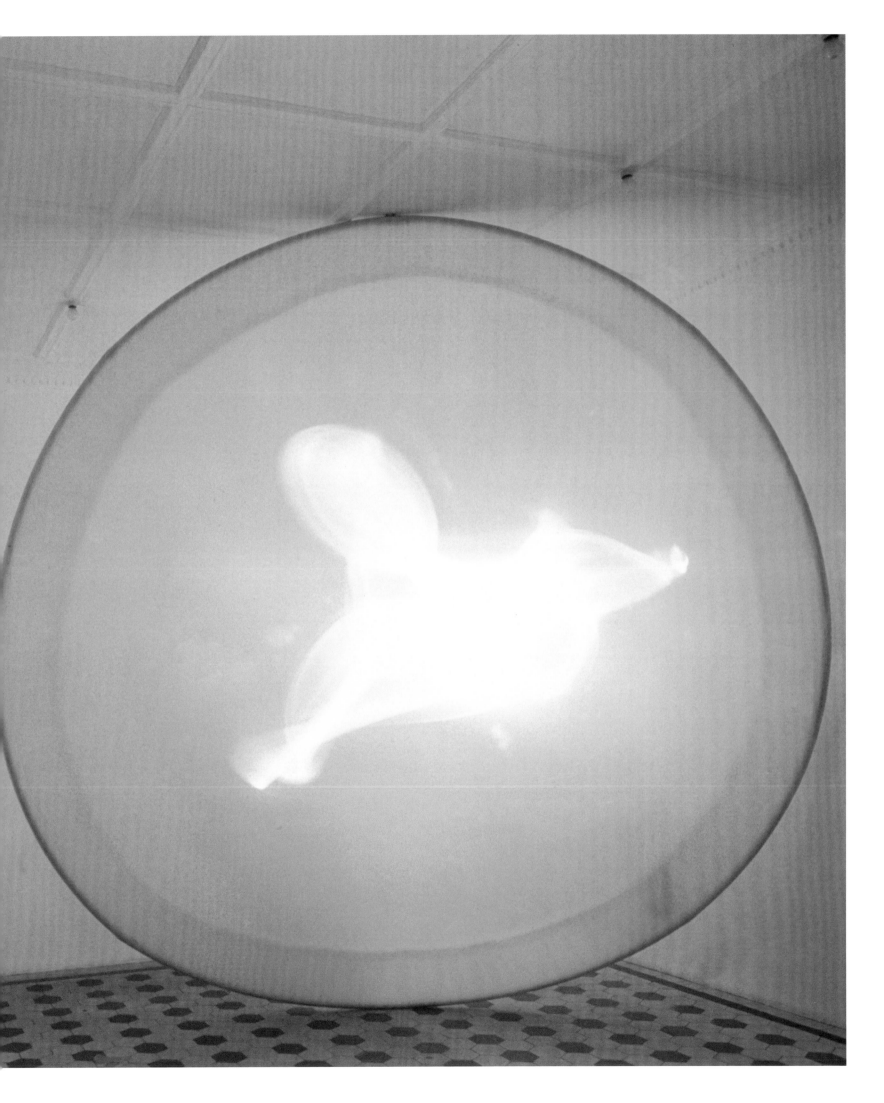

43

44

45

47–50

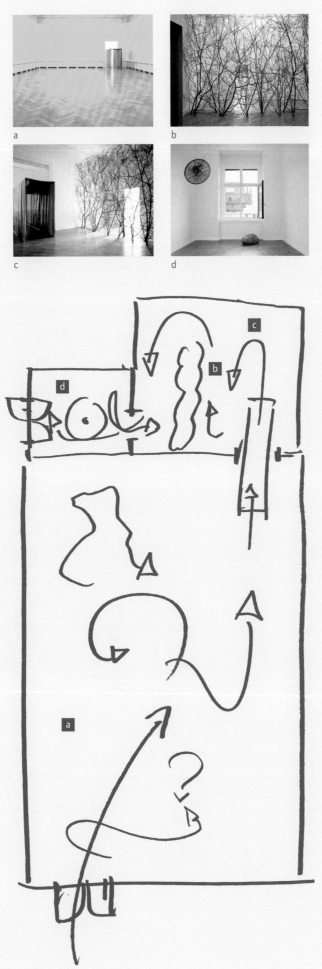

a

b

c

d

51–54
The curious garden, 1997
Installation views at the Kunsthalle Basel, Switzerland, 1997. Monofrequency lights, plastic sheet, metal, hedge, stone, fan, and cable. Private collection, courtesy neugerriemschneider, Berlin

This installation comprised several distinct environments through which the visitor passed sequentially. A large gallery bathed in yellow monofrequency light transitioned into a second room via a rectangular tunnel lined with blue plastic sheeting. The color of the sheeting only became visible after the visitor entered the next room, which was flooded with natural light. A blackthorn hedge blocked direct access to the final gallery. There, a fan—suspended from the ceiling and propelled by the blade's movement—circulated fresh air coming through an open window, beneath which was placed a single boulder. To exit the installation the viewer had to double back through each space.

55
The island series, 1997 (EXH.)
Fifty-six framed chromogenic prints. Each from 6 3/8 x 16 1/2 in. (16 x 42 cm) to 11 x 16 1/2 in. (28 x 42 cm); 92 1/4 x 141 in. (234.3 x 358.1 cm) overall. Private collection

The artist traveled around the islands surrounding Iceland to make this series of prints. He sequences these distinct land formations according to size, with the tallest islands appearing in the bottom row.

56–67
Erosion, 1997
Installation views at the 2nd Johannesburg Biennale, South Africa, 1997. Suction filter, water, hose, and pump. Private collection

Using a pump, the artist empties a reservoir into the streets of a city, altering the urban landscape. Pedestrians must renegotiate their normal routes in order to avoid unexpected pools of water swelling in gutters, on streets and sidewalks, and in other public areas.

68–70
The very large ice floor, 1998
Installation views at the 24th Bienal de São Paulo, 1998. Water, ice machine, metal, and plastic foil. Courtesy the artist; Tanya Bonakdar Gallery, New York; and neugerriemschneider, Berlin

Ice covers a shallow basin on the floor. As viewers walk over the ice, its surface texture changes over the course of the exhibition.

71
Ventilator, 1997 (EXH.)
Installation view at the 1st Berlin Biennial, 1998. Altered fan and cable. Collections of Peter Norton and Eileen Harris Norton, Santa Monica, California

Attached to a cord and suspended from a ceiling, an electric fan erratically circulates in space, propelled only by the force of air it generates.

72–77
Green river, 1998
Installation views in Bremen, Germany, 1998 (pl. 72); Los Angeles, 1999 (pl. 73); Stockholm, 2000 (pl. 74); Tokyo, 2001 (pl. 75); Moss, Norway, 1998 (pl. 76); and the Southern Fjallaback Route, Iceland, 1998 (pl. 77). Uranin and water. Courtesy the artist; Tanya Bonakdar Gallery, New York; and neugerriemschneider, Berlin

The artist performed this outdoor intervention in a number of different locations. Without public announcement, he poured an environmentally safe green dye into the waterway of each locale. Propelled by natural currents, the color traveled throughout the river's passages, dramatically altering the appearance of the landscape along the way.

78
Double sunset, 1999
Installation view in Utrecht, Netherlands, 1999. Xenon lamps, steel, and scaffolding. Courtesy the artist; Tanya Bonakdar Gallery, New York; and neugerriemschneider, Berlin

A giant, yellow steel disc tops a building in an urban location. At dusk, when it is illuminated by stadium lights, viewers could mistake it for a setting sun. The disc is placed in close geographic proximity to where the sun naturally sets, so that from a distance two suns appear to sink toward the horizon.

79–80
Waterfall, 1998
Installation views at the Kunsthalle Köln, Cologne, 1998. Steel, water, pump, aluminum, foil, scaffolding, hoses, and wood. 354 1/3 x 354 1/3 x 236 1/4 in. (900 x 900 x 600 cm). Courtesy the artist; Tanya Bonakdar Gallery, New York; and neugerriemschneider, Berlin

Evoking the sight and sound of a natural waterfall, this work can be adapted to interior or exterior locations. Water rushes loudly down a tower of scaffolding, then is pumped back to the top.

81
Ice pavilion, 1998
Installation view at the Reykjavík Art Museum—Kjarvalsstadir, 1998. Steel, sprinkler, and water. 118 1/8 x 196 7/8 x 196 7/8 in. (300 x 500 x 500 cm). Courtesy the artist; Tanya Bonakdar Gallery, New York; and neugerriemschneider, Berlin

A sprinkler and a punctured garden hose line the top of a simple steel structure. Standing outdoors, the work is contingent upon a cold environment. Over time, cascading icicles form through the metallic netting that covers the structure. In warmer weather pools of water accumulate beneath the pavilion.

82–83
Your compound view, 1998
Installation views at the Reykjavík Art Museum—Kjarvalsstadir, 1998. Mirror foil, aluminum, and wood. 126 x 118 1/8 x 315 in. (320 x 300 x 800 cm). Reykjavík Art Museum—Kjarvalsstadir

A monumental hexagonal kaleidoscope made of wood and lined with foil stands within an exhibition space. One end rests on the floor and is wide enough for viewers to enter, while the opposite end narrows to form an eyehole. Ambient light enters both openings, exploding into hexagonally patterned reflections inside. From the large end, the view through the kaleidoscope resembles an insect's compound eye.

84
The inner cave series, 1998 (EXH.)
Thirty-six framed chromogenic prints. Each 14 x 20 1/2 in. (35.5 x 52 cm); 99 3/4 x 140 1/2 in. (253.4 x 356.9 cm) overall. Collection of Ruth and Carl Pite

A grid six rows high by six columns wide pictures the openings of various Icelandic caves—sites where the earth transitions from an invisible interior to a visible exterior.

85–87
Your natural denudation inverted, 1999
Installation views at the Carnegie Museum of Art, Pittsburgh, 1999. Scaffolding, wood, steel, rubber, water, and steam. Courtesy the artist; Tanya Bonakdar Gallery, New York; and neugerriemschneider, Berlin

Installed within a large outdoor courtyard, this site-specific work changed according to the seasons. Leaves and snow accumulated in a large, shallow, water-filled basin that was fitted to the stepped levels of the courtyard and built around the trees. A pipe running from the building's internal heating system released plumes of hissing steam at the basin's center. From inside the museum, the viewer gazed through the windows at a picturesque, contrived landscape.

88–93
Room for all colours, 1999
Installation views at De Appel, Amsterdam, 1999. Halogen lamps, color filter foil, projection foil, and dimmer. Collection of Christian Boros, Berlin

A reflective panel is mounted in front of a wall, leaving the mechanical elements visible for viewers passing into adjacent spaces. Light is projected through tinted filters onto the screen from behind, bathing the entire room with a changing chromatic spectrum. A dimmer controls the intensity of the light over time. When a new hue floods the gallery, the viewer sees its complementary color as an afterimage.

94

Spiral pavilion, 1999
Installation view at the 48th Venice Biennale, Italy, 1999. Stainless steel. 102 3/8 x 236 1/4 x 236 1/4 in. (260 x 600 x 600 cm). Kunsthalle Bielefeld, Germany

Inspired by the natural spiral of the double helix, an interior tunnel leads to an opening in the pavilion's uncovered center. The illusion of crisscrossing patterns obscures the viewer's ability to differentiate between foreground and background.

95

Reversed waterfall, 1998
Installation view at the Stiftelsen Wanås Utställningar, Knislinge, Sweden, 2000. Water, steel, wood, PVC, foil, and pump. 122 5/6 x 109 1/2 x 36 in. (312 x 278 x 160 cm). Thyssen-Bornemisza Art Contemporary (T-B A21), Vienna

The artist erects a stepped, metal scaffolding indoors or in a natural setting. Fonts on each of the four levels direct water up the frame and into a square basin on the next story, reversing its gravitational flow. A rudimentary piping system recirculates the water to the base of the structure.

96

The drop factory, 2000
Installation view at the Zentrum für Kunst und Medientechnologie, Karlsruhe, Germany, 2001. Stainless steel and aluminum mirrors. 255 7/8 x 413 3/8 x 413 3/8 in. (650 x 1,050 x 1,050 cm). Courtesy the artist; Tanya Bonakdar Gallery, New York; and neugerriemschneider, Berlin

A geodesic dome rising more than twenty feet high in an exhibition space, this work is constructed of triangular mirrored panels fitted into a stainless-steel frame. Both sides of the panels reflect the dome's respective exterior and interior spaces.

97

1 m³ light, 1999
Installation view at the Zentrum für Kunst und Medientechnologie, Karlsruhe, Germany, 2001. Halogen lamps, tripods, and fog machine. 39 3/8 x 39 3/8 x 39 3/8 in. (100 x 100 x 100 cm). Private collection

Three lamps are affixed to each end of four metal stands placed in a square precisely one meter apart in a darkened space; the beams of light they emit form the outline of a cube. Fog released into the gallery volumetrically fills the empty space.

98

Your position surrounded and your surroundings positioned, 1999
Installation view at Dundee Contemporary Arts, Scotland, 1999. HMI lamps, aluminum, steel, and transformers. Fundació "la Caixa," Barcelona

Two light machines stand in a darkened gallery. Each consists of a powerful lamp, a propeller, an aluminum sheath, and a mechanized masking device. The heat from the light causes the propellers to turn inside both machines, rotating their sheaths. Thin, vertical openings in the aluminum cast lines of white light onto the surrounding walls. As the lines circle the gallery, the masking devices adapt the height of each beam according to the room's architectural features.

99

Your intuitive surroundings versus your surrounded intuition, 2000
Installation view at the Art Institute of Chicago, 2000. Fluorescent tubes, control unit, and projection foil. La Colección Jumex, Ecatepec de Morelos, Mexico

The artist suspends a row of fluorescent bulbs from a gallery ceiling, with a translucent white screen placed below to diffuse the light. A control unit adjusts the gradation over time, simulating the changing light levels of a cloudy day.

100–103

Your now is my surroundings, 2000
Installation views at Tanya Bonakdar Gallery, New York, 2000. Mirrors, metal, and concrete. Collection of Martin Z. Margulies

Originally a site-specific installation, this project involves removing the glass from a room's gabled skylight, exposing the space to the elements and allowing the noise of the city to enter. Four walls are constructed to match the dimensions of the skylight, then lined with mirrors just above eye level. The mirrors infinitely reflect the skylight's metal frames, the sky, and the adjacent buildings, blending the interior and exterior spaces.

104–6

The movement meter for Lernacken, 2000
Installation views in Lernacken, Malmö, Sweden, 2000. Stainless steel, glass, and lamp. Tower 497 1/4 x 157 1/2 x 157 1/2 in. (1,263 x 400 x 400 cm); pavilion 113 3/8 x 354 1/3 x 354 1/3 in. (288 x 900 x 900 cm). City of Malmö, Sweden

The artist made this permanent light tower for a coastal site near the border between Sweden and Denmark. Rising more than forty feet high, dozens of twisting metal tubes spiral up to the open top, where a light fixed across from a band of colored glass panels creates a spectral light show for nighttime motorists on the nearby Øresund Bridge. Approximately a quarter of a mile away stands a related pavilion comprising six freestanding stainless-steel structures— each a grid of equilateral triangles—that form a pinwheel shape. Sunlight bouncing off the colored panels (some mirrored) produces intricate patterns throughout the day.

107–8

Seeing yourself sensing, 2001
Installation views at the Museum of Modern Art, New York, 2001. Glass and mirror. Courtesy the artist; Tanya Bonakdar Gallery, New York; and neugerriemschneider, Berlin

For this site-specific installation, the artist replaced the windows in the museum's entrance hall using glass panes with mirrored stripes. The thin silver strips reflected fragments of the interior space while the transparent ones permitted a view of the courtyard.

109

The aerial river series, 2000 (EXH.)
Forty-two framed chromogenic prints. Each 15 3/4 x 23 5/8 in. (40 x 60 cm); 106 x 182 in. (269.2 x 462.3 cm) overall. San Francisco Museum of Modern Art, gift of Helen and Charles Schwab

Documenting the variability of the natural landscape, this series includes multiple views of the Markarfljót River in Iceland. The first image, in the upper left corner, shows the river's mouth; the pictures then progress horizontally toward higher elevations, concluding at the mountain peaks where the stream originates.

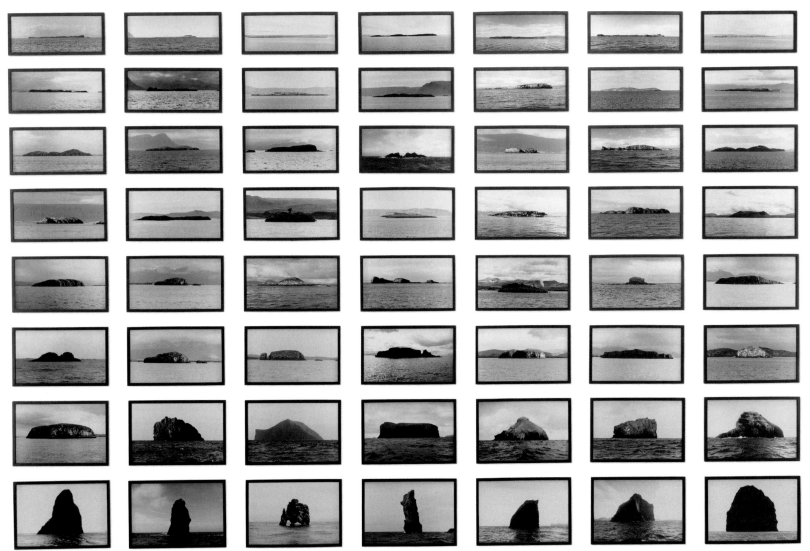

56–67

68

69

70

72

73

74

75

76

79

80

82

83

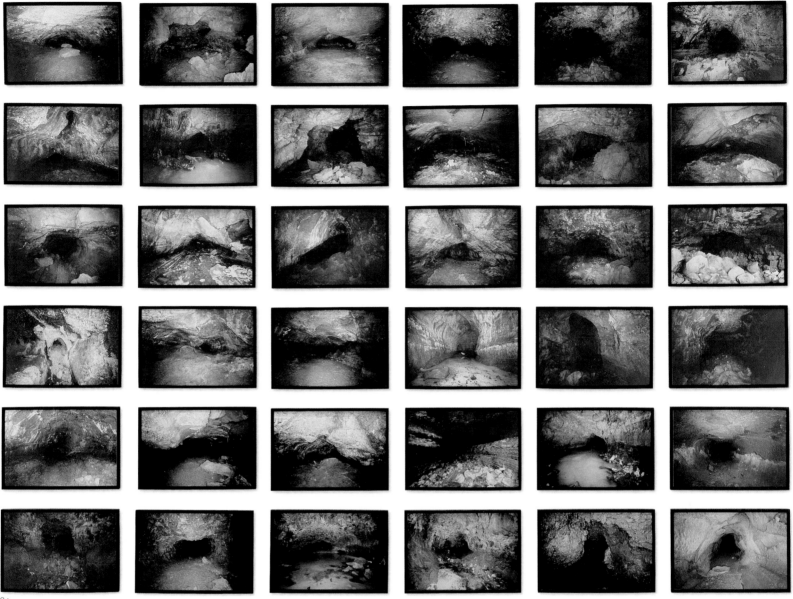

86

87

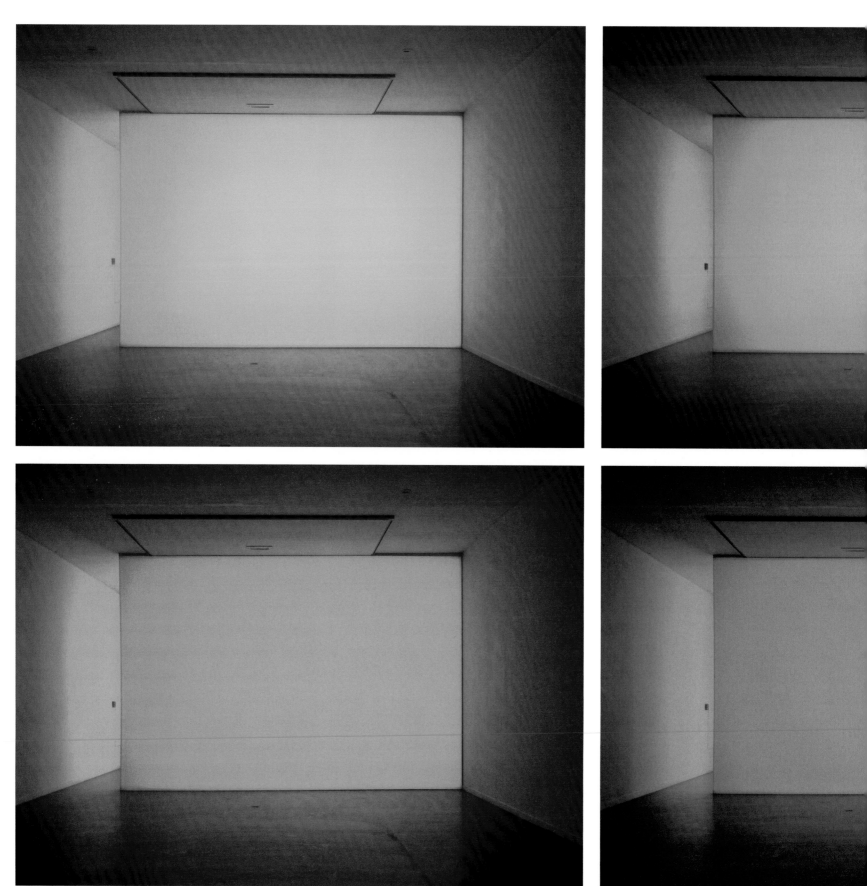

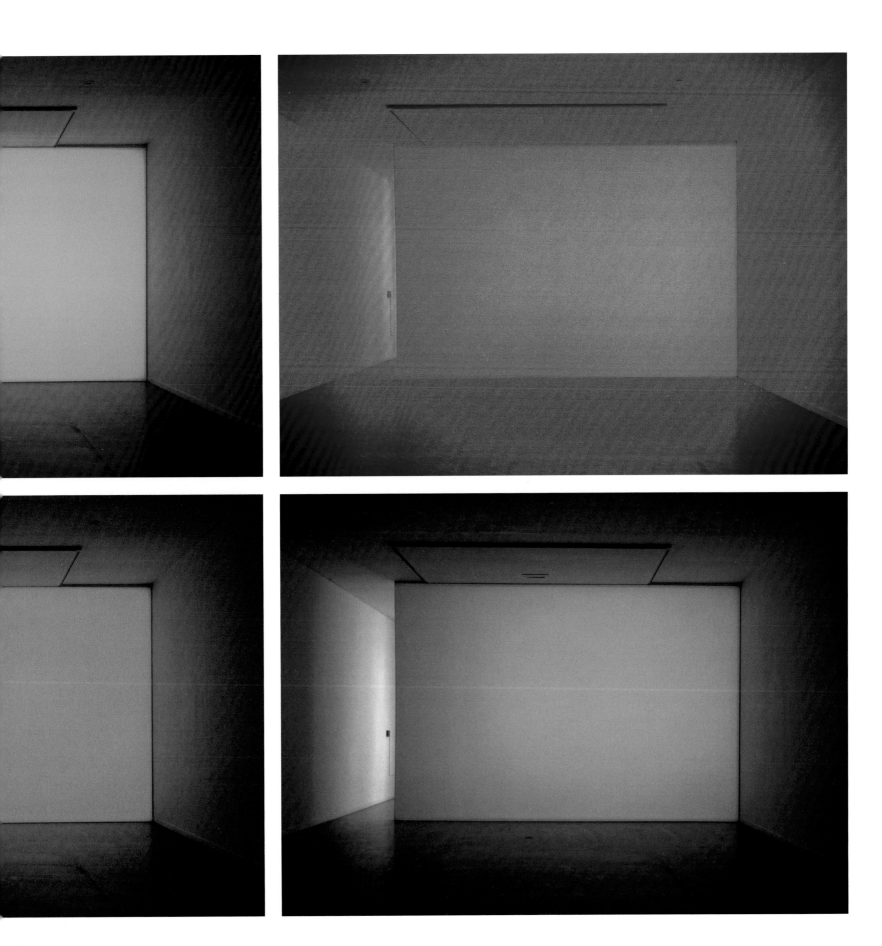

94

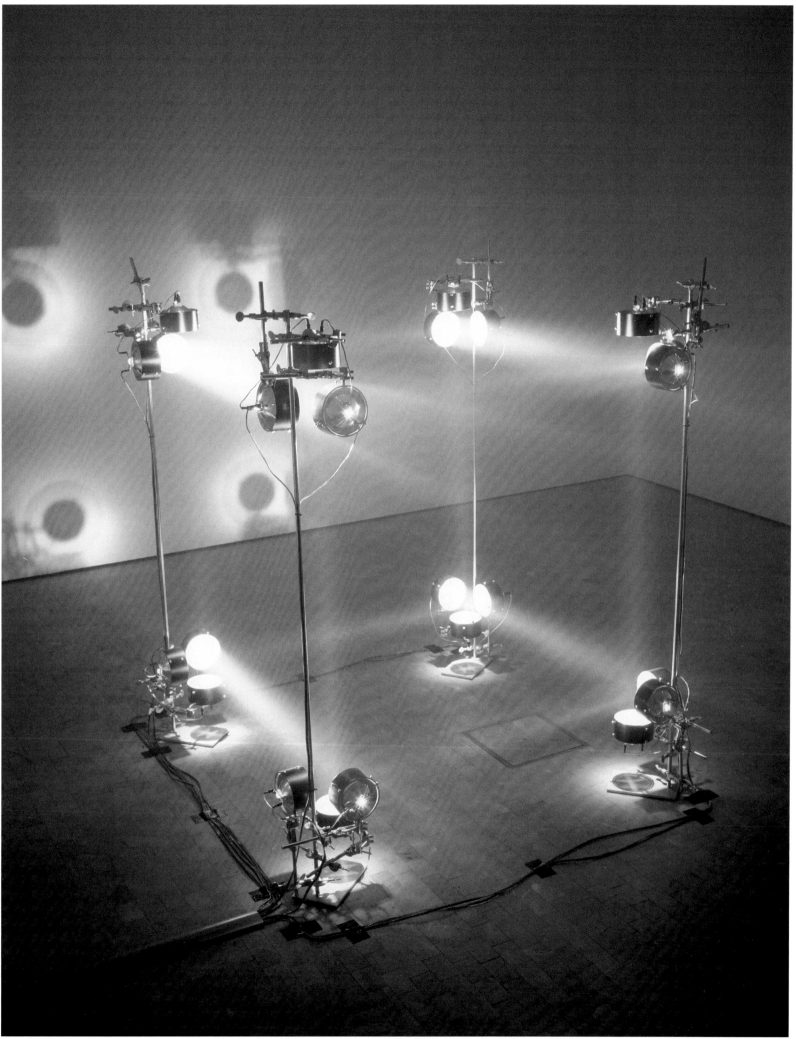

99

100

101

102

104

105

106

107

108

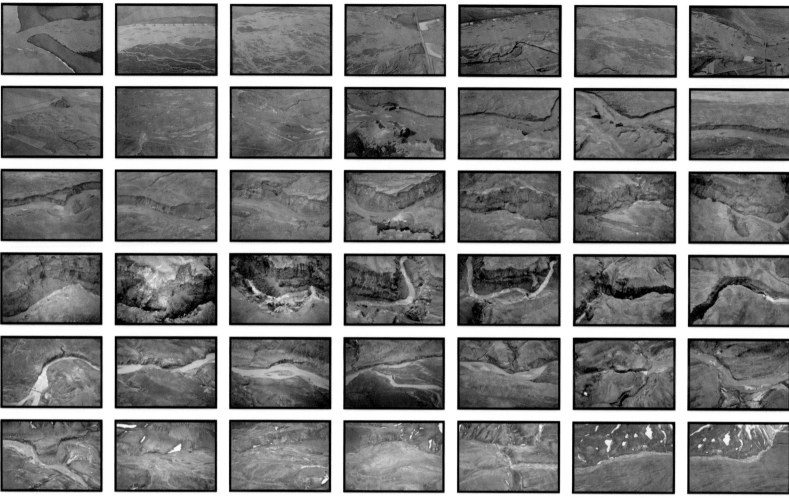

109

a

b

c

d

110–21

The mediated motion, 2001
Installation views at the Kunsthaus Bregenz,
Austria, 2001. Water, wood, compressed soil,
fog machine, metal, foil, duckweed, and
shitake mushrooms. Courtesy neugerriemschneider, Berlin

Responding directly to the museum's architecture, this installation used natural materials and
distinctive transitions to elicit unsteady physical
states in viewers navigating the building's four
levels. Shitake mushrooms (on the first floor)
and floating duckweed (on the next) grew and
changed during the course of the exhibition.
Each environment was connected by narrow
walkways and stairs; one flight was built over
the existing steps and brought the spectator
uncomfortably close to the ceiling. The viewer
was further disoriented by a subtly inclined
floor of compressed earth and a shaky, fog-
enshrouded suspension bridge. The journey
came to an abrupt end at the far side of the
bridge, where a dead end forced the visitor
to turn around and descend.

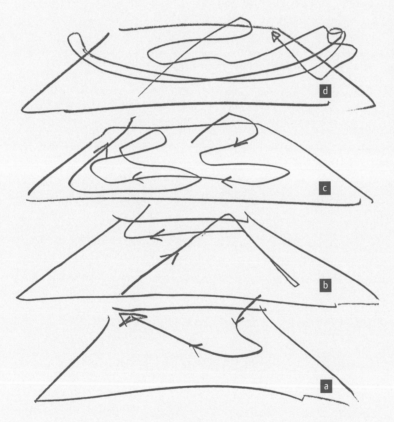

d

c

b

a

110

111

112

114

115

116

119

120

121

HELIOTROPE

Daniel Birnbaum

Each time that there is a metaphor, there is doubtless a sun somewhere; but each time that there is sun, metaphor has begun.

—Jacques Derrida[1]

Olafur Eliasson's art is not complete without you; in fact, you are part of it. His works are not self-sufficient objects in the usual sense; rather, they are environments— productive arrangements, heterogeneous apparatuses—awaiting your arrival. Indeed, they need you. To a certain extent that is, of course, true of every work of art, since all aesthetic experience requires an experiencing subject. But in Eliasson's case the contribution of the active viewer is so central to the works that one might wager the claim that this very activity is what they are about. You belong to them, and they belong to you. The nature of this mutual belonging, which cannot be grasped in terms of mere possession, is the primary theme of this essay. It is my belief that one must understand this relationship as a kind of reciprocal creation process.

In his preface to the second edition of *The Critique of Pure Reason,* Immanuel Kant spelled out the so-called Copernican revolution that placed the experiencing subject at the very center of all epistemological inquiry:

> We here propose to do just what Copernicus did in attempting
> to explain the celestial movements. When he found that he
> could make no progress by assuming that all the heavenly bodies

revolved round the spectator, he reversed the process, and tried the experiment of assuming that the spectator revolved, while the stars remained at rest. We may make the same experiment with regard to the intuition of objects.[2]

This metaphor provides an interesting point of reference with regard to Eliasson's art. His work—heliotropic to the core, as I will elaborate below—depends as much upon the position of the viewer as upon the cosmic elements of light, heat, and moisture. *Beauty* (1993; pls. 5, 31), a key early work that Eliasson has re-created in several versions, defines the basic parameters that recur from installation to installation: an emphasis on perception and the viewer's active involvement in the process. Tiny drops of water sprinkle down from a perforated hose, creating a liquid curtain; a lamp sends rays of light through the water to produce a rainbow in the room. The overtness of the technical setup is typical of Eliasson's art. Unlike other artists who deal with light and perception (James Turrell being one relevant point of comparison), Eliasson makes no attempt to conceal how he produces his effects. When you enter *Beauty* the hose and electric light are immediately visible. The work has the evasive quality of quickly shifting weather— take one step in either direction and the whole thing is gone, like a gentle breeze or sunlight reflecting off a passing vehicle. There are no secrets, just a fascinating optical phenomenon to behold. Instead of tempting us to look for veiled gadgetry, the installation confronts us with the thing itself: the fact that light and water in combination can produce color. And with the fact that it takes a viewer—an embodied subject located in space—for the phenomenon to appear. The people next to you, standing a few feet away, may not quite get what you are talking about. It could very well be that all they see is a perforated hose and a primitive lamp that bears no resemblance to the sun.

Your black horizon (2005; pl. 123), presented on the island of San Lazzaro as part of the 2005 Venice Biennale, is a more recent example of the artist's heliotropic speculations. You enter an elegant wooden pavilion (pl. 122) consisting of a kind of patio and an exhibition space that measures nearly two thousand square feet.[3] First you see nothing; there is only darkness. All you know is that you are ascending some kind of ramp. Ahead of you a light emerges, and you walk right into it. Your eyes must adjust before you get a full view of the situation. You realize that you are surrounded by a thin, horizontal line of light. You can walk along the line (which is in fact a slit in the wall letting out a glow, the source of which initially remains hidden), or you can position yourself at the very center of the space and rotate, thus getting the full experience of a horizon that seems miles away. Once the initial sense of disorientation is gone, you become attentive to subtle shifts. The quality of the light changes slowly: it gets warmer, more reddish, then chills off into bluish shades of white. The artificial horizon reproduces the light of the lagoon surrounding the island, but it condenses an entire day into fifteen minutes so that every viewer can experience the full range of color and

122
Adjaye/Associates
T-B A21 Pavilion, Venice, Italy, 2005

123
Olafur Eliasson
Your black horizon, 2005
Installation view at the 51st Venice Biennale,
Italy, 2005. LED lights, steel, and control unit.
Courtesy Thyssen-Bornemisza Art Contemporary
(T-B A21), Vienna

brightness from sunrise to sunset. Concentrating on the luminous line triggers strange physiological effects in your eyes, and you notice a second line—a kind of visual echo—that travels upward and fades away. Then a new one appears and starts to wander. The color of this drifting afterimage is hard to determine, but perhaps it really is black, as the title of the work indicates. And it is certainly *your* horizon, in the sense that it is triggered somewhere inside you, behind your eyes rather than in front of them. The intriguing but slightly disturbing lines in your visual field are of your own making. They are out there, but the black sun is obviously in your head. The very distinction between inside and outside suddenly seems rather blurry, and you feel the urge to compare notes with other viewers. Through an introspective mode you are thus driven beyond yourself. This is the kind of sociability, grounded in reflection, that is typical of Eliasson's art, which is never solely about social interaction. It is never only about private experience either. It is always about both.

"All works of art produce a model of sociability," writes Nicolas Bourriaud in *Relational Aesthetics*. "So there is a question we are entitled to ask in front of any aesthetic production: 'Does this work permit me to enter into dialogue? Could I exist, and how, in the space it defines?'" Some artworks are more democratic than others, he declares: "May I simply remind you, for the record, that the forms produced by the art of totalitarian regimes are peremptory and closed in on themselves."[4] It seems to me that Eliasson's art represents an approach that is all about engaging the viewer. His works suggest a model of sociability that not only permits the viewer to enter the dialogue but takes this dialogue as its very point of departure. His installations are dialogical in composition and democratic in their very structure. They are about sharing.

In "The Distribution of the Sensible" the French philosopher Jacques Rancière outlines an approach to politics and aesthetics that focuses on "the manner in

124
Carsten Höller
Test Site, 2006
Installation view at the Tate Modern, London, 2006. Stainless steel and Makrolon. Courtesy the artist

which the arts can be perceived and thought of as forms of art *and* as forms that inscribe a sense of community."[5] Every artistic articulation involves a distribution of shared experience and is thus a figure of sociability or community. In what sense can an artwork be political? More specifically, in what sense can, say, a sculptural work by Eliasson really be said to be democratic? The arts, says Rancière, can "only ever lend to projects of domination or emancipation what they are able to lend to them, that is to say, quite simply, what they have in common with them: bodily positions and movements, functions of speech, the parcelling out of the visible and the invisible."[6] An artwork can be political because there is an aesthetics at the very core of political life. This "has nothing to do with . . . the 'aestheticization of politics'" typical of the twentieth century, the "age of the masses."[7] Rather, aesthetics here should be understood in Kantian terms, as the "*a priori* forms determining what presents itself to sensory experience"—in other words, as the system of delimitations of time and space articulating that which members of a community share.[8] On the basis of this "primary aesthetics," Rancière explores the question of artistic practice—"ways of doing and making"—in order to discover exactly "what they 'do' or 'make' from the standpoint of what is common to the community."[9]

If each work of art produces a form of sociability, it also suggests a model of political life that starts from such immediate and tangible things as physical location, the position from which one speaks, and the concrete "parcelling out of the visible and the invisible."

What, then, is relational aesthetics? The most straightforward definition is probably the one offered by Bourriaud in the glossary that concludes his book. It is, he declares, an "aesthetic theory consisting in judging artworks on the basis of the inter-human relations which they represent, produce or prompt."[10] This seems to imply that the theory, in principle, can be applied to any work of art or aesthetic phenomenon: an abstract painting hanging in a classic white-cube gallery, a modern ballet production, or even a punk concert. Of course, Bourriaud makes no secret of the fact that he has developed the theory in response to works produced by a group of artists of roughly his own generation who, it would seem, attribute to social interaction a newly prominent function. For relational artists social exchange is not just a side effect or a backdrop, it is at the very center of their work. What they produce, says Bourriaud, are "inter-human experiences" and "relational space-time elements." For today's art, he adds, this "relational field" plays as important a role as mass production did for Pop.[11] Social interaction is not only the starting point and the outcome; it is also what this art is *about*. Exhibitions of work by artists such as Liam Gillick, Dominique Gonzalez-Foerster, Douglas Gordon, Carsten Höller (see pl. 124), Pierre Huyghe, Philippe Parreno, and Rirkrit Tiravanija all "construct models of sociability suitable for producing human relations, the same way architecture literally 'produces' the itineraries of those residing in it."[12]

Bourriaud, who does not discuss Eliasson's art, mentions meetings, invitations, casting sessions, appointments, encounters, various types of collaborations, games, festivals, parties, and further forms of conviviality as examples of "aesthetic objects" that take on the role traditionally played in art by images and objects. Tiravanija, perhaps the most convincing example of an artist who enacts "relational procedures," often describes his sculptures and installations as models. He creates stages, platforms, and spaces that can be understood as offerings to the exhibition visitor. In 1996, for example, for the exhibition *Untitled (Tomorrow Is Another Day)* at the Kölnischer Kunstverein in Cologne, Germany, he built a true-to-scale replica of his New York apartment that could be inhabited around the clock. Often Tiravanija offers food, frequently rice and curry (see pl. 125). One gathers and enjoys the meal with others. In 1996, at the Neue Kunst Halle St. Gallen, Switzerland, he installed a working sound studio that was made available to local music groups as a practice space. And for his 2001 exhibition at the Portikus in Frankfurt, Germany, he built a large stage platform intended for various cultural activities. During the course of the show there were concerts, readings, and workshops; an editorial office for a magazine was set up as well as a bar. Each Tiravanija work is a proposal that can be adapted, altered, or further

125
Rirkrit Tiravanija
Untitled (Pad See-ew), 1990/2000
Performance at the San Francisco Museum of Modern Art, 2000. San Francisco Museum of Modern Art, gift of Connie and Jack Tilton

126
Rirkrit Tiravanija
A Retrospective (Tomorrow Is Another Fine Day), 2004
Installation view at the Museum Boijmans Van Beuningen, Rotterdam, Netherlands, 2004

developed in new contexts. So what remains when the show is over? The artist's 2004 mid-career survey, titled *A Retrospective (Tomorrow Is Another Fine Day)* (pl. 126), displayed no objects, just empty plywood simulacra of gallery spaces in which he had worked. Walking through the void one encountered performances and recorded sound-tracks, including one scripted by the science-fiction writer Bruce Sterling ("Imagine living in an art gallery. No, don't try, that's unimaginable").[13] Tiravanija's art takes place between people. There is very little room for subjective expression or for forms of interi-ority associated with the first-person perspective. Things are out there, between the visitors of the exhibition. Collective activities thus precede the introspection of the single subject. A first-person stance emerges only belatedly, when the action is over and one is left to one's own devices. The artist's empty retrospective, for instance, seemed haunted by a past existing only as a rumor—or rather many conflicting rumors. "Like an insane person he builds replicas of rooms and apartments that have been in his life," wrote Gavin Brown some years ago in what remains an important text on Tiravanija.[14] What, then, does one take away from a Tiravanija show? Not even the rice and curry remain. "Ultimately," says Brown, "it is Rirkrit's melancholia."[15]

In Eliasson's case it is usually the other way around. His works inspire a reflective stance, reminding the viewer of his or her own position as an experiencing, bodily being and of the subjective condition of all interactions with the world (and with other embodied subjects). If Eliasson is a relational artist, then it is perhaps more in Rancière's sense than in Bourriaud's. He is no doubt more interested in art as a way of distributing the sensible, and in the politics involved, than in games, festivals, or parties. His "phenomenological" point of departure—the insistence on a first-person perspec-tive—never locks the single subject into a solipsistic position. The world we share is still there, and so are other people. Eliasson's art helps us realize general truths: the deeper one gets into oneself, the more obvious it gets that the very core of subjectivity is dialog-ical. Phenomenology is one of those terms so variously abused in the discourse of con-temporary art that they usually don't mean much of anything. Eliasson's work, however, could be said to represent a phenomenological approach in a stricter sense of the word. Kant's Copernican revolution, as further developed by Edmund Husserl, insists on the active role of the subject in all forms of experience and, ultimately, in the very concept of reality. All possible experience of the world depends on an experiencing subject, even when the thing being experienced is understood to be independent of the perceiving mind. Accordingly, Eliasson takes great care to make the active role of the viewer appar-ent. His very titles suggest that the works are part of—or even a product of—the beholder's conscious life. *Your strange certainty still kept* (1996; pls. 14, 42), *Your spiral view* (2002; pl. 174), and *Your activity horizon* (2004; pls. 209–11) belong to the person seeing them. They belong to you and me.

Eliasson's debt to phenomenological philosophy has been pointed out by numerous critics and by the artist himself, who in his own statements often returns to the writings of Husserl and Maurice Merleau-Ponty. An emphasis on a meaning-bestowing, embodied subject is, of course, relevant to any artistic practice that focuses on the active role of the perceiver. More specifically, however, a theme that links Eliasson's work even closer to Husserl and his disciples is the notion of alterity: the fundamental difference that cuts right through the subject and its ability to be "other" to itself. Time and intersubjectivity are closely associated in Husserl's phenomenology. The reflective subject returns to itself in search of a sphere of original givenness. At the foundation of its own being it finds the "living present," which upon closer inspection turns out to be not a zone of monolithic self-presence but a heterogeneous origin. The present is permeated by absence and otherness. Only when letting in that which is other—nonpresence in the temporal sense as well as that of another subject—can it remain as it is. Approaching the most fundamental level of consciousness, Husserl discovered the impossibility of reducing that which is other than presence, since presence itself represents a kind of othering.[16] The same theme reappears in the work of Merleau-Ponty, rephrased in terms of the alterity of the "flesh" of embodied subjectivity. For Merleau-Ponty, otherness is inscribed in the body. Since the flesh is never transparent to itself, it introduces otherness into the very core of that which is mine, and it is precisely because it is also my flesh that there can be alter egos, other *myselves*. Intersubjectivity is established on this primordial level. Indeed, at the very foundation of *ourselves* we find *others*.[17]

Again, Eliasson's works belong to you and me. But who are you and who am I? When the artist installed *Your sun machine* (1997; pls. 47–50) at Marc Foxx Gallery in Los Angeles, he added nothing to the space (at least nothing that was not in some sense already there). If anything, he subtracted from it, cutting a hole in the roof and letting the dazzling California sunlight flood in. Rematerialized as a vibrating patch on the floor, the distant celestial body became physically present—you could see it move. But *Your sun machine* is not just an artwork about the fiery body at the center of the solar system; it is also a piece about you. Things out there may appear to be moving, but of course it's the other way around: your own activities make things appear as they do. The sun floats across the gallery floor because you yourself are traveling across the universe at incredible speed, standing on this tiny planet of yours. One may get the impression that Eliasson's art is all about nature, and more precisely the powerful natural phenomena of his native Iceland: wind, water, light, and fire. However, the entirely new sensations his installations create are not natural, if *natural* is meant in the sense that experience has been purified of all artificial ingredients. If there is purification here, it is an effect of some mechanical process, as in *The curious garden* (1997; pls. 51–54), in which one room of the Kunsthalle Basel, Switzerland, was filled only with light. As the light was restricted to the yellow spectrum, however, the entire space was bathed in a lemony glow. In an uncertain era of new technologies and mediated subjectivity, the focus on perception in Eliasson's work is certainly visionary,[18] and it is clearly influenced by utopian minds such as Buckminster Fuller, but there is nothing radically futuristic or high-tech about his projects. This suggests that he views the mechanical quality of perception not as something that pertains only to today's situation, but rather as something fundamental to human experience. In fact, Eliasson's works cannot be grasped in terms of a distinction between the mechanical and the biological. "Instead," as Jonathan Crary contends, "a nature/culture duality is dissolved within a single field in which machine and organism are not separable."[19]

To a certain extent you produce the work. But in turn you are produced as a subject by the environments the artist constructs. "It could perhaps be called a relationship of co-production," says Eliasson. "As an example I might say: when someone walks down a street she produces the street and is, simultaneously, produced by the street."[20] Is it the intentionality of the active viewer who enters the work of art and fully explores its most extreme possibilities that determines the limits of what it means to be a subject? Or is it the work itself that defines the parameters of new forms of subjectivity, perhaps involving modes of awareness that dodge the framework of phenomenology? Such are the questions that constitute the ultimate horizon of any investigation of Eliasson's art from the perspective of possible subjectivities.[21] Who is the subject established (constructed, assembled, or taken for granted) in Eliasson's works—these sometimes abstract yet visceral machineries of perception and kinesthetic experience? Each installation seems to give rise to its own set of problems and then set them in motion.

Indeed, at the heart of Eliasson's practice is the desire to introduce time as a key element. The importance of thinking about artistic interaction with the world in temporal terms is a key theme of "Vibrations," his most systematic attempt to date to articulate a role for creative practice in contemporary society. What he calls "the reintroduction of time" is just the first step in a strategic attempt to break down the "governing dogma of timelessness and static objecthood," making possible an individual relationship with the world based on personal engagement.[22] The theoretical framework of "Vibrations" does not necessarily give phenomenology the last word. Its privileging of the effects of waves and vibrations may be seen as an attempt to position phenomenology as a philosophy with legitimate but limited reach. "If the individual is simply—and passively—produced by the space, she fails to mobilize the critical potential embodied in the situation," writes Eliasson, emphasizing the fact that the subject is not given as a stable structure once and for all, but is actually constituted by forces from the outside.[23]

Continuing this line of thought, one might end up with a kind of experimental constructivism, one that finds inspiration in Walter Benjamin's declaration that the human perceptual apparatus, far from being a natural given, is historically and technologically conditioned. In some of the most progressive and daring essays of the

1930s, Benjamin envisioned a new form of subjectivity in sync with the latest technologies of mechanical reproduction—a collectivized subjectivity that had left behind traditional notions of creativity and aesthetics in order to renegotiate the function of art in terms of (socialist) politics and new modes of mass production and distribution.[24] Of the "necessary and ultimately liberating" integration of the human subject and the technology of cinema, Rosalind Krauss writes, "Not only was film to release men and women from the confines of their private spaces and into a collective realm . . . but it was to infiltrate and restructure subjectivity itself, changing damaged individual experience into energized collective perception."[25] She cites Benjamin, who obviously saw this reconstruction of subjectivity as a moment of emancipation and compared it to the act of breaking out of jail: "Then came the film and burst this prison-world asunder by the dynamite of the tenth of a second, so that now, in the midst of its far-flung ruins and debris, we calmly and adventurously go traveling."[26] Benjamin's constructivist approach toward the question of a future subject—full of optimism and difficult to reconcile with the melancholic gaze and interest in obsolescence typical of the majority of his writings—bears certain similarities to more recent speculations concerning new constructions of the self, admittedly less collectivist but carried forward through a similar rhetoric of liberation.[27]

Who (or what), then, emerges? In recent critiques of humanist notions of subjectivity, the plural mode of being has become a key issue: "The subject does not disappear; rather its excessively determined unity is put in question. What arouses interest and inquiry is its disappearance (that is, the new manner of being which disappearance is), or rather its dispersal, which does not annihilate it but offers us, out of it, no more than a plurality of positions and a discontinuity of functions (and here we re-encounter the system of discontinuities, which, rightly or wrongly, seemed at one time to be characteristic of serial music)."[28] What interests me here is not so much disappearance as a manner of being, but rather the "system of discontinuities" that represents so many different modes of appearance or emergence. Eliasson is hardly one of those artists who dreams of the ultimate disappearance of the self. On the contrary, he is interested in an empowered self: an active subject capable of forming him- or herself through engagement with the environment. Once we have liberated ourselves from traditional notions of subjectivity, the plurality of positions and discontinuity of functions open up a spectrum of diverse subject constructions. Is there any resolution to these inquiries? Perhaps Eliasson would claim that there is no such thing as phenomenology, only phenomenological problems. That is why the investigation must be ongoing; each problem demands its own forms of attention. Therefore, while some of Eliasson's projects have a spectacular quality, such as *By means of a sudden intuitive realisation* (1996; pls. 43–44), in which a jet of water illuminated by a strobe light appears frozen into a series of solid bodies, others may be as simple as *Erosion* (1997; pls. 56–67), for which the artist set a huge amount of water (more than five gallons per second) flowing down a street in Johannesburg, South Africa, or *The very large ice step experienced* (1998; pl. 127), a minimalistic row of ice blocks left to melt slowly on a lawn in a Paris suburb. Other works construct incredibly elaborate apparatuses, perceptual and kinesthetic machineries that let a subject emerge and unfold in accordance with varying distributions of time and space. Neither nature nor the machine but the perceiving subject's relation to its heterogeneous environment—this would seem to be Eliasson's recurring theme.

127
Olafur Eliasson
The very large ice step experienced, 1998
Installation view in Nanterre, Paris, 1998.
Water, foil, and wood. Courtesy the artist;
Tanya Bonakdar Gallery, New York; and
neugerriemschneider, Berlin

It is no coincidence that problems of temporality play a crucial role in any attempt to come to grips with subjectivity; a long line of writers has located the anxiety elicited by time at the very heart of the subject. Commenting on the Kantian idea of the "self-affection" of time as the most original form of self-awareness, Merleau-Ponty concludes, "It is of the essence of time to be not only actual time, or time which flows, but also time which is aware of itself."

This turning back of time toward itself, an original temporal fold, traces out interiority and represents the very "archetype of the relationship of self to self."[29] This original form of becoming a subject can only be grasped as a kind of architecture of time. Late in life, Gilles Deleuze elaborated a theory of subjectivity that employs phenomenological terminology and reintroduces the topologies of transcendental philosophy: "Time becomes a subject because it is the folding of the outside and, as such, forces every present into forgetting, but preserves the whole of the past within memory: forgetting is the impossibility of return, and memory is the necessity of renewal."[30] The ultimate exteriority, the absolute Outside, cannot be understood in spatial terms, but rather as a temporal dimension. Time affects itself, and through this autoaffection it folds, producing interiority: an inner realm of reflexivity. Thus, the Outside is twisted, folded, or doubled to create an Inside. Is there perhaps another fold in time after that experienced by the subject as we know it? A fold (or "superfold") after man?

Though Eliasson never deconstructs the framework of humanism to suggest posthuman forms of life, he does deploy devices that destabilize the position of the meaning-bestowed subject (the viewer). Ina Blom has pointed out the simultaneous presence of a sophisticated "phenomenology of perception" and all-encompassing "media machines" in Eliasson's works.[31] His artificial environments thus frame the very idea of the subject within a different kind of philosophy, one that no longer sees the first-person perspective of phenomenology as a self-evident starting point. The

128
Olafur Eliasson
Light lab (test I), 2006
Installation view at the Portikus, Frankfurt,
Germany, 2006. Monofrequency lights and wood.
Courtesy the artist; Tanya Bonakdar Gallery, New
York; and neugerriemschneider, Berlin

Copernican revolution, which established the subject as a sun around which objects revolve, is superseded by another revolution: both subject and object are found to be relative to the apparatus producing the epistemic structure that makes the distinction appear so crucial. In work after work, Eliasson stages scenarios that make the viewer aware of him- or herself as an I/Eye. You see yourself see, and suddenly a kind of inversion takes place—you are seen by the work rather than just seeing the work.

As Eliasson's career progresses, a recurring solar fascination is becoming increasingly clear. This is evident in the artificial rainbow of *Beauty* and the rotating patch of sunlight in *Your sun machine* as well as in his succession of synthetic suns, the most massive of which was at the center of *The weather project* (2003; pls. 1–2, 15, 196–97) at the Tate Modern, London. This heliocentric drive (explored recently and systematically as part of the ongoing "solar laboratory" project that started at the Portikus in the spring of 2006 [see pl. 128]) seems to have little to do with recent theoretical or artistic developments, and a lot to do with ancient speculations concerning vision and the power of the mind.[32] Philosophy as such seems to have started as a kind of sun dance;

the tropes of language itself turn toward the celestial light. Writing about heliotropism as the foundation of all philosophical metaphors in "White Mythology," Jacques Derrida spells out the solar obsession in Platonic discourse: "There is only one sun in this system. The proper name, here, is the nonmetaphorical prime mover of metaphor, the father of all figures."[33] Is the sun the original metaphor or is it the anchoring point of all philosophically relevant metaphors? Eliasson is not a historian of Western philosophy or a theorist specializing in philosophical language, but with impeccable intuition he has grappled with this cosmos in work after work, creating visual scenarios that stage the sun and the eye in the most dramatic fashion. Sometimes the sun is black. Occasionally the eye is blinded. You move in and out of roles: you are the sun; you are the flower turning its face toward the heavenly body; you carry the darkness of the eclipse inside you. Derrida's essay, though written nearly forty years ago, reads like a manifesto of Eliasson's artistic endeavor: "If the sun is metaphorical always, already, it is no longer completely natural. It is always, already a luster, a chandelier, one might say an artificial construction, if one could still give credence to this signification when nature has disappeared. For if the sun is no longer completely natural, what in nature does remain natural?"[34] That, I believe, is what Eliasson, today's chief manufacturer of suns, would ultimately want to know.

NOTES

1. Jacques Derrida, "White Mythology: Metaphor in the Text of Philosophy" (1971), in *Margins of Philosophy*, trans. Alan Bass (Chicago: University of Chicago Press, 1982), 251.

2. Immanuel Kant, *The Critique of Pure Reason*, 2nd ed., trans. J. M. D. Meiklejohn (Adelaide, Australia: eBooks@Adelaide, 2004), etext.library.adelaide.edu.au/k/kant/immanuel/k16p/k16p2.html.

3. The structure housing *Your black horizon* was designed by the British architect David Adjaye.

4. Nicolas Bourriaud, *Relational Aesthetics*, trans. Simon Pleasance and Fronza Woods with Mathieu Copeland (Dijon, France: Les presses du réel, 2002), 109.

5. Jacques Rancière, "The Distribution of the Sensible," in *The Politics of Aesthetics: The Distribution of the Sensible*, trans. Gabriel Rockhill (London and New York: Continuum, 2004), 14.

6. Ibid., 19.

7. Ibid., 13.

8. Ibid.

9. Ibid.

10. Bourriaud, *Relational Aesthetics*, 112.

11. "This said," notes Bourriaud, "we find ourselves, with relational artists, in the presence of a group of people who, for the first time since the appearance of Conceptual Art in the mid-sixties, in no way draw sustenance from any re-interpretation of this or that past aesthetic movement. Relational art is not the revival of any movement, nor is it the comeback of any style" (ibid., 44).

12. Ibid., 70.

13. Bruce Sterling, "Tomorrow Will Be Another Fine Day," in *Rirkrit Tiravanija: A Retrospective (Tomorrow Is Another Fine Day)*, by Bruce Sterling et al. (Rotterdam, Netherlands: Museum Boijmans Van Beuningen), 36.

14. Gavin Brown, in *Supermarket: Rirkrit Tiravanija* (Zurich: Migros Museum für Gegenwartskunst, 1998), 72.

15. Ibid.

16. See Edmund Husserl, *Cartesian Meditations: An Introduction to Phenomenology*, trans. Dorion Cairns (The Hague, Netherlands: M. Nijhoff, 1969), particularly the fifth meditation's exploration of the notion of intersubjectivity and its relationship to time.

17. See Maurice Merleau-Ponty, *Phenomenology of Perception*, trans. Colin Smith (London: Routledge, 1962), 433.

18. As suggested by Jonathan Crary in "Olafur Eliasson: Visionary Events," an essay for *Olafur Eliasson: The Curious Garden*, the catalogue accompanying the Basel show (Basel: Kunsthalle Basel / Schwabe & Co., 1997).

19. Ibid., n.p.

20. Olafur Eliasson, "Vibrations," in *Olafur Eliasson: Your Engagement Has Consequences; On the Relativity of Your Reality*, by Olafur Eliasson et al. (Baden, Switzerland: Lars Müller Publishers, 2006), 65.

21. I draw here upon ideas first developed during a 2003 seminar at the Städelschule in Frankfurt, Germany, and published in my book *Chronology* (New York: Lukas & Sternberg, 2005).

22. Eliasson introduces the acronym *YES* ("Your Engagement Sequence") to denote a fifth dimension that individualizes the subject's relationship with time and space (*Olafur Eliasson: Your Engagement Has Consequences*, 62–63).

23. Ibid., 67.

24. See Walter Benjamin, "The Work of Art in the Age of Mechanical Reproduction," in *Illuminations*, ed. Hannah Arendt, trans. Harry Zohn (New York: Schocken, 1969).

25. Rosalind Krauss, "'The Rock': William Kentridge's Drawings for Projection," *October* 92 (Spring 2000): 30.

26. Benjamin, "The Work of Art in the Age of Mechanical Reproduction," 236.

27. For a discussion of the subject and its "disappearance," see Maurice Blanchot, "Michel Foucault as I Imagine Him," trans. Jeffrey Mehlman, in *Foucault/Blanchot*, by Michel Foucault and Maurice Blanchot (New York: Zone Books, 1987).

28. Ibid., 76.

29. Merleau-Ponty, *Phenomenology of Perception*, 426.

30. Gilles Deleuze, *Foucault*, trans. Séan Hand (London and New York: Continuum, 1988), 108.

31. See Ina Blom, "Bright Shadows: A Conversation between Olafur Eliasson and Ina Blom," in *Olafur Eliasson: Your Engagement Has Consequences*, 177.

32. For the large glass roof of the Portikus in Frankfurt, Germany, Eliasson has developed *Light lab (test I–XII)* (2006–8), an ambitious installation project in twelve chapters, all relating to solar phenomena. The Portikus, which is part of Frankfurt's Städelschule Art Academy, has arranged a related series of philosophical seminars exploring the nature of light from scientific, poetic, and philosophical points of view.

33. Derrida, "White Mythology," 243.

34. Ibid., 251.

SURFACE TENSIONS: OLAFUR ELIASSON AND THE EDGE OF MODERN ARCHITECTURE

Henry Urbach

Around midday, when the sun became visible outside, there was some commotion in the exhibition hall. The splendor of the colored glass ornament was so enhanced by the sun that one was at a loss for words to praise this wonder of color. Many visitors shouted repeatedly, "Delightful! Wonderful! Great! Incomparable!"

— Paul Scheerbart[1]

Paul Scheerbart's futuristic novel of 1914, *The Gray Cloth and Ten Percent White*, meditates on the rise of glass architecture, positing a future in which the modernist fantasy of total design has reached its apotheosis. The story's protagonist, architect Edgar Krug, circumnavigates the globe with his wife, Clara, constructing wildly varied and vibrantly colored glass buildings wherever he goes: a high-rise exhibition and concert hall in Chicago, a retirement complex for pilots in Fiji, a museum of ancient weapons in Malta. To maximize the impact of these colorful buildings, Krug demands that his wife wear only gray clothes containing ten percent white. Her compliance has the effect the architect desires, revealing the buildings' splendor by contrast and securing his fame worldwide.

At the advent of Modernism, and alongside the rise of air travel and *Weltpolitik*, the link between globalization and glass architecture had already become an object of critical inquiry for writers and designers. The modern embrace of clear plate-glass construction would lead, in Scheerbart's fictional account as well as radical design practices of the time, to a counterproposal: an effort to saturate glass buildings with color, a quality that more functionalist strains of Modernism would fail to sustain. To give one important example, Bruno Taut's Glass Pavilion (pl. 129), built in Cologne for the Werkbund Exhibition of 1914, refracted light through its faceted cupola and translucent block walls to illuminate a seven-tiered chamber lined with glass mosaic. Progressive aphorisms by Scheerbart—"Glass brings a new era," "Building in brick only does us harm," "Colored glass destroys hatred"— were literally inscribed on the pavilion's surfaces.

129
Bruno Taut
Glass Pavilion, Cologne, 1914

Nearly a hundred years later, among other contemporary artists and designers seeking to revitalize the constructed surfaces of modernity, Olafur Eliasson has recently and nimbly begun to make his mark. His sizable studio employs many specialists, including more than ten architects who collaborate with professional design firms on projects around the globe, and the roster of Eliasson's recent work with public architecture is impressive to say the least. He has proposed a set of spatial interventions for the Hirshhorn Museum and Sculpture Garden in Washington, D.C., and is developing significant built elements for the Icelandic National Concert and Conference Center in Reykjavík in addition to installations on an architectural scale for the new Opera House in Oslo and the concert hall of the University of Southern Denmark in Sønderborg. He has completed an architecturally inflected work for the Palazzo Grassi in Venice, Italy, as well as *The blind pavilion,* a structure first presented atop the Danish Pavilion at the 2003 Venice Biennale and now situated on an island near Reykjavík. Other design-related projects include *Your mobile expectations* (2007; pl. 130), which sheathes a hydrogen-powered BMW race car with layers of ice to reflect upon the relation between the automotive industry and climate change.

Eliasson's ongoing investigation of space and design follows on his idea of the studio as a laboratory that generates, in his own words, "interdisciplinary dialogues between art and its surroundings, an example being architecture."[2] Shifting part of his practice to an intermediate zone between art and architecture, Eliasson assumes a position from which he can critically investigate the codes that give each field its disciplinary coherence and identity. He presses at the habits of each—an artist works like this, an architect works like that—to posit a new and vital terrain between the two. Within this expanded field, Eliasson articulates a tension between two modes of making: what we might call the projective impulse of architecture—an effort to realize some sort of imagined and desired condition—and a more interpretive, phenomenological approach to making art that seeks to reveal what already exists. In many of Eliasson's projects, built elements, whether constructed by him or by others, have the quality of found material awaiting further elaboration. He teases each surface he makes or

130
Olafur Eliasson
Study (2006) for *Your mobile expectations*
(BMW H₂R Project), 2007
Installation view at Studio Olafur Eliasson, Berlin,
2006. BMW H₂R chassis, net, ice, and cooling unit.
55 1/8 x 220 1/2 x 94 1/2 in. (140 x 560 x 240 cm).
Courtesy the artist

activates, challenging it to open itself toward new and
dynamic forms of experience.

In Eliasson's work, the dialogue
between art and architecture is often pursued along the
surfaces and edges of buildings. The wall or facade
becomes, in many of his projects, a site for establishing
uncommon forms of visual experience and a newly
complex relationship between viewer and architecture.
Built works, following Eliasson's interventions, shed
their stasis and assuredness—their stubborn objecthood—
to become, instead, a more tentative, shaky set of rela-
tionships that unfold over time. He makes surfaces that appear to unmake themselves
or, more precisely, continue to make, unmake, and remake themselves again and again
in the eyes of their beholders. Eliasson often attains this result by using materials that
exploit both the dynamic and chromatic qualities of light, orchestrating an interplay
of tectonic elements, light, color, and viewer that transforms each.

Luminous substances, prismatic shapes, reflective surfaces: these are
some of the tropes that recur when Eliasson's practice approaches architecture. Their
persistence may be seen as an extension of his ongoing body of work with kaleidoscopic
forms in sculpture. Among his early efforts to translate this research into an architectural
mode is *Quasi brick wall* (2002; pls. 165–66), a modest project built on the grounds of
the Fundación NMAC in Cádiz, Spain. Here, in a park setting, Eliasson constructed a
freestanding wall of unusually shaped clay blocks covered with small pieces of mirrored
stainless steel. As sunlight meets its many reflective surfaces, the wall gathers images
of sky, ground, and the surrounding landscape, releasing multiple optical effects that
depend on weather conditions, viewer position, and light. Numerous examples of kaleidoscopic structures and surfaces exist in Eliasson's body of work (see, for example, pls.
82–83, 175, 220–21), and it is worthwhile to reflect briefly on the origins of the kaleidoscope as a way to understand its significance for a late modernist art practice concerned
with architecture.

The kaleidoscope was invented in 1816 by the Scottish scientist Sir
David Brewster, whose work "A Treatise on the Kaleidoscope" was published three years
later. Named by combining the Greek words for beautiful *(kalos)*, form *(eidos)*, and
watcher *(scopos)*, the new device constructed an enclosed landscape for visual pleasure
that was as artificial as it was wondrous. Early kaleidoscopes contained loose pieces of
colored glass within a rotating tube, with angled mirrors and lenses creating complex,
mesmerizing patterns. Kaleidoscopes became extremely popular, especially in America;
as they stimulated the eyes of those who looked inside, they participated in the expan-
sion of quasi-aesthetic experience, transferring the mimetic imperative and transformative

aspirations once reserved for painting and sculpture into a more popular, participatory mode. Held directly to the eye, a kind of prosthetic device for visual pleasure, the kaleidoscope offered people an experience as absorptive and artificial as it was fleeting, and it required an act of attentive viewing to enact its magic.

Let us speculate that Eliasson endeavors to make buildings kaleidoscopic and, with that, to open architecture to a more active and vital mode of experience. Consider *Your wave is* (2006; pls. 223–25), a project commissioned for the facade of the Palazzo Grassi on Venice's Grand Canal, now home to the art collection of French entrepreneur François Pinault. Here Eliasson introduced a lightweight yet monumental web of luminous fiber that hovered nearly five feet in front of the historic facade, with crisscrossing lines running vertically from cornice to waterline. Eliasson's three-dimensional veil glowed by night, reflecting its light onto the moving water of the canal. The project reinterprets the Vitruvian *firmitas* of the original edifice and returns it to us as a kind of stage set, a work in progress that must constantly perform its own representational effects. Eliasson has literally caught the building in the web of its own complex historical reinventions, including its most recent rebirth as a center for the presentation of contemporary art.

Eliasson staged a more spatially complex intervention with another Venice project, his transformation of the Danish Pavilion for the 2003 Biennale (pls. 176–94). Various devices—including kaleidoscopic sculptures, ramps, a monochromatic yellow chamber, and a camera obscura—created a sequence of uncanny effects as viewers moved through interior and exterior spaces, ultimately arriving at a pavilion atop the roof terrace. This circular structure, with walls made of canted, geometric planes of opaque black and clear glass, simultaneously promised and frustrated a panoramic view of the surrounding gardens. The pavilion was later moved from Venice to a windy hilltop on Videy Island, where it now frames and interrupts views across the rural landscape and toward the skyline of Reykjavík (see pl. 131). This is a structure that has been designed specifically to reveal how it mediates between the viewing subject and the viewed world.

131
Olafur Eliasson
The blind pavilion, 2003
Installation view on Videy Island, Iceland, 2005.
Steel and glass. 98 1/2 x 295 1/4 x 295 1/4 in.
(250 x 750 x 750 cm). Private collection

Among many projects now on the boards, Eliasson's proposal for the Icelandic National Concert and Conference Center in Reykjavík (2009; pls. 132–33), designed in collaboration with Henning Larsen Architects, stands out as especially promising. Eliasson has devised a semitransparent skin that produces luminous chromatic effects. The south facade is composed of large prismatic volumes, nearly seven

132–33
Olafur Eliasson in collaboration with
Henning Larsen Architects
Renderings (2007) of Icelandic National
Concert and Conference Center,
Reykjavík, projected opening 2009

feet high, made of steel frame covered with clear and color-filtering glass. These volumes, whose complex shape derives from the form of basalt columns, register extreme seasonal differences in sunlight and change as viewers move around the building.

With the Reykjavík project Eliasson seeks to create what he has called "a visually negotiable structure." If successful on these terms, the building will never cease to change appearance, always presenting instead a dynamic convergence of space, time, and light coordinates. Dramatic shifts in transparency, reflection, and color will render the building surface kaleidoscopic rather than a static and stable carrier of meaning, as is more traditional in historical Modernism. It is not difficult to imagine people reacting to this building as Scheerbart's fictional crowds did, declaring utter delight, albeit with a diminished sense of how colored glass might enact a new social order.

Eliasson's proposal for the lobby of the new Opera House in Oslo (2008; pl. 134), designed by Snøhetta, operates on a more intimate, interior scale. Lightweight, lattice-like screens veil existing concrete walls, dematerializing these built elements. (The lattice also recalls the fishnet pattern of *Your wave is*; indeed, another kaleidoscopic aspect of Eliasson's work is the way in which he continually recombines fragments and

134
Olafur Eliasson
Rendering (2005) of foyer installation, Opera
House, Oslo, projected opening 2008

135
Dan Graham
Two-way Mirror Cylinder Inside Two-way
Mirror Cube and Video Salon, 1989–91
Installation view at Dia Center for the Arts,
New York, 1991. Glass, steel, wood, and rubber.
96 x 432 x 432 in. (243.8 x 1,097.3 x 1,097.3 cm).
Collection of Dan Graham and Marion
Goodman Gallery

forms from past projects into new arrangements.) LED lights, set into the floor as well as behind the mesh screens, will be programmed by the artist to create changing optical effects over the course of the evening. Another surface, built of mirrored glass, penetrates the facade of the building, half inside and half out, to elaborate further visual complexity through the entry sequence.

Eliasson's walls advance a project initiated by Dan Graham in the late 1970s. In Graham's glass pavilions, many built with two-way mirrored panels, shifts in daylight and viewer position enact myriad optical effects, continually modulating relative degrees of transparency and reflection along the structures' inner and outer surfaces (see pl. 135). They envelop viewers in disorienting spaces of doubling, flattening, and reversal, thereby challenging and complicating perceptual and social relationships in space. Like Graham, Eliasson holds a mirror up to architectural practice and a century of modern glass construction and offers a provocation instead. He extends Graham's groundbreaking project in numerous ways, including a move toward more monumental, urban-scale projects and a commitment to producing a greater variety of visual effects. Perhaps the most significant difference, and the one most likely to captivate crowds and provoke architects to rethink their ways, is the transformation of the facade into a kaleidoscopic device, a surface capable of producing delirious chromatic effects that have, quite simply, not been seen before.

Throughout much of Modernism, color has been viewed as a kind of other, a decorative or ornamental category not on par with structural or representational priorities. Where architects have pursued transparency, especially, they have usually limited color to monochrome, and the idea that a building could actually change color has not held much credibility. As David Batchelor argues in *Chromophobia*, color has been negligently or forcefully purged from many Western aesthetic practices, either by linking it to something alien (foreign, Eastern, feminine) or by relegating it to the realm of the superficial and cosmetic.[3]

In Eliasson's project for Reykjavík, as with others now in development, color returns with a vengeance to activate the transparent glass surface. Where modernist architects sought to purify the surfaces they offered to the world, Eliasson aims to render them complex, impure, and engaging. These are enriched walls, edges that are lined with nuance and surprise. Eliasson thus invites us to experience architecture in a deeply unexpected way: with wonder. In this respect he allies his work with some of the more significant reinventions of the facade in recent memory, including Jean Nouvel's 1987 Institut du Monde Arabe in Paris, where the entire southern wall is composed of mechanical oculi that open and shut like camera lenses, and Diller Scofidio + Renfro's Blur Building (pl. 136) on Lake Neuchâtel, constructed for the 2002 Swiss Expo and fitted with more than thirty-one thousand spray nozzles that engulfed the structure in a cloud of fog and mist.

Throughout the last century, architects have usually charged facades with the imperative to be honest, transparent, direct, orderly, appropriate, contextual, reflective, layered, or expressive. But how often have walls been imbued with sufficient complexity and nuance to provoke awe? By recognizing and manipulating the potential of the architectural surface, Eliasson takes the discourse a step forward. It is not against gray clothing with ten percent white that his built works radiate; it is against the banality of so many buildings that have abandoned wonder as a touchstone of modern design.

136
Diller Scofidio + Renfro
Blur Building, Yverdon-les-Bains, Switzerland, 2002

What remains to be seen, as Eliasson advances this architectural and urban line of investigation, is how "visually negotiable" structures might unfold to become more complex spatial provocations, and how their wondrous effects might be channeled further to reveal more fully the transformative potential of architecture. For the moment, we have a gesture of real force and a reminder to architects that facades can, quite simply, do more. This is what Scheerbart imagined a hundred years ago: a challenge to modern architecture that was largely forgotten and reaches us, in our times, as part of the incomplete project that is modernity.

NOTES

1. Paul Scheerbart, *Das graue Tuch und zehn Prozent Weiß* (The Gray Cloth and Ten Percent White, 1914), published in English as *The Gray Cloth: Paul Scheerbart's Novel on Glass Architecture*, trans. John A. Stuart (Cambridge, MA: MIT Press, 2001), 3.

2. This and subsequent quotations by the artist are from an interview with the author at Studio Olafur Eliasson, Berlin, June 2006.

3. See David Batchelor, *Chromophobia* (London: Reaktion Books: 2000).

Mieke Bal

We're metaphors. We always come in the colour and shape of your imagination.
—Femi Osofisan[1]

Water Time

Some time ago I went to Rotterdam to see Olafur Eliasson's installation *Notion motion* (2005; pls. 4, 137, 226–33) at the Museum Boijmans Van Beuningen. I don't often travel to another city on a Sunday afternoon, but I am fond of the Boijmans and was attracted by Eliasson's work, so I decided to go.

Notion motion, as exhibited at the Boijmans, is an ensemble of three rooms or spaces or events connected by a single long wall. In each space, the viewer is caught up in a semidarkness where light "happens"—changes and moves—thanks to the impossibility of water remaining entirely still in the presence of living creatures. The first room I entered contained a shallow pool of water, slightly moving, its tiny, symmetrical waves projected onto the wall behind it. Over the water a suspended object hovered. Every so often this object, a sponge, was dumped into the water with a splash that, from within the stillness this piece inspired, sounded like a violent shot.[2]

As a consequence of the fall of the sponge the water changes, as does the reflection. The middle of the pool turns into a mouth, then an oyster, a flower opening up, perhaps a face. Moving quickly at first, then slowly widening, the circular ripples of water begin to calm down, returning to tiny waves before the viewer has seen enough. Slow, yet too fast. Holding my breath, I waited for the next drop of the sponge. It came, yes, but I had to adapt my impatience to its rhythm and wait, unable to influence the pace of the machinery. Later I looked at the installation from the back and saw a cut in the wall that resembled a framed painting. An image, an event; a frame, a stretch of time.

In the second space, waves of water appeared on a narrow band at the bottom of the wall. The horizontal isolation of the tiny movements made the waves suggestive of writing in an unknown script. The desire to see turned into the desire to read, to decipher water language. Turning around, I saw the same waves, larger, on a farther wall, but now shadows of people disturbed their quiet beauty. To see the waves properly at full scale was not possible unless I accepted the presence of other people's bodies. People were cast within the waterscape.

The contribution of moving bodies to what we can see of moving water was even more prominent in the third space. Here the floor had some uneven boards, beneath which something invisible and beyond the visitor's control had to happen. The movement of people walking on these boards set off machinery that produced motion, but only marginally. This realization made people want to make more movement, to jump on the boards, but nothing much happened as a result. In the first room, time was what effected transformation and was the element to which the visitor had to submit; here it was an a priori decision concerning the scope of the visitor's impact: subtle but not spectacular, modest yet inevitable. One could not see the reflected water here without making it move, but the game was not in one's own hands. The materiality of light became visible as that of the walls faded, while anthropocentric self-importance was kept at bay.

Inside this intimate, quiet, and delightfully playful space, I remembered standing once on the Canadian side of Niagara Falls, inside the grotto. Behind the eternally thundering wall of water I realized the brevity of human existence. I also realized the power of water: its violence, beauty, and autonomy. Schooled, like most of us, in the Romanticism that lingers within postmodernity, I could not help thinking of the sublime and its cliché icon, Caspar David Friedrich's painting *Wanderer above a Sea of Fog* (ca. 1817; pl. 138). But nothing I had ever read about the sublime connected with this experience. The falls made me think of every inundation, every transgression of water over dikes, of streamlined, canalized rivers and straightened coasts. This mighty wall of water reaffirmed that autonomy, nature's vengeance on human bossiness. Later, the 2004 Indian Ocean

137
Olafur Eliasson
Notion motion, 2005 (EXH.)
Installation view at the Museum Boijmans Van Beuningen, Rotterdam, Netherlands, 2005. HMI spotlights, tripods, water, foil, projection foil, wood, nylon, and sponge. Museum Boijmans Van Beuningen, on loan from the H+F Mecenaat

138
Caspar David Friedrich
Wanderer above a Sea of Fog, ca. 1817
Oil on canvas. 37 3/8 x 29 1/2 in. (94.8 x 74.9 cm).
Hamburger Kunsthalle, Hamburg, Germany, on
permanent loan from the Foundation for the
Promotion of the Hamburg Art Collections

tsunami, Hurricane Katrina 2005—the new icons of water's might—would insinuate themselves.

Rather than soliciting the experience of the sublime, then, Eliasson's installation brings water closer to humans. There is no imminent danger, no sense of self-inflicted doom, yet the work is powerfully political. Accidents become small, modesty-inducing, purposeful acts; time, no longer eternal yet beyond our control, becomes a responsibility; not too bright, artificial but on and in water, light—the best draughtsman imaginable— becomes material, almost heavy. At the Boijmans, the paintings hanging near one of the entrances to the installation offered a refuge, a safe haven from an engagement I neither could nor wished to escape, that felt intrusive into the deepest recesses of "me." It transformed my sense of self-in-place, my very capacity of perception, of seeing light and its materiality.

But then, this happened inside a museum. The simple fact that *Notion motion* was accessible only by way of traditional paintings triggered an understanding of (art) history that I must bring to bear on Eliasson's installation. If only to gauge the meaning of his body of work, we must clear away this historical perspective, lest we fall into the trap of declaring his art either unique or merely part of a tradition—in both cases disempowering it.

The surroundings of an artwork are not indifferent to its meaning and its power, and few artists drive this point home more clearly than Eliasson, whose exhibition titles, with their frequent second-person pronouns, include *Your intuitive surroundings versus your surrounded intuition* and *Surroundings surrounded*. He even subtitled one recent book "Your Engagement Has Consequences: On the Relativity of Your Reality." It does, indeed: willy-nilly, every exhibition is an installation of sorts, hence a work of installation art, and thus engages its viewers spatially.

It may be more or less successful qua installation—indeed, the curator may or may not pursue the affiliation between exhibition and installation—but Julie H. Reiss's assertions about installation also inevitably hold true, at least in principle, for the larger and more heterogeneous ensembles that are exhibitions:

> There is always a reciprocal relationship of some kind between the viewer and the work, the work and the space, and the space and the viewer. . . . One might add that in creating an installation, the artist treats an entire indoor space (large enough for people to enter) as a single situation. . . . The spectator is in some way regarded as integral to the completion of the work.[3]

Exhibitions are what installations explicitly seek to be: "critical habitats," to recycle Emily Apter's felicitous concept.[4] For this reason, I begin my essay with a response to *Notion motion* in its temporary habitat, which is critical in the precise sense of disentangling, and

139
Pieter Claesz
Breakfast, 1636
Oil on panel. 14 1/8 x 19 1/4 in. (36 x 49 cm).
Museum Boijmans Van Beuningen, Rotterdam,
Netherlands

140
Willem Claesz. Heda
*Still Life with Oysters, Roemer, Lemon, and
Silver Tazza*, 1634
Oil on panel. 16 7/8 x 22 1/2 in. (43 x 57 cm).
Museum Boijmans Van Beuningen, Rotterdam,
Netherlands

go on to consider the relationships that it establishes with its environment—in space and
in time—as emblematic of the larger exhibition.

Herein lies a paradox I cannot escape. Though Eliasson's work imposes
the installation's meaning as mise en abyme of the museum, it is radically *not* an instance
of, or even a variation on, the tradition of landscape painting. Between the depicting kind
of representation and his installation of elements such as water lies a gap that no theoretical
perspective can bridge: Eliasson emphatically does not offer representations, though his art
engages the pervasiveness of representation in our visual surroundings. His work is full of
images that offer possibilities for seeing things in them, but he does not re-present in the
sense of depicting them according to a model. There is a difference between portraying
a landscape from elsewhere on canvas and creating a landscape on the spot and in the
moment; this quality of "surroundings surrounded" thus implicates the sense of space itself.
Experience is at the heart of this approach, and although the experiences the works induce
are artificial, isolated from "life" outside the gallery as it is the mission of "art" to propose,
something real happens during the brief suspension of disbelief that transforms the subject's
sense of self. This change emerges from an experience of space that is profoundly unsettling.
No longer measurable and external, space, here, is a subjective sensation of being-in-time.

As a result, the historical context or frame is no longer thematic or
anchored in landscape; it is philosophical and aesthetic. The new affiliation I would
therefore propose for Eliasson's work is with the baroque. By this I do not mean seventeenth-
century painting and sculpture—or, more pertinently perhaps, architecture—but a sensibility that never went away, only moved underground when more classical tendencies
took over. It is a baroque we have seen reemerge with Gilles Deleuze and "his" Henri
Bergson (the latter also a favorite of Eliasson's). Baroque is the name of a relationship
between subject and surroundings, or reality, that is neither relativist nor nominalist
but literally *engaging*.[5] Considering the work as baroque requires a sense of history that
breaks through the linearity of evolutionism, and is instead anchored in memory. This
opens the way to the political in this art—the sense that subjects must engage with their

environments, neither detached nor immersed but active, on innovative, creative, and responsible terms.

From landscape to light, from space to body, and by means of baroque politics, Eliasson brings his work to bear on its relationship with the viewer and, in turn, the viewer's relationship with the environment. At the same time, however, that environment speaks back. This seems appropriate in a discussion of art that is, above all, relational. The final paradox, then, is this: Eliasson makes powerful statements, proposals for reenvisioning the world; he suggests that we must learn to see it differently rather than change it. This is a call for modesty, for abandoning the utopian passion for a changeable world. Yet the modesty involved in this limitation is precisely what is most profoundly political about his work.

Landscape to Light: Out of Eden

Since *Notion motion* is all about light and water, water as light, it makes sense to see Eliasson's installation in the context of painting's keen interest in light and, especially in the Low Lands, its effect on water.[6] Outside the installation, the light on the skin of a herring in Pieter Claesz's *Breakfast* of 1636 (pl. 139) seemed to shine more brilliantly than I had ever seen it do. But it was not only the almost excessive sheen that struck me. The shining skin appeared to be a body turned inside out. It glossed Willem Claesz. Heda's still lifes (see pl. 140), with their characteristic lemon peels, which I had always seen as a classical device boasting the mastery of the artist, foregrounding his skill in

depicting the inside and outside of an object in one curling move. Now, however, that inside-out game seemed to reference the larger problem of surface and vision, suggesting that seeing is itself an act of being inside and outside at the same time. And Dutch light—light *on* and, to an extent, *in* water—had something to do with that.[7]

The Boijmans's collection here skips two centuries. Hendrik Willem Mesdag's painting *North Sea During a Storm* (1885; pl. 141), near the seventeenth-century still lifes, looked freshly restored, with a pristine surface of paint as light. The success of the painter's rendition of light on water, however, served to accentuate a failure inherent in the medium: the menacing storm so naturalistically evoked by the touch of the brush and the simple whites of the paint asked for the waves to move, but they did not. Frantically, I imagined, the spectator moves her eyes to compensate for the unnatural stillness of the paint, which glisters so fiercely that the light on the water seems to roar. The semidarkness of the storm further highlights—literally—the light that the dark water appears to push up from beneath its surface.

Juxtaposed with the Boijmans's collection, Eliasson's high-tech installation incongruously rivals the venerated tradition of Dutch painting. It claims a place in

141
Hendrik Willem Mesdag
North Sea During a Storm, 1885
Oil on canvas. 55⅛ x 71¼ in. (140 x 181 cm).
Museum Boijmans Van Beuningen, Rotterdam, Netherlands

that tradition while gently mocking it, without derision. This double relationship is anchored in the radicalization his work implies: no longer representing movement, relying on the viewer to mimic it, the installation makes it "real." The viewer is inside movement yet also makes it. Suddenly there is that tension, that unsettling sense of the self as necessarily related to "your intuitive surroundings" (of which the painters could only create the illusion). Yet, in spite of the presence of actual water, nothing is real. The rivalry does not concern the sun and the sea; all of this is artificial, theatrical.

Only because of this framing environment did the installation initially make sense as a landscape—specifically, a water-and-lightscape. Many of Eliasson's works entertain a contentious relationship with landscape. *Moss wall* (1994; pl. 30), for example, uses real moss in the way *Notion motion* uses real water, but denaturalizes the moss by isolating it and growing it vertically. Instead of being an element of the natural environment—something that we often literally walk on, that we use as a doormat—the humble plant becomes an impediment, a boundary beyond which we cannot see. It precludes vision from penetrating the distant beyond and thus corrects the tendency to ignore what is close at hand. Many Eliasson works deploy light as their tool, medium, and image. *Round rainbow* (2005)—a disc piece quite similar to *Colour space embracer* (2005; pls. 212–13)—engineers, with ostentatious artifice, the color effect of another conventional trigger of the sublime, speaking to the relationship of light and water as a miracle worker for vision. Such works refer to, inherit, comment upon, recast, and innovate what traditional art appreciation knows as "landscape." Paradoxical as it may seem, discussing these three-dimensional installations, in which no paint is involved, as or in relation to landscape is a first step toward understanding their historical position.

Landscape is a genre of figurative painting. It is also a material reality of "nature," arranged for humans. Petra Halkes formulates its principles tersely: "Traditional landscape paintings have generally shown scenery, a vista, a prospect; the land is laid out before the viewer with geometric clarity. Foreground, middle ground, and background are organized according to the principles of perspective and are demarcated by the edges of the picture plane."[8] Due to its exposure along the width of the wall and its expansive inside spaces, *Notion motion* is a bit of a landscape itself. By means of such allusions to the genre, it manages to question profoundly common conceptions of landscape. Eliasson's works may sometimes suggest landscape, but more frequently they "do" landscape through intervention. And landscape, both the natural scenery so named and the painterly genre, is bound up with the history of philosophy: its dual history reflects changing conceptions of humanity's place in the environment.[9]

"Landscape" seems a relevant frame for Eliasson's works—not because they are landscapes (many are not), but because they perform interventions in what we have naturalized as landscape. In this sense, they intervene not just in the natural environment, but also, more importantly, in our conception of it, our position in relation to it.

The term *landscape* indicates a humanized relationship with nature, whether this relationship is one of self-affirmation through dominion or conquest or, on the contrary, a desire to transcend and efface the self in the face of nature. Both attitudes come from a fundamental discontent with the limitations of human existence. It is this dissatisfaction that Eliasson's work questions, and endeavors to remedy by empowering subjects to be more responsive and responsible. Attempts to separate the two appearances of landscape (as outside and as representation) are themselves entangled in preconceptions—either in attitudes such as those just mentioned or in the very paradox of their coexistence.[10]

Notion motion alludes to this problematic by insisting that the genre of landscape painting does not rest on a distinction between nature and culture, but instead evidences the impossibility of making such a distinction. The word *landscape* implies an arrangement of the environment by the human gaze, whether it leads to the landscaping of nature or to its representation in painting. Eliasson's installation cuts through the dichotomy between representation and reality. It is a radical arrangement, all thought out and technologically mise en scène—pure artifice. Though the light shines on real water, the work drastically severs the relationship between "real" and "natural." As a result, we come to realize that the idea of landscape, instead of enabling humans to bypass representation, catches us within a web of representational strategies and resulting events, subtracting from the experience any easy distinction between the two. In short, real water is not natural.

The impossibility of representational innocence can be detected in traditional landscape as well. The historically changing yet durable status of this tension is important, for it shows in two traditional topoi frequently associated with landscape. Both are foregrounded by light on and in water. Both shimmer through Eliasson's installation, specifically in the ostentatious tension between "real" and "natural" (controlled movement and the randomness of water made to move by mechanical devices in conjunction with visitor behavior).

One of these topoi is the myth of the garden of Eden as the precultural space of innocence; the other is the idea of the sublime. *Notion motion* invokes, considers, and ultimately rejects both. The installation deploys theatrical means, with the pleasure of artifice that entails, to offer—to perform and stimulate—in-depth reflection that can be properly called philosophical. Eliasson's work, without falling into the many traps of representation as imitation, unmoors, by means of fictitious environments, the position of humans in the environment called nature. Catching this philosophizing in the act, then, we are able to see how each piece contributes to what the ensemble most profoundly points out: that art "thinks"—not illustrating prior thoughts but actually cogitating. And since this thinking requires the participation of viewers, the task of provisionally completing the thought befalls the visitor, helped as she is by the curator. If one is tempted to position this work art historically, the way in which it thinks makes such positioning necessarily philosophical.[11]

In opposite ways, Eden and sublimity each foreground the near-desperate attempt to imagine and theorize humanity as distinct from nature—a distinction the concept of landscape presupposes and represses. Eden stands for an idealized state of humanity before the "fall," the awareness of life's limitation, its finitude. The fall into reality. Religion calls it sin: the sin of transgressing rules. Psychology calls it adulthood: the knowledge needed to compensate for death through procreation. Our obsession with time as chronology and progress calls it prelapsarian: *before* the fall, before the end of timeless bliss, before, also, the fall of the sponge that disrupts the infinite, gentle waves reflected on the wall in *Notion motion*. "Before," or in fantasies of infinitude, we were happy in a safely enclosed garden that had everything we needed. The chronology implied by "before" is a problem of consciousness, awareness, and relationality. "Eden" is an enclosed space of "before," from which humans were expelled "after."

Today, with increasing anxieties about borders (academic borders between disciplines as well as political borders between nations) and, most worrisomely, anxieties concerning the preservation of borders as the basis of constructions defining inside and outside, "us" and "them," it seems opportune to reflect on the childish fantasy involved in the myth of paradise. Ambivalence toward nature doubtlessly incites a desire for a protected, enclosed, Edenic nature. Eliasson's *Moss wall* makes the point ironically: You want enclosure? Here you have it: an impenetrable wall beyond which you cannot see. The wall contradicts the two meanings of landscape, as vista and as representation, term by term, both equally radically.

The three spaces of *Notion motion*, however, are both enclosed and open. Each proposes a different sense of the motion of light on water and of our bodily relationship with that motion, yet each communicates with the others. Literally, the spaces are contiguous, connected by a narrow opening. Figuratively, each addresses the same issue: what we see when our body sees light on water. With this dialectic of space as both open and closed, Eliasson acknowledges the tension inherent in the ideology of Eden. To the extent that he engages the relationship between humans and nature, he also inevitably engages the politics of boundaries, borders, and transgression inherited from the Eden fantasy.[12]

Of equally great social and artistic relevance is the need to reflect critically on the sublime—an idea that many of Eliasson's works invoke and reject. The sublime is a flirtation with the absence of enclosures such as those offered by Eden. Eliasson alludes to this longing in *Moss wall*'s systemic opposites, *I only see things when they move* (2004; pl. 198), *Sunset kaleidoscope* (2005; pls. 220–21), *Yellow*

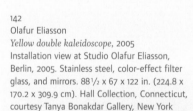

142
Olafur Eliasson
Yellow double kaleidoscope, 2005
Installation view at Studio Olafur Eliasson,
Berlin, 2005. Stainless steel, color-effect filter
glass, and mirrors. 88½ x 67 x 122 in. (224.8 x
170.2 x 309.9 cm). Hall Collection, Connecticut,
courtesy Tanya Bonakdar Gallery, New York

double kaleidoscope (2005; pl. 142), and *Beauty* (1993; pls. 5, 31); the Tate Modern's Turbine Hall almost condemned him to come to terms with this issue for *The weather project* (2003; pls. 1–2, 15, 196–97).[13] Yet, by taking manifestations of the sublime literally and showing its ideological mechanisms (among other means, through overt acknowledgment of the art's technological mechanisms), these works undermine sublimity's possibility— and, indeed, its desirability. In the experience of the sublime, supposedly, the near-overwhelming might of nature, absent firm enclosures and boundaries, revises the relationship between humans and the environment. But this starting point, seemingly opposite from Eden, is deceptive.

143
Olafur Eliasson
Your colour memory, 2004
Installation view at the Arcadia University Art Gallery, Glenside, Pennsylvania, 2004. Wood, stainless steel, fluorescent lights, color-filter foil, control unit, and projection foil. 127 1/8 x 208 5/8 x 349 1/4 in. (323 x 530 x 887 cm). Astrup Fearnley Museet for Moderne Kunst, Oslo

The sublime experience occurs at the moment one is confronted by the power of nature, in danger of being overwhelmed by it, and comes out victorious, thanks to rationality. In Immanuel Kant's version, the greatest thrill of the sublime experience is that in spite of the threat—indeed, after the subject has gone or worked through it—reason wins. Hence, while Eden is based on a chronological "before," sublimity's time is an "after." As Gayatri Spivak has pointed out, Kant's argument needs the firm establishment of a limit—between rational men and those he considers limited cases of humanity.[14]

Eliasson's work teases us with the association. As Jonathan Crary, one of the first contemporary critics to have drawn attention to embodied modes of vision and their historical emergence, wrote apropos of Eliasson's *Your colour memory* (2004; pl. 143), this association is one of many traps the work proposes. Crary argues that the indeterminate and ineffable qualities of the installation are "conditions out of which other events might tentatively occur, out of which communication, interpersonal exchange, and provisional forms of understanding might be possible."[15] I concur with Crary's resistance to sublimity as a framework for Eliasson's art, and also with the direction in which the author seeks alternatives—forms of understanding and (or in) interpersonal communication. Still, I consider the very status of the contested concept— hence, the temptation to bring it to bear on the work—a reason to probe further why it is not applicable, yet seems such an obvious association that it comes up regularly in criticism on the artist. In line with Eliasson's own manifest attitude toward what he critiques, I feel compelled to take the association seriously; discarding it too quickly would miss a crucial point in his political posture. Indeed, the collusion between Eden and sublimity, as bound together in Eliasson's deployment of the relationship between humans and nature, deserves closer scrutiny.[16]

The point I wish to make is that the collusion between the myths of Eden and sublimity breaks through the apparent opposition of the two. I seek to understand it in the connection between two art-historical topoi: color and the detail. Color, in an art-historical tradition Svetlana Alpers has discussed at length apropos of Peter Paul Rubens, has often been considered in ideological terms (specifically gendered feminine); so has, according to Naomi Schor, the detail.[17] Eliasson's work with color as uncertain, changing, subject-created, and insubstantially dependent on light—most famously in *Your colour memory, Room for one colour* (1997; pl. 178), and *360° room for all colours* (2002; pls. 167–72)—can be seen as critically engaging such limited and essential-

izing views. In terms of the discussion of landscape, it is also important to realize that he conducts this debate by creating critical habitats for the experience of color. Moreover, in *Notion motion* the painterly richness of the reflections is produced in black and white, which is yet another way of destabilizing the perception of color.

144
Olafur Eliasson
Yellow corridor, 1997
Installation view at the ARoS Aarhus
Kunstmuseum, Denmark, 2004. Monofrequency
lights. Collection of Pat and Juan Vergez

Although many of Eliasson's works do engage color in color, never is color concrete or self-evident. Some of his most subtle elaborations of color simultaneously engage the tension between presentation and representation. *Moss wall*, obviously, recalls that color cannot be stable since it is organic (in this work "really") and hence has a life in time. The reflections inside and outside *The drop factory* (2000; pl. 96) continually import and export color as visitors put themselves in the picture, fractured and multiplied as they are by the segments of the dome. *Yellow corridor* (1997; pl. 144) and *360° room for all colours* immerse visitors in that same color instability. And *Beauty* most emphatically underscores the instability of color. Inside the dark space of this installation, each visitor must take up a unique spatial position to see a rainbow appear in the curtain of water. This exquisite vision connects the primal scene of color perception both to scarcity (each viewer can only see it from a precise angle) and to a widely diffused cliché. Moreover, the work's title draws attention to the bond between color and three conceptions of beauty, all liable to illusion and abuse: nature, art, and femininity.

The question of the detail is one that the historical baroque posed to Renaissance art; what seemed a commentary on the marginal and its temporal variant, the fleeting and the accidental, rapidly took over the entire field of vision. In *Notion motion*, the detail of the round, mouthlike shape that immediately follows the plunge of the sponge extends to the far corners of the frame until it fades away, yet its memory leaves traces long after the water has returned to its normal state. Elsewhere in the installation, the writing of light on and with water comments on the detail as crucial to perception yet unstable and fugitive. As if questioning, with Jacques Derrida, the stability of writing, the finely drawn waves elude any attempt to distinguish permanence from presence and stillness from movement.[18] Instead the work posits a Bergsonian continuum of time and space that depends on the subject, whose very involvement and implication "make" time and space.[19]

In the context of the opposing philosophical—or, rather, ideological—conceptions that have such a predominant status in contemporary Western culture, it is worth noting that the sublime and Eden have different problems with the detail. In the former, rational man wrestles his way out of his status as a mere detail in the landscape: tiny man conquers infinite nature, and reason turns the tables in the precarious power relationship. In the latter, man is unreasonably forbidden to eat a detail (what is one piece of fruit, one tree among so many?), but that detail, once absorbed, turns out to be overwhelming, regulating life beyond individual human existence.[20]

Is it a coincidence—a subjective, idiosyncratic response on my part—or a more fundamental speech act of *Notion motion* that the first figure produced by the sponge's fall is a mouth? The mouth's associations are plentiful: creaturely embodied existence, foodscapes, eroticism and its presence in advertising, speech in its embodied status as act.[21] Eden is not necessarily the first that comes to mind, but the biblical story's insistence on eating as transgression is certainly powerful. Spivak, citing Raymond Williams, uses the term *pre-emergent* to describe meanings that remain marginal yet are persistent once they have been made to matter.

I retain Spivak's term here, again, in its literal sense, for the mouth in the water's reflection is visible only for a fleeting moment: first as pre-emergent (if one already has mouths on one's mind, so to speak), and then passing through the shape of a flower before widening into disappearance, lingering only as an afterimage. This temporal aspect of *Notion motion* is key to the *experience*, not the result, of the compulsion to associate. And experience, not a feature or a thing, is what defines the sublime. When considered in its temporality, sublimity is nearly overwhelming, an experience of finitude in the face of infinitude—yet crucially, in the end, mastery is restored. By referencing the mouth as a site of transgression (a mouth we must "perform," as we catch it in its pre-emergent state and cannot hold on to it as it fades), the fall of the sponge questions Eden and the sublime in one rapid move. Eliasson's work does not simply recuperate the traditional distinctions of art (i.e., color and detail), but engages, answers, and makes tangible Spivak's critique of Kantian sublimity as the boundary of what it is to be human.

By virtue of being housed in a museum, processed by visitors as "art" and thereby slowing down the experience, *Notion motion* offers Edenic shelter and enclosure. The artist contemplated this protective tendency of art exhibitions in an interview with Daniel Birnbaum: "Looking out of the window might work in the same way as being inside a museum, where everything is presented as if it's isolated from its time, history, and context."[22] All of Eliasson's works, in vastly different ways, demonstrate that if we take—or, rather, give—the time these installations require to *work*, such protection is unnecessarily defensive and limiting. His art, by complicating ideological engagements with nature that rest on the boundary between humanity and nature, resists contemporary misreadings of Kant that turn the experience of the sublime into a feature of the object. Eliasson's most sublime work, *The weather project*, rejects the concept rigorously, as it also displays its own mechanism of deception. As a result of its temporality and experiential nature, the sublime, in its modified and perhaps thereby contradictory form, is rigorously on the order of the performative. But the empowering effect of performance de facto undermines the sublime; it is no longer something that happens to us but something that we actively "do." The initial state of terror is unnecessary, Eliasson seems to suggest, if we are able to shed our obsession with the dichotomy between nature and culture.[23]

Eliasson's disenchanted use of mechanical devices and theatrical effects to produce the "nature effect," along with his obvious activism against an autonomist conception of installation art, binds reflection on the sublime to performativity. The viewer is in charge of performing *Notion motion*; the installation subjects her body to the dictatorial temporality of nature as the waves restore themselves to regularity. The desire to hold on to the fleeting figuration is itself a bodily experience, rendering vision tactile. But by taking the viewer seriously as an embodied subject rather than a "pure" brain or eye, Eliasson ultimately rejects the sublime experience. Instead of conquering nature with reason, the installation keeps the precariousness alive, hovering between the separate bodies of the viewer and the frame of reflections, on the one hand, and the temptation to merge them, on the other. Instead of a threat, nature constitutes a challenge; instead of being nearly overwhelming, it is engaging. Unlike Eden, *Notion motion* undermines delimitation.

Perhaps, then, Eliasson's work, especially when it alludes to landscape yet keeps it at bay, contributes to a different kind of landscape—a performative one, embodied via acts of landscaping and resulting in what Ernst van Alphen would term *landscapishness*: an engagement with "your intuitive surroundings" rather than the colonization of a prestructured prospect.[24] In this performative landscape, boundaries are acknowledged but made transgressable and unstable. Here boundaries can be suspended without threat; here boundaries are spaces, not the refusal of space. (As Inge E. Boer would have it, they become spaces of negotiation and contestation.)[25] One reading of Eliasson's art would posit the works themselves as boundaries—as terrains or playgrounds that would separate if we were ever to stop playing in and with them. In this sense, the artist is invested in keeping viewers actively engaged by the works as long as possible—long enough, that is, for them never to be able to return to an ideological state of separation.

Eliasson's work is thus philosophically profound and open; by way of the metonymical metaphor of landscape, the nature of that philosophical contribution becomes visible. In an Adornian negative dialectic between Eden and the sublime, the installations allow and facilitate a reflection on the relationship between, on the one hand, the individual who has been the target of Western art and, on the other, the environment, whatever we consider it to be: nature, that which lies outside the home and family, "impure" art, or cultural "others." This relationship, the artist seems to suggest, can be rethought, free of any pervasive sense of threat.

So not only has Eliasson taken a place in the tradition of landscape painting, he has become a major performative philosopher. The shift entails a reversal of historical outlook. It takes us back to the dialectic of detail and whole—the white tips of the waves, for example, in Mesdag's stormy sea. Spatially, *Notion motion* overtakes the environment of which it was initially only a detail and recasts its elements (hence the sense of recent cleaning with the Boijmans's paintings). Temporally, then, it reverses the notion of history as chronology that is so dear to the humanities and specifically to art history. Now the present moment, that Sunday afternoon in Rotterdam, becomes the starting point, the origin from which all else—the skin of the herring, the tips of the waves in Mesdag's painting—evolves. Similarly, *Notion motion* is now the starting point for a new imaginary of nature, one in which neither Eden nor sublimity, neither their entanglements nor their obsessive distinctions, has a place.

Space to Body: In Time

The dialectic of detail and whole is foregrounded by the relationship between the building as a whole, its other displays, and the exhibition of Eliasson's works—many of which function, in turn, as installations, reiterating that dialectic. In other words, upon entering the museum the visitor is immediately surrounded and surrounding; incapable of visually colonizing it, he or she is instead absorbed within a tripartite installation: of the entire museum, including its permanent collection; of the Eliasson exhibition; and of the works within the exhibition. At the San Francisco Museum of Modern Art, for example, rather than taking the elevator to the top floor, occupied in its entirety by Eliasson's works, the visitor can enter the exhibition by way of a bridge suspended across the circular skylight at the center of the atrium, over which one of Eliasson's tunnel pieces has been installed (see pl. 145). Although this entrance is perfectly safe, its visual precariousness prepares

145
Olafur Eliasson
Rendering of *One-way colour tunnel*, 2007 (EXH.)
Stainless steel, color-effect acrylic, and acrylic
mirrors. 100 3/4 x 70 7/8 x 413 3/8 in. (256 x 180 x
1,050 cm). Courtesy the artist; Tanya Bonakdar
Gallery, New York; and neugerreimschneider, Berlin

the visitor for an experience in which viewing is multisensorial, space moves, and time is unpredictable. This means of entering the exhibition broaches the question to which the discussion of landscape and its traditions led us in the previous section of this essay: the relation of space to the body entering it, surrounded by it and intuitively surrounding it at the same time. The bridge literally embodies the relationality that the works seek to perform; the tunnel is the bridge's counterpart.

According to Annelie Lütgens, twentieth-century Light and Space art began to deploy four fundamental tenets as early as the 1920s, when László Moholy-Nagy began his experiments with light sculptures (see pl. 146).[26] Eliasson's art, like Moholy-Nagy's, makes space a coordinate of movement, compels perception to realize its dynamic nature, theatrically stages this realization by means of machinery, and activates the viewer's participation beyond the mere act of looking. Add movement and time to this list, and three related antecedents—Light and Space art, early modernist attempts to represent the passage of time, and the historical baroque—vie for his attention and submit to his preposterous acts of recasting, restaging, and transforming.[27]

146
László Moholy-Nagy
Light Prop for an Electric Stage (Light-Space Modulator), 1930
Aluminum, steel, nickel-plated brass, other metals, plastic, wood, and electric motor.
59 1/2 x 27 1/2 x 27 1/2 in. (151.1 x 69.9 x 69.9 cm).
Busch-Reisinger Museum, Cambridge, Massachusetts

To assess the radical position of Eliasson's art as a philosophy of space—a Bergsonian, "extensible" space made concrete—its landscapishness remains relevant. When seen within the framework of a larger exhibition, as a performative landscape, *Notion motion* is an Eden waiting to happen, its devastating consequences temporarily held in check. Small in scale compared to the building as a whole, it is an enclosed space where everything is possible and time shifts gears. The work here poses, with great urgency, the question of limitations. Between support and light, solid and liquid, two and three dimensions, vision and touch, the water's reflections recall the difficulty and the fulfilling result of giving up the certainty of distinctions.

It is the spatial work performed by the installation that the metaphor of landscape brings to the fore. As a typical struggle with space, landscape is by definition anchored in the ambivalence that results from the impossible yet desired distinction between humanity and culture, on the one hand, and nature outside, on the other. Why such a distinction is desirable is easy to imagine: as natural catastrophes never fail to bring home, nature refuses to be mastered. It can be destroyed, as humanity seems set upon doing, but never controlled.[28] Of all the arts, architecture most keenly works with this distinction and its impossibility in tandem. A building is a delimitation between its human inhabitants and the world outside, but it is also an integral part of the environment from which it cordons off its interior. If, then, the interior space is visually extended outward by means of windows, the building is making manifest what it has been all along: no more than a parergon, an ambiguous frame that is part of what it delimits.[29]

The paradoxes of limits and control help us see how exhibitions are, in addition to all the other things I have mentioned, also reflections on space and its relation to the body—in movement, hence in time. Eliasson's specific demonstration of collaboration and tension, contrast and resonance, inside and outside, derives its power primarily from an exceptionally full deployment of the analogy between space and parergon. This is the sense in which his art is baroque. Beyond that, as a true "theoretical object," his SFMOMA survey rethinks the exhibition as a cultural practice; a new space not only underlies its production of spatial experience, but also emerges from it.[30]

Baroque, as I have extensively discussed primarily apropos of Caravaggio, is a mode of embodied thinking that considers how being "enfolded" in what one is seeing affects what one sees, and how embodying is a way of fully grasping what is outside the self. It is a way of considering the relative importance of unpresuming elements through a process of wavering scale, of articulating engagement as a way of knowing, and, finally, of understanding the self/other dialectic that threatens to conflate the subject and object of knowledge.[31] Term by term this description applies to Eliasson's work, which I consider, therefore, to be a prime example of baroque thought. But he also undermines the traditional expressions of these terms, primarily by rejecting any simple notion of representation. (He does not deny representation outright, however; he implicates it by way of the fugitive associations each viewer brings to the work.) One of the tendencies of his revised baroque is the incommensurability in scale between the world and his art, which is nevertheless firmly anchored in synecdoche. In this respect *The weather project* is exemplary, but *Notion motion* also makes scale radically ungraspable by means of reflection.

These baroque features remain couched in an utterly artificial yet real relationship to the natural environment, emphasizing the work's impossible, antirepresentational landscapishness. The viewer standing at the beginning of SFMOMA's catwalk, overlooking the enormous open space to be crossed, experiences just how secure retinal perception can flip to bodily insecurity. The tunnel piece on the catwalk is a brilliant curatorial intervention that foregrounds the way exhibitions are installations, and how curatorial practice cannot be separated from artistic agency. The bridge truly bridges, but, as a Derridian parergon, it bridges a boundary that does not separate. Nature beyond Eliasson's landscape remains visible as well as influential, primarily through the glass of the round skylight.

This sends us back to the consideration of light. Entering the exhibition over the catwalk, the visitor is instantly aware of the tremulous unpredictability of natural light, and is thus prepared for a very different experience of light inside the galleries. Eliasson's light works rely on the metaphors of cinema and theater to set up a competition between the architect's natural light and the extreme artificiality of the light the artist must deploy to make his spaces possible. The arts he references are equally artificial, yet they counter the distinction between fake and natural upon which the very idea of artifice is based. The light coming through the skylight is the live version of that light that has intrigued and inspired generations of painters and their viewers.[32]

Of all of the aspects of nature, volatile light is the least easy to master; it is also nature's least threatening element. Yet it is indispensable, especially in relation to visual art. In art exhibitions, light is a powerful tool for articulating visibility. To surrender an entire installation to the vagaries of light, allowing water and visitors' bodies to make drawings on a dematerialized wall, then, is a bold and, at first sight, humble decision. It suggests the surrender of the tool, of the power to dominate that artificial light creates. It is a decision to unfix what artificial light can fix, and instead to accept differences in light, hence visibility and even, as suggested above, shape. But while alluding to the sublime, such a decision also entails confidence in the art displayed. The serendipity that may emerge from light's volatility is a gift to the artworks.

And, I hasten to add, vice versa. Serendipity embodies the attitude of nonmastery and willingness to engage with nature that lies at the heart of Eliasson's art. Chance in combination with landscape creates a sense of space that comes to and, at the same time, emanates from the body: an effective way of binding together the two meanings of landscape (representation and vista). The architecture's vulnerability to chance effects of light, made tangible in the walk over the bridge, brings serendipity to bear on the photographs, sculptures, and installations in the exhibition. It remains, that is, as an afterimage, flickering in the light that is disturbed and enhanced by the presence of the body.

Light is not the opposite of materiality. Rather, Eliasson's rich exploitation of light achieves a reconciliation of matter and light; he invites us to experience the very materiality of light itself. Light, if taken seriously as a material element and not just as a tool for visibility, can become extraordinarily artistic—affective and effective, moving beyond representation instead of serving as its handmaiden.

Countering the postminimalist, postmodernist refusal of figuration and contrived narratives are the exuberant forms set in motion by the fall of the sponge and the movement of bodies through and on space. Eliasson's works bring to bear on the space they constitute (and that houses them) something that goes against the landscape tradition: a sense of nonmastery, of the implication of the body, of the vulnerability of skin exposed to nature. Here, alternative forms of space are emerging.

When it comes to the political nature of vision, primarily but not exclusively anchored in the tradition of perspective, the embodied nature of looking cannot be overemphasized. Representations of space, of which the landscape is only one strand, have long tended to disincarnate the gaze; alternatives, especially in late-twentieth-century painting, have proposed to abandon the omniscient point of view that commonly characterizes landscape. It is in relation to the ideologies invested in perspective that Eliasson's work turns from the third person—the grammar of perspective—to the second. Ina Blom wrote in this context about the artist's tendency "to eschew the frontality of the purely visual for the ambient and indeterminate effects of the total-surround environment as experienced by some 'you.'"[33] This "some 'you'" is indeterminate by definition, and that is why this form of address is so important. The position of "you" is interchangeable and constantly changing. It is also the position from which any "I" must be recognized and validated: without "you," no "I" is possible. But the "you" does not need to be a person. Space, the artworks intimate, is also a "second person," indispensable to sustain the subject. (This interchange between "you" and "I" takes place over time; therefore a certain narrativity is also indispensable, even in the least figurative of works.)[34]

"Second-personhood" is at the heart of Eliasson's art. This is why the utterly lonesome experience of sublimity must be kept at bay. Instead, this work is nothing if not communicative. For Eliasson, space—moving beyond Bergsonian thought—is not only an always-extensive emanation from the subject, but first of all an *address*. The production of space does not lie in the "I" but in the "you," where space and the other come together. The only way to make a case for this is to under-stand the self in the here and now as the anchor of an unusual obsession with the performativity of a different kind of time-space, one that is disrupted and subsequently elongated and either almost totalized or annihilated—that is, to use Mikhail Bakhtin's term, a *chronotope*. The Russian literary theorist used this word to foreground the indissoluble bond between time and space, the two dimensions in which, at any given moment, (real or fictional) subjects are located. In his most succinct wording, chrono-tope refers to "the intrinsic connectedness of temporal and spatial relationships that are artistically expressed."[35]

Wherever and whenever you are—at home, in the street, in a gallery—you are caught in time-space coordinates that, like invisible strings, attach your body to an indelible here and now that is different from any other combination of moment and place. No one else can ever be there then, because *you* occupy that position. A split second later, one foot shuffle farther down the street, and the moment has passed; the place is given over to the anonymous others who inhabit the world, share its space, and traverse its duration. You don't notice it, but the strings are there; they act, inscribe your presence, and register it in an encounter between your sense perceptions and the world. Nothing seems more natural. In linguistics, the strings that shape the subject in this way are called *deixis*: words such as *I* and *you* that define personhood, *here* and *there* that situate the speaker in space, *now* and *then* (or *yesterday* and *tomorrow* as distinct from *today*) that locate the event in time.[36]

The positions carved out by these words are fundamental to the forma-tion of subjectivity. In visual art, uniquely, the place of the "I," initially occupied by the viewer, must be exchanged with that of the work: the "I" becoming its "you" when it appears to address you. Unlike in speech, the work is an object; this address is thus a fiction. But, as great literature and advertising have taught us, fiction is truer than life—

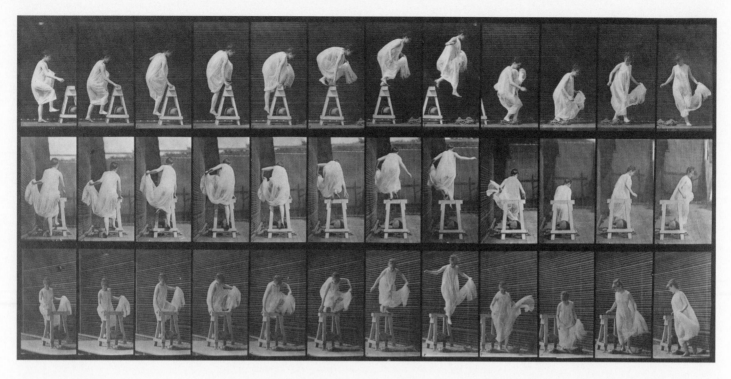

147
Eadweard Muybridge
Woman Jumping over a Barrier, 1887
Collotype. 8 x 12 in. (20.3 x 30.5 cm). San
Francisco Museum of Modern Art, gift of
Frederick P. Currier and Amy McCombs

or at least indispensable to it. It is important to keep in mind that Eliasson, so rigorously focused on the experience of seeing the world (differently) and using materials such as water, plants, and light, nowhere claims to present his environments as real or natural. At the same time, he questions and revises the uniqueness of the chronotope I just evoked.

This is worth attempting, since the tragic condition of existence is that the uniqueness of our chronotopes generates both dependency and loneliness. We make them livable through the small deceptions of continuity. Both space and time appear to envelop us smoothly, moving along as we move along with them, displacing the horizon and extending duration so that we seem to be on solid ground, enfolded in the capsule of time that we need to do our little and big things. We know that death awaits us at the end, but that is always later. Our experience of moving through space-time is normalized; we don't have to think about it, which leaves us free to do other things—until, of course, something happens. Eliasson's creation of space, often but not exclusively by means of light, endeavors to make us fall—to allude to the Eden myth once more—out of our habit-worn chronotopical certainties. The viewer must surrender her baggage of visual knowledge in order to *see* what is *here now*—and, on that basis only, experience time.

Some of the associations prompted by Eliasson's works appear to oppose others: minimalist sculpture versus exuberant painting; inconspicuous materials that blend into their surroundings versus strongly self-aware environments distinct in color, texture, and scenography; integration in the environment yet always emphatically fictional. Suddenly, the viewer falls out of her chronotope. This is impossible, of course. Yet, on some level, this is exactly what happens. Fiction is, indeed, truer than life.

To recover the preposterously historical light this work casts on the past, I propose to look back to early modernism, the time of Bergson—another baroque

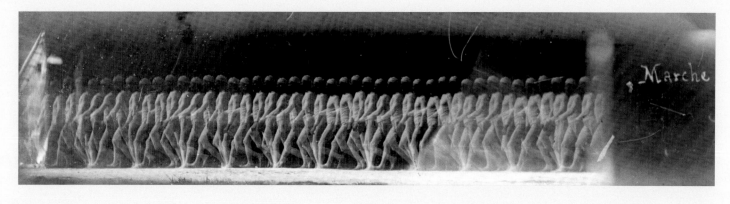

148
Etienne-Jules Marey
Demeny Walking, 1883
Glass photographic plate. 4 x 13¼ in.
(10.2 x 33.7 cm). Collège de France

era. A century and a half ago, Eadweard Muybridge and Etienne-Jules Marey conducted experiments with the newly invented photographic camera. Both attempted, in radically different ways, to record movement, that crossover of the body between time and space (see pls. 147–48). Though historians have credited Muybridge and Marey with the invention of the image of movement that led to the moving image of cinema, in fact neither achieved this. Whether a comic-strip succession of separate frames (Muybridge) or a recording of different spatial positions within barely legible single frames (Marey), the result is the utter stillness of the image. Their documents of the different positions the body can occupy in space remain poignantly mute and immobile—there is literally no space for time. As it happens, both photographers could only conduct their experiments because they relinquished, suppressed, or denied the strings of deixis.

The film historian Mary Ann Doane has brilliantly analyzed the tensions between memory, time, and legibility in the work of Marey as well as his younger contemporary Sigmund Freud.[37] The underlying issue is space and its indissoluble yet incompatible relationship with time. The problem, she points out, is how to *store* continuity—the continuity that defines time, at least according to Bergson. Like Freud, Bergson was obsessed with the storage of time in the storage that is memory, but, unlike the inventor of psychoanalysis, he did not see memory in terms of the individual. For him it was both material and social; in opposition to the photographers' experiments, he theorized memory in contrast to, rather than as a form of, perception. "To *picture* is not to *remember*," he famously wrote.[38]

If Bergson—and Marey—struggled to understand the continuity of duration, the British philosopher Bertrand Russell, like Muybridge, foregrounded discontinuity. Not coincidentally, Russell was also fascinated by the possibility of perception from unoccupied spatial positions. Eliasson, obviously, would not seek to join him in this attempt, but the artist does demonstrate a keen awareness of the difficulty of maintaining continuity in spatial experience. In *Beauty*, for example, he sets movement not *in* time but in opposition to it. Movement is indispensable to achieve the experience of the rainbow, but the two immediately destroy each other. He thus casts a new light on the deictic experience in the chronotopic world. One string appears to be broken—almost. The work functions almost like an experimental video: in order to isolate a single frame of the so-called moving image, the viewer is caught in the right position and then animates it. The installation locks her up in that fleeting instant that we are never aware of, slowing it down as a frozen action. There is duration, but it is not the one that was already there—not the "natural" duration that keeps us going as if nothing in the world could disturb us. In contrast to the stillness of *Beauty*, *I only see things when they move* functions as one of Eliasson's most Muybridgean/Mareyan works. Brilliant colors move around the room as the lamp that produces them rotates. The instability of color makes color the overwhelming environment, but the colors require the viewer's presence to exist.[39]

In *Beauty*, one elementary unit of the chronotope—the moment/place where a viewer can see the rainbow—brings the flow of space in duration to an arbitrary, serendipitous halt. In contrast, *I only see things when they move* conditions visibility on continuous movement, but from Muybridge one must hop over to Marey and risk losing legibility. *Beauty* isolates a slice of space in time: the impossibly unique place where all colors are visible as well as legible, in the deictic sense of being attached to one's sense of space. This tiny atom of time-space sits in the dead time of the anonymous, unspectacular interval that "happens" between the ticks of a watch or the flashes of a lighthouse— the metaphor that informs the title of an important publication on Eliasson's light works.[40]

Beauty's spatial requirement is an unspectacular intervention in space-time, consistent with the project of disrupting chronotopic deixis. The suspended moments in which one manages to perform space "rightly" accrue an incredible intensity of suspense. Like the scene of a crime, the place where the interval happens is pregnant with eventful potential. Yet the slowdown that follows does not lead to the climax such intensity would have us expect. On the contrary, it stretches out the arbitrary moment in which nothing really happens. Thus, this elongated temporality serves no purpose in our expectation of narrative spectacle; it releases us from the moment without leading us elsewhere.

Nor is that moment the object of representation. It is graven on the visitor's brain, an afterimage at the very moment it happens, modified and recycled, perhaps, but not portrayed. For the place of the object of presentation is already taken. The viewer who happens on this moment—unaware that the world is about to shift, just living on—is in charge of performing the space-temporality that is *prearranged* for her. In this respect, the obvious continuity of Eliasson's work with the preoccupations of Muybridge and Marey draws through modernism upon the baroque aesthetic in its misrecognized focus on the nonspectacular.[41]

Eliasson stops the viewer in his tracks, leaving him to wonder about the purpose, for example, of the loose, displaced elements of his likeness in the broken reflections of *Yellow double kaleidoscope*. Anywhere but in a gallery these fragments would appear to be the result of chance, negligence, or error, resulting in a dystopic self-image. But here they fold back onto themselves. Visitors, broken and vanishing, seem to be attempting to flee their chronotopes; suddenly, the here and now has lost its innocence, its naturalness. The smooth flow of time has come to an end. Yet the experience is exhilarating in its address to space as "you" and "you" as space.

Conversely, the cubes and screens of light in *Remagine* (2002; pls. 160–62) consist of pure space. There is no matter, only light; no figuration, not even by association—just squares, flat and three-dimensional. Imagine anew, make an image again, and your space is yours. The creation of space from empty cinema screens and perfect cubes without color—or, given that they are white, harboring all colors—is utterly simple and mysterious at the same time. Disorienting the visitor in their game between two and three dimensions, these shapes welcome the (visual, imaging) imagination. The sharp delineation seems to be an attempt, comparable to that of the near-interruption of time, to question the flow of space without falling into the trap of atomization via measurement.

Teasingly promised but never quite actualized, this potential disruption of temporal and spatial continuity addresses and modifies issues probed by modernism, early cinema, and the endless proliferation of photographic images. To this proliferation Eliasson adds millions of images, but not storable ones.[42] Through a new, disenchanted manipulation of duration, these works position themselves at the other end of the long twentieth century—in other words, *post* the modernism of Muybridge and Marey, of Bergson and Russell, of Gauguin and Freud. But, as we know, *post* does not simply mean "beyond"; it means "through," "critical of" as well as "indebted to," "in complicity with" yet "attempting to twist away from" that modernism I have evoked here through a few of its most brilliant representatives.

The issue around which the contemporary artist reenvisions the relationship between time, space, and the subject that informed the modernist quest is the natural preeminence and consistency of deixis. The difficulty of theorizing the storage of time in a legible manner that does not fix it—turning time into space—is neither denied nor deplored. Instead, the artist *almost* ruptures the bond between time and space in order to facilitate a separate, self-reflexive encounter with each of the chronotope's elements. Eliasson's works examine, in their own distinctive ways, the conditions of readability in terms of the authenticity of the subject. The way in which he stretches out indivisible temporalities, shifting time away from its "natural" space so that our belatedness becomes the primary condition of existence, is, again, most clearly demonstrated in *Notion motion*.

Between the Freudian subject, whose unconscious is timeless yet archives the traces of time that memories constitute, and the physical, instrumental body of perception, the subject held up and together by the strings of deixis is bent down when one of its coordinates flounders—even if, to use a relevant phrase, *temporarily*. The natural habitat has a hole in it. That hole is what makes the habitat unnatural, what untangles it from habit so as to allow it to become critical. Space (the gallery) is still there, but it loses its anchoring function because time—the slowing-down factor that hampers perception—is no longer self-evident. There is still duration, for the artist, like Bergson, believes in the value of its fiction, and art making entails complicity with that fiction. Duration is thus aggrandized, enlarged like the image of murder in Antonioni's 1966 film *Blowup*, until it reaches "natural" size and becomes unreadable. As a result, it courts Russell's disbelief in continuity. But the "opaque thisness" of the moment remains both stubbornly empty and irreducibly material.[43]

The most incisive effect of these works is that they reinvent deixis, whereby the subject yields her individual "authenticity" to a disenchanted, contemporary sociality. In her theory of the formation of subjectivity and the place of the body therein, Kaja Silverman argues: "One's apprehension of self is *keyed* both to a visual image or constellation of visual images, and to certain bodily feelings, whose determinant is less physiological than social."[44] This statement explains how the relationship between the individual subject and the culturally normative image is bodily without being innate or anatomically determined. Eliasson's insistent interrogation of the indexical relationship between image and viewer solicits such bodily interaction from within subjectivity and the outside culture. At the same time he enforces the mutuality of that relationship: the "you" and "I" as interchanging, in time, all the time. In this, the work is preposterously baroque, and it is that baroqueness that constitutes its political force.

Light Politics

This brings me to the phrase I have chosen for the title of this essay. In an article on Eliasson's relationship to politics, Molly Nesbit has this to say: "He explained that for him and for his generation the hope of actually changing the world did not exist. But he did say that if the idea of changing the world had come to seem outmoded, the idea of seeing the world differently, or more deeply, was still vital, still critical, still burning." For me, a child of 1968, this distinction between changing the world and seeing differently harks back to the disappointment of discovering that society was not, after all, "makeable." Yet it also leaves me uneasy, as if seeing were not also an act. But then Nesbit continues:

> To try to see the world differently, one needed to change one's own position. The change would need to be physical and mental. Sometimes the sensuous experience of a new sight alone could throw the world open anew. It could be a matter of taking steps to see by a different light.[45]

From disenchanted modesty, the specificity of art as political has now become almost immoderately ambitious. If Eliasson can make good on this goal, every visitor will exit his exhibitions transformed, mentally and even physically, for having gone through the sensuous experiences generated by the work. Between mental and physical, however, a mediation must be brought about.

How does that mediation work? In the statement by Silverman quoted above, the issue is feeling: how does the subject *feel* his or her position in space? What we call feeling is the threshold of body and subjectivity in space. The idea has two components, which together constitute the basis of political art as Eliasson proposes it: feeling and its affective status, and deixis as spatial. With the latter, external images are attached to the subject's bodily existence; she is "locked up" in the external world—in the dark space of *Beauty* or in the image of rippling water in *Notion motion.* In the musical sense of the word *key*, the external images and the body are adapted and harmonized; one is set into the tonality of the other. But *to key to* can also be understood through the notion of code: the key to understanding, comprehending, communicating between individual subjects and the culture at large—a communication in which "abstract space" is practiced.

This keying of the subject into cultural space is utterly material. Elizabeth Grosz makes a similar point about the relationship between cities and bodies. She draws a distinction between the tropes (she calls them models) of causality, considering that humans make or "cause" cities rather than just being keyed to them as if by fate, and the analogy between bodies and cities, finding both problematic. As an alternative, she offers the trope of a "fundamentally deunified series of systems and interconnections, a series of disparate flows, energies, events or entities, and spaces, brought together or drawn apart in more or less temporary alignments."[46] The temporal shadow that characterizes the perception of the rainbow, projecting an event we arrive too late to witness, encompasses and illuminates just such a spatiotemporal flow, temporarily and provisionally conflating the subject's body with the space it occupies. Similarly, the fragmentation produced by the reflections in Eliasson's *Your spiral view* (2002; pl. 174), *Yellow double kaleidoscope,* and *The drop factory* makes this deunification inescapable. The point of their equally inescapable beauty—the harmony despite the fragmentation—is comparable to the way in which the artist alludes to sublimity without endorsing it: the haunting beauty of the kaleidoscope, for example, detaches or even detoxes us from the need for unity.

The usefulness of "carrying along" this connotative use of a crucial concept from semiotics becomes obvious when Silverman, writing about the bodily basis of the ego—that is, about proprioceptivity (the sensation of the self from within the body)—asserts that it is the "egoic component to which concepts like 'here,' 'there,' and 'my' are keyed."[47] Here she uses the concept of deixis to theorize the construction of subjectivity in language. Strictly speaking, by placing deixis "within," "on," or "at" the body, she decisively extends language to include spatial experience, as do Eliasson's titles.

Not only, then, is language unthinkable without physical involvement, one can even argue that words cause pain and harm or arouse sexual and other excitement, and that bodily effects thus form an integral part of linguistics.[48] Conversely, this proprioceptive basis for deixis comprises more than just words: it includes the muscular system and the space around the body, the space within which it fits as within a skin. Abstract space becomes a concrete place within which the subject, delimited by his skin, is keyed in—a space he perceives and of which he is irrevocably part. Silverman uses the phrase "postural function" to refer to this place of the keyed subject. The reflection and the shadow—both effects of light on bodies, of bodies on space—can be taken as allegories of this postural function's outward movement. As if to insist on this point, Eliasson attempts to show the inside and outside of the body simultaneously. The kaleidoscopes, the tunnel pieces, and *The drop factory* demonstrate this possibility as well as its cost—fracturation of the self. The body, to recycle Lacan's phrase, is scattered into bits and pieces. It holds together quite miraculously, not in spite of its distinction from but because of its suturing to space.

Eliasson's bold decision to name his works in deictic terms endorses a refusal to sever language from space. No longer restricted to the domain of language, deixis is a form of indexicality, one that is locked into (or keyed to) the subject. This form of deixis provides greater insight into types of indexicality in which the postural function of the subject—its shaping from within—sends back, so to speak, the images that enter from without, this time accompanied by affective "commentary" or "feeling." But the relationship between Eliasson's work in three dimensions and this theory of psychic space is "thickened" by a sense of quotation that cannot be reduced to chronology, and can only be construed as engaging psychoanalytic thought as the site where the philosophy of space joins the theory of bodily subjectivity.

As we have seen, Eliasson's works quote a variety of visual discourses, including the Romantic landscape; the philosophical tenets of baroque sculpture and painting; modernist attempts to grapple with memory, movement, and time; and installations by earlier Light and Space artists. At the same time, however, recognizing these precedents is beside the point. The works' diffuse citationality posits in rather broad strokes the cultural chronotope from within which they seek to disrupt the specific chronotope of each viewer. For, they seem to say, only when confronted with its fragility can we ultimately access our subjectivity. Which, finally, brings me to the politics of Eliasson's art. On the basis of the simple fact that this is real water and *its* light, I would suggest that the work's political import rests upon its repositioning of human beings in the environment. Perhaps unexpectedly, this political thrust operates by means of feeling.

Feeling space: the other half of this phrase concerns affect. Affect, writes Charles Altieri, "comprises the range of mental states where an agent's activity cannot be adequately handled in terms of either sensations or beliefs but requires attending to how he or she offers expressions of those states." Affects, he continues, "are ways of being moved that supplement sensation with at least a minimal degree of imaginative projection."[49] He then proceeds to rank the affects hierarchically:

> Feelings are elemental affective states characterized by an imaginative engagement in the immediate processes of sensation. Moods are modes of feeling where the sense of subjectivity becomes diffuse and sensation merges into something close to atmosphere, something that seems to pervade an entire scene or situation. Emotions are affects that involve the construction of attitudes that typically establish a particular cause and so situate the agent within a narrative. . . . Finally, passions are emotions within which we project significant stakes for the identity that they make possible.[50]

From this short taxonomy it is clear that mood is the affective domain where artwork and viewer can most easily share the diffuse sense of subjectivity. Hence, if Eliasson elects a light mood—in all senses of the word—this choice must be decisive, including with regard to the political work the pieces perform.

But what makes mood, here, more suitable than the other affects? In writing on war and death, Silverman offers an illuminating distinction between fear and anxiety. This distinction can help us understand two things: it explains why mood is more effective than the other affects, particularly emotion, and it clarifies why Eliasson's works are able to affect us profoundly and why they are thereby politically effective. According to Silverman,

> Fear is the affect through which we apprehend the "nothing" in the mode of a turning away. Anxiety is the affect through which we apprehend it in the mode of a turning toward. Fear fails to reconcile us to the nothing, because it always *represents* the attempt to specify or concretize the nothing. Anxiety, on the other hand, "attunes" us to it, because it is the affect par excellence of the *indeterminate*.[51]

This passage explains the political import of Eliasson's bypassing (but constant invocation) of representation. The thrust is to create a mood appropriate to the disasters the world is staging and representing through media such as television, thus stripping them of affect. To create a mood, in other words, that helps us determine how to respond to them. Eliasson's installations rely on both representational reticence and the exuberant staging of a mood light enough to empower the subject. Staging, here, takes a particularly theatrical form, in which the discrepancy between mood and events, rather than the representation of the latter, enters the viewer's affective capacity.

For this bodily, sensuous political affect, then, critical engagement with the traditions that the work invokes with critical intimacy—such as Eden and the sublime—leads to what Apter calls, in her definition of critical habitat, an "ecologically engaged conceptualism." The word *conceptualism* might suggest, wrongly, that this art is disembodied. On the contrary, like much contemporary conceptual art, it is fully, exceedingly bodily. Instead, the term refers to the constructedness of the embodied relationality it produces.

For art to be politically effective, I have argued, it must be effective aesthetically.[52] Rather than addressing singular causes (however important they may be), art "works with" affect, here inflected as mood, to compel visitors to address the causes that constitute the "you" of the art environment. For example, I suggested early in this essay that Eliasson's art implicates the anxiety about boundaries represented by Eden. For me, that issue "performs" the politics of borders: the wall in Israel, the fence along the southern border of the United States, the borders of fortress Europe. Attributing that cause to this art, however, would be a severe, even contemptuous misrecognition of its political force. Eliasson's work, clearly, is much more invested in the issue of environment than in the notion of migrancy in the post/neocolonial condition. But to say, therefore, that his politics address concern for the environment—that he is an activist, for example, for Greenpeace—would, again, demonstrate a devastating blindness.

Instead of promoting such singular, punctual causes (the importance of which I am far from underestimating), the political work this art performs is attributed as a task to the visitor. The art offers liberation from the myths of our culture and the indifference promoted by representation. Thus it clears space—to use the key noun—for a relationality that is based on, for lack of a better word, an "I"/"you" exchange across the cultural borders beyond which otherness commences. *Care* might be the operative word: recognition of and attention to people and (or rather in) space—which is always, to an extent that includes culture, nature. The tool is the experience in and of time that empowers visitors to take historical responsibility for the past in the present. This is why Eliasson's works make memory, in its intertwined multiple registers, a form of temporal deixis; they key us into the past like that classical example of deixis, "yesterday." Not to let it enslave us in unproductive guilt and the resulting powerless indifference, but to enable us. Hence the light mood.

This is why, in order to work politically, Eliasson's art needs to stage a fictitious space for its experiences and experiments. Reluctant to espouse the discourse of political art as manifesto, this work is much more effective, aesthetically and thereby politically, because it does not pronounce upon the world, but considers how seeing it differently is already changing it. To sum up this art's politics, I end with an appeal to the artist by paraphrasing the subtitle of one of his books, which is only acceptable because he is so emphatically opposed to intentionalism: *your engagement has consequences on the relativity of your reality.*

NOTES

1. Antigone's crew, in *Tègònni, an African Antigone*. See Femi Osofisan, *Recent Outings: Two Plays* (Ibadan, Nigeria: Ọpọn IFA Readers, 1999), 27. This passage was brought to my attention by Astrid van Weyenberg, a PhD candidate at the Amsterdam School of Contemporary Analysis.

2. Additional photographs of the Boijmans installation of *Notion motion* may be found in *Olafur Eliasson: Your Engagement Has Consequences; On the Relativity of Your Reality*, by Olafur Eliasson et al. (Baden, Switzerland: Lars Müller Publishers, 2006).

3. Julie H. Reiss, *From Margin to Center: The Spaces of Installation Art* (Cambridge, MA: MIT Press, 1999), xiii.

4. Emily Apter, "The Aesthetics of Critical Habitats," *October* 99, no. 1 (Winter 2002): 21–44. Apter defines a critical habitat as "art informed by geopolitics; by an ecologically engaged conceptualism; . . . that critiques the relationship between media and environment and explores forms of global identification" (22). I will return to this concept later in my essay.

5. For an in-depth discussion of this concept, see my *Quoting Caravaggio: Contemporary Art, Preposterous History* (Chicago: University of Chicago Press, 1999).

6. One recent book on the artist is solely devoted to his works with light (*Olafur Eliasson: Your Lighthouse; Works with Light 1991–2004* [Wolfsburg, Germany: Kunstmuseum Wolfsburg; Ostfildern-Ruit, Germany: Hatje Cantz, 2004]); in it one finds an essay in which an entire tradition of Light and Space art, mostly German, serves as a context for Eliasson's work (Annelie Lütgens, "Twentieth-Century Light and Space Art," 32–40). The critic Carol Diehl places his work in the tradition of twentieth-century light art in her article "Northern Lights," *Art in America* 92, no. 9 (October 2004): 108–15. Both texts are, so to speak, illuminating. Peter-Pim de Kroon's 2003 documentary *Hollands licht* (Dutch Light) was also on my mind as I strolled through the galleries of the Boijmans's permanent collection.

7. Of course, Eliasson knows light on water from his own Nordic background. There is no reason to suppose that he would have been particularly interested in Dutch light. It is just that Dutch light is the temporary host environment, where I, as a visitor to this installation, came from and went back to, overdetermined by my own Dutchness. There is nothing "natural" about this environment. Only "art"—that attempt to slow the pace of everyday life, making room for experience and reflection—can establish such a relationship between the temporary work and its ad hoc environment. It is because I had walked through the museum's collection of old masters, with its landscapes and seascapes, still lifes and genre paintings, that Eliasson's laboratory of unknown experience fell in with this tradition.

8. Petra Halkes, *Aspiring to the Landscape: On Painting and the Subject of Nature* (Toronto: University of Toronto Press, 2006), 3–4.

9. In these paragraphs I reformulate and extend thoughts published in "A l'est d'Eden / East of Eden / Ten Oosten van Eden," in *Marthe Wéry: Les couleurs du monochrome*, ed. B.P.S.2 Projects (Tournai, Belgium: Musée des Beaux-Arts de Tournai, 2005), 35–104, 119–27. To avoid overburdening this essay with footnotes, I have not indicated further references to that text.

10. The literature on landscape is immense; I cite here only a few references relevant to the remainder of this essay. For an excellent study of the subject, see Petra Halkes, *Aspiring to the Landscape* (PhD diss., University of Leiden, 2001). In 2006 Halkes published a substantially revised version (see note 8). The relationship between landscape and (imperial) power is analyzed in *Landscape and Power*, ed. W. J. T. Mitchell (Chicago: University of Chicago Press, 1994). On landscape and death, see Louis Marin, "Towards a Theory of Reading in the Visual Arts: Poussin's *The Arcadian Shepherds*," in *Calligram: Essays in the New Art History from France*, ed. Norman Bryson (Cambridge: Cambridge University Press, 1988), 63–90. On landscape and its relation to history, see Simon Schama, *Landscape and Memory* (New York: Knopf, 1995).

11. On Eden, see Carolyn Merchant, "Reinventing Eden: Western Culture as a Recovery Narrative," in *Uncommon Ground: Toward Reinventing Nature*, ed. William Cronon (New York: W. W. Norton & Co., 1995), and chapter 5 in my *Lethal Love: Feminist Literary Readings of Biblical Love Stories* (Bloomington: Indiana University Press, 1987). On the sublime, a good introductory text is Peter de Bolla, *The Discourse of the Sublime: Readings in History, Aesthetics, and the Subject* (Oxford: Basil Blackwell, 1989). In-depth reflection on the sublime can be found in various publications by Jean-François Lyotard, who seemed to be obsessed by the sublime in relation to extreme situations; see, in particular, "Presenting the Unpresentable: The Sublime," *Artforum* 20 (April 1982): 64–69; "The Sublime and the Avant-Garde," *Artforum* 22 (April 1984): 36–43; and *The Postmodern Condition: A Report on Knowledge*, trans. Geoff Bennington and Brian Massumi (Minneapolis: University of Minnesota Press, 1984). The idea that art thinks has been popularized by the work of the French art historian/philosopher Hubert Damisch (e.g., *The Origin of Perspective*, trans. John Goodman [Cambridge, MA: MIT Press, 1994], and *A Theory of /Cloud/: Toward a History of Painting*, trans. Janet Lloyd [Stanford, CA: Stanford University Press, 2002]). For a presentation of Damisch's major books in light of this idea, see Ernst van Alphen, *Armando: Forms of Memory* (Rotterdam: NAi, 2000), and *Art in Mind: How Contemporary Images Shape Thought* (Chicago: University of Chicago Press, 2005).

    The role of the curator in the overall philosophical effect of an exhibition cannot be overestimated, but I cannot engage this topic enough here to do justice to it, beyond the analogy of exhibition to installation. For background to this remark, see my *Double Exposures: The Subject of Cultural Analysis* (New York: Routledge, 1996) and "Exhibition as Film," in *Exhibition Experiments: Technologies and Cultures of Display*, ed. Paul Basu and Sharon MacDonald (Oxford: Blackwell, 2006).

12. See Karl Figlio, "Knowing, Loving, and Hating Nature: A Psychoanalytic View," in *FutureNatural: Nature, Science, Culture*, ed. George Robertson et al. (London: Routledge, 1996), 72–85.

13. *The weather project* also raises the issue of scale (on which more later). Its dimensions (approximately 88 feet high, 74 feet wide, and 510 feet long) cast it as perhaps the largest interior work in contemporary art.

14. See Gayatri Chakravorty Spivak, *A Critique of Postcolonial Reason: Toward a History of the Vanishing Present* (Cambridge, MA: Harvard University Press, 1999), chapter 1.

15. Jonathan Crary, "Your Colour Memory: Illuminations of the Unforeseen," in *Olafur Eliasson: Minding the World* (Aarhus, Denmark: ARoS Aarhus Kunstmuseum, 2004), 223. For Crary's general observations on the subject of vision, see *Techniques of the Observer: On Vision and Modernity in the Nineteenth Century* (Cambridge, MA: MIT Press,1990).

16. This for reasons similar to my attachment to the art-historical discourse invoked by the Rotterdam installation.

17. See Naomi Schor, *Reading in Detail: Aesthetics and the Feminine* (New York: Methuen, 1987).

18. See Jacques Derrida, *Of Grammatology*, trans. Gayatri Chakravorty Spivak (Baltimore: Johns Hopkins University Press, 1976).

19. On space and time, see Henri Bergson, *Matter and Memory* (1911), trans. Nancy Margaret Paul and W. Scott Palmer (London: Allen & Unwin, 1970), 126. An explanation of the way Eliasson's work engages Bergsonian ideas is offered by Marianne Krogh Jensen, "With Inadvertent Reliance," in *Olafur Eliasson: Minding the World*, 119–28. The artist himself has stated an interest in the French philosopher; he selected an excerpt from Bergson's *Creative Evolution* (1907) as his "Artist's Choice" in *Olafur Eliasson*, by Madeleine Grynsztejn et al. (London: Phaidon, 2002), 112–20.

20. On marginality, see Jacques Derrida, *Margins of Philosophy*, trans. Alan Bass (Chicago: University of Chicago Press, 1982). On the detail, a founding study is Schor's *Reading in Detail* (see note 17). On the detail as specifically aesthetic, see Daniel Arasse, *Le détail: Pour une histoire rapprochée de la peinture* (Paris: Flammarion, 1992).

21. On embodied existence, see Norman Bryson, *Looking at the Overlooked: Four Essays on Still-Life* (Cambridge, MA: Harvard University Press, 1989). On foodscapes, see Rick Dolphijn, *Foodscapes: Towards a Deleuzian Ethics of Consumption* (Delft, Netherlands: Eburon, 2004).

22. Grynsztejn et al., *Olafur Eliasson*, 9.

23. Not coincidentally, as with color and the detail, there is a gendered aspect of the sublime as a struggle for (masculine) mastery, which the "feminine" shapes in the water after the fall of the sponge might also evoke by counterpoint. I am not attributing any of this to the artist's intention, even if I am confident he would be sensitive to this aspect. A feminist attempt to save the sublime from romantic obsolescence can be found in Christine Battersby, *The Phenomenal Woman: Feminist Metaphysics and the Pattern of Identity* (New York: Routledge, 1998).

24. See van Alphen, *Armando*.

25. In *Uncertain Territories: Boundaries in Cultural Analysis* (Amsterdam: Rodopi, 2006), Inge E. Boer elaborates a notion of boundaries not as separating but rather as creating a space for contestation, mediation, and new understanding.

26. Lütgens, "Twentieth-Century Light and Space Art." Light and Space is a strand with which Eliasson's work is obviously affiliated but to which it is not reducible. For more on his art's commonalities with—and innovations upon—work coming out of the Light and Space movement of the 1960s and 1970s, see Pamela M. Lee's essay in this volume.

27. In *Quoting Caravaggio* I propose a notion of preposterous history, in which a chronologically later artwork can transform our understanding of that which came before.

28. See Neil Evernden, *The Social Creation of Nature* (Baltimore: Johns Hopkins University Press, 1992).

29. With the term *parergon* I wish to recall Jacques Derrida's important text *The Truth in Painting*, trans. Geoff Bennington and Ian McLeod (Chicago: University of Chicago Press, 1987). In their own ways, of course, all of the venues for the Eliasson exhibition will fulfill the same function.

30. A theoretical object is an object that, when experienced or analyzed, compels the emergence of theoretical ideas. The term was used by Hubert Damisch to argue that art is not mute, silent, or stubbornly visual only. See van Alphen, *Art in Mind*.

31. See *Quoting Caravaggio*, 8. I borrow "enfolded" from Gilles Deleuze, *The Fold: Leibniz and the Baroque*, trans. Tom Conley (Minneapolis: University of Minnesota Press, 1993).

32. Needless to say, this work with light to shape and make things—to create three-dimensionality through spatial engagement—is a key tenet of the baroque's best painters, such as Caravaggio and Rembrandt.

33. Ina Blom, "Beyond the Ambient," trans. Bram Opstelten, *Parkett*, no. 64 (May 2002): 20.

34. I find a first indication of the relevance of "second-personhood" in the titles Eliasson has given many of his works—as opposed to, for example, those of David Reed, who paints in the second person, as it were, but generally numbers his canvases rather than titling them. Not coincidentally, Reed's paintings are essentially light paintings, and his colors are as artificially constructed as Eliasson's. The connection with a nonfigurative painter may seem far-fetched. However, I do not consider it insignificant that, in addition to using light, highly artificial color, and a general second-personhood, both Eliasson and Reed have worked over the space of the historical palace that is occupied by the Neue Galerie am Landesmuseum Joanneum in Graz, Austria. Compare Eliasson's *Die organische und die kristalline Beschreibung* (The organic and crystalline description, 1996; pl. 46), with Reed's *Mirror Room for Vampires* of the same year, in *David Reed Paintings: Motion Pictures*, by Elizabeth Armstrong et al. (La Jolla, CA: Museum of Contemporary Art San Diego; New York: Max Protetch Gallery, 1999), 18. Both works foreground the color

blue: Eliasson's in combination with yellow, Reed's with pink. And in spite of creating paintings, Reed is heavily invested in representing motion.

35. M. M. Bakhtin, "Forms of Time and of the Chronotope in the Novel," in *The Dialogic Imagination: Four Essays by M. M. Bakhtin*, ed. Michael Holquist, trans. Caryl Emerson and Michael Holquist (Austin: University of Texas Press, 1982), 84. For a discussion of this concept's relevance to contemporary culture, see Esther Peeren, *Bakhtin and Beyond: Intersubjectivities and Popular Culture* (Stanford, CA: Stanford University Press, 2007).

36. This view was famously put forward by the French linguist Emile Benveniste in *Problèmes de linguistique générale*, vol. 1 (Paris: Gallimard, 1966), translated by Mary Elizabeth Meek as *Problems in General Linguistics* (Coral Gables, FL: University of Miami Press, 1971). According to Benveniste, deixis, not reference, is the essence of language. The notion that the subject is not autonomous has been advanced in other disciplines as well. In psychoanalysis, the dependence of the subject on the other is theorized in terms of a mother/infant dyad ruptured by the function of the father, who represents the third person of the world and its rules of conduct, breaking into the "I"/"you" dyad as the "he" becomes "I" in turn. In social theory and (its) philosophy, the concept of care is probably the most adequate equivalent. Art history reflects on the consequences of this dependency in its theorizations of response. I believe it is useful to take the linguistic version as literally as possible, especially in the case of an artist who is so deeply engaged with space and whose titles alert us to the special relevance of second-personhood.

37. See Mary Ann Doane, "Temporality, Storage, Legibility: Freud, Marey, and the Cinema," *Critical Inquiry* 22 (Winter 1996): 313–43.

38. Bergson, *Matter and Memory*, 126.

39. For Bertrand Russell's thinking on the perception of time, see "On the Experience of Time," *The Monist* 25 (1915): 212–33. For a brilliant exposition of Russell's ideas, see Ann Banfield, *The Phantom Table: Woolf, Fry, Russell, and the Epistemology of Modernism* (Cambridge: Cambridge University Press, 2000). Banfield proposes an alternative, even opposing view of modernist literature and its subject-centeredness. Paradoxically, in spite of the closeness of Eliasson's work to Bergson's thinking, one can bring the Russellian approach to bear usefully on the artist's work, since it complicates the currently fashionable facility in thought about continuity.

40. See *Olafur Eliasson: Your Lighthouse*. The watch and lighthouse metaphors come from an extraordinary, though ultimately unsuccessful, little book by George Kubler, *The Shape of Time: Remarks on the History of Things* (New Haven, CT: Yale University Press, 1962). Kubler was a disciple of Henri Focillon, another early theorist of time (see *The Life of Forms in Art* [1934], trans. Charles Beecher Hogan and George Kubler [New York: Wittenborn, 1948]).

41. As Derek Jarman so convincingly demonstrated in his film *Caravaggio* (1986), the object of representation is not the holy scene from the Bible, but the drab posing session in the artist's studio, where the neighborhood poor or street urchins make a few lire but can hardly conceal their sense of chronotopical displacement. See Derek Jarman's *Caravaggio: The Complete Film Script and Commentaries* (London: Thames & Hudson, 1986).

42. See Walter Benjamin, "The Work of Art in the Age of Mechanical Reproduction," in *Illuminations*, ed. Hannah Arendt, trans. Harry Zohn (New York: Schocken, 1968), 217–52. On the proliferation of images and the storage problem this entails, see Allan Sekula, "The Body and the Archive," *October* 39 (Winter 1986): 3–64.

43. I borrow "opaque thisness" from Friedrich A. Kittler, *Discourse Networks 1800/1900*, trans. Michael Metteer with Chris Cullens (Stanford, CA: Stanford University Press, 1990), 211.

44. Kaja Silverman, *The Threshold of the Visible World* (New York: Routledge, 1996), 14 (my italics).

45. Molly Nesbit, "I Am the Tiger," in *Olafur Eliasson: Minding the World*, 141.

46. Elisabeth Grosz, "Bodies-Cities," in *Sexuality and Space*, ed. Beatriz Colomina (Princeton, NJ: Princeton University Press, 1992), 248. Beyond the general idea of deunification, however, I find her description of the situation too all-encompassing to be useful here.

47. Silverman, *Threshold of the Visible World*, 16.

48. See Judith Butler, *Excitable Speech: A Politics of the Performative* (New York: Routledge, 1997).

49. Charles Altieri, *The Particulars of Rapture: An Aesthetics of the Affects* (Ithaca, NY: Cornell University Press, 2003), 47. This definition is remarkable for its negativity, as the book in which it appears is entirely devoted to promoting the affects as an aesthetic.

50. Ibid., 48.

51. Kaja Silverman, "All Things Shining," in *Loss*, ed. David L. Eng and David Kazanjian (Los Angeles and Berkeley: University of California Press, 2003), 235 (my italics). The first part of this quotation paraphrases Martin Heidegger's "philosophy of mortality" (Silverman, 341) in *Being and Time*, 228–35. Silverman adds a note explaining the multiple connotations of the German word *Stimmung*, which means "mood" as well as "attunement," including in the musical sense. Importantly for this understanding of Heidegger's philosophy, he characterized mood as the attunement of Dasein to something else. In a similar vein, Eliasson stages mood in his installations, presenting its possibility without representing it.

52. See my "The Pain of Images," in *Beautiful Suffering*, ed. Mark Reinhardt, Holly Edwards, and Erina Duganne (Chicago: University of Chicago Press; Williamstown, MA: Williams College Museum of Art, 2006).

TOWARD THE SUN:
OLAFUR ELIASSON'S PROTOCINEMATIC VISION

Klaus Biesenbach and Roxana Marcoci

Over the last fifteen years Olafur Eliasson has experimented with a range of lighting effects, from reflected daylight to artificial monofrequency sources. Probing the cognitive aspects of what it means to see, his installations and sculptures based on mechanisms of motion, projection, shadow, and reflection have come to embody a protocinematic approach—a practice that explores the space between photography and film. Eliasson creates complex optical phenomena using simple, makeshift technical devices: colored bulbs bathe a room in yellow light, for example, turning everything inside duotone; strobes illuminating a thin curtain of falling water cause the eye to freeze the droplets in midair, producing a screen of crystalline forms that evokes early "flicker films." By emphasizing the formal components of light- and movement-capturing media, Eliasson converts the classic apparatus of film into material for new perceptual propositions.

According to the *Oxford English Dictionary*, the word *cinematic* is derived from the French *cinématique,* meaning "the geometry of motion." Eliasson's spatially transformative projects involve geometry as well as optics, while also conveying an indelible sense of filmic event and narrative. This is due to the fact that projections are not just images induced by light but also by the imagination, closer to the workings of *mise-en-image* than to mere retinal impressions. The medium of photography likewise speaks to the artist's general interest in light, temporality, movement, sequence, and perception. It is no coincidence that Eliasson's pictures of landscapes filled with arctic light—from telescopic aerial shots of rivers to close-up views of glaciers—are assembled in sequential grids that reinforce a filmic narrative. A reconsideration of protocinematic precedents, including the interchanges between still and moving images, optical processes, and narrative structures, thus opens an interpretive avenue into Eliasson's work. This path is paved by two distinct artistic lineages: on the one hand the unconventional optical techniques and social analyses of the 1920s Neue Optik, or New Vision, generation of artists, among them El Lissitzky, László Moholy-Nagy, Hans Richter, Man Ray, and Marcel Duchamp; and on the other the situational aesthetics advanced by James Turrell, Gordon Matta-Clark, Robert Smithson, and Anthony McCall in the 1970s.[1] Transforming the art object from static image to protocinematic projection, these artists not only marked a radical break with the regime of one-point perspective that had prevailed in Western culture since the Renaissance, but also expanded the traditional viewing space to include active participatory fields. As such, they drew attention to the conditions and complexities of perception both within the framework of institutional display and in outside surroundings. The understanding that perception (the nomadic point from which the world is experienced) does not exist in and of itself, but rather is embodied in a social situation, was a primary concern of all these artists, and it is also at the core of Eliasson's practice today.

By the early 1920s, the most ambitious currents of avant-garde thought were being expressed through artworks that bore the obvious influence of photography, cinema, and other light-based media. In 1922 Lissitzky developed his *Prouns*, abstract paintings of translucent and opaque planes, some of which were intended to be rotated or hung in any direction.[2] At the same time, Moholy-Nagy was investigating the pictorial forms of glass architecture in his *Transparents*, constructions that tackled the interplay between mass and void. Both artists also began to look into the intelligibility of lighting effects transposed from photography. Light served variously as an agent of social transformation in Lissitzky's architectonic projects, which celebrated constructivist ideas amid the rhetoric of socialist Soviet culture; as a building block in Moholy-Nagy's kinetic sculptures, which relied upon a novel conception of space and the vocabulary of "the 'new world' of post-war German reconstruction"[3]; and as a technical starting point for the artists' parallel experiments with multiple exposures and photograms (pictures made by exposing objects placed on photosensitive paper to light). Taken as the *Kunstwollen*, or "artistic will," of modernist culture, the new medium of light mapped the entire field of optical, spatial, and social expression. The camera, furthermore, enabled Lissitzky and Moholy-Nagy to introduce visual experiences that highlighted the altered realities of an era transformed by landmark scientific discoveries, from Thomas Edison's development of incandescent electric light to Max Planck's quantum theory and Albert Einstein's theory of relativity. The ethos of the time is perhaps best summarized by Lissitzky: "The (painted) picture fell apart together with the old world which it had created for itself. The new world will not need little pictures. If it needs a mirror, it has the photograph and the cinema."[4]

In 1925, two years after he joined the faculty of the Bauhaus school in Weimar, Germany, Moholy-Nagy published an influential book titled *Painting, Photography, Film*—part of a series that he coedited with Bauhaus director Walter Gropius—in which he asserted that photography and cinema heralded a "culture of light" that had overtaken the most innovative aspects of painting. Moholy-Nagy extolled photography—and film by extension—as the paradigmatic medium of the future. In an aphorism that the critic Walter Benjamin soon espoused, the artist noted: "It is not the person ignorant of writing, but the one ignorant of photography who will be the illiterate of the future."[5] Out of his interest in photograms and his examination of the movement of objects and light through space, Moholy-Nagy conceived *Light Prop for an Electric Stage (Light-Space Modulator)* (1930; pl. 146), a mobile light mechanism constructed of metal, wood, and transparent plastic screens organized around pivoting rods. When set in motion by its electric motor, this kinetic object throws a variety of light patterns into the surrounding space, materializing its creator's goal of "painting with light."[6] The *Light Prop* substantiated a shift in the Bauhaus from a medieval notion of craft to a more industrialist approach that identified the machine (not just the light-space modulator, but also devices such as the camera and film projector) as "the spirit of the century."[7] Moholy-Nagy's sculpture also became the subject of his only abstract film, *Ein Lichtspiel schwarz weiß grau* (A Lightplay Black White Gray, 1930; pl. 149), which synthesized his attempt to visualize the act of seeing from multiple viewpoints. Eschewing a fixed, predetermined perspective, the film's spatially expansive imagery assumes a mobile viewer whose gaze is no longer channeled or punctual. The idea of perception as a confluence of the phenomenal and the social ensued from Moholy-Nagy's association with the political *Volkstheater* of the Weimar-era dramatist and director Erwin Piscator, with whom the artist collaborated on stage designs in the late 1920s. Together with Bertolt Brecht, Piscator was a foremost exponent of epic theater, which emphasized political context rather than emotional content. This brand of theater relied on scenographic techniques developed by Moholy-Nagy that radically remapped the space of the stage using mechanized sets and projected film, turning the passive onlooker into an engaged participant.

The ideas developed by Lissitzky and Moholy-Nagy—particularly the value they placed on aesthetic experimentation with light sources and the social potential of visual agency—are significant to Eliasson's work. Since 1990 Eliasson has produced hundreds of light installations, sculptures, and photographs that focus the viewer's attention away from the object and toward the processes of perception. For example, in *Beauty* (1993; pls. 5, 31), an early installation consisting of a light whose rays are projected through sprinkling water to produce a rainbow, the viewers' movements in

149
László Moholy-Nagy
Stills from *Ein Lichtspiel schwarz weiß grau* (A Lightplay Black White Gray), 1930
16mm film, 6 min. Courtesy the Estate of László Moholy-Nagy

space allow them to see the different colors of the spectrum. Each move engages the work in ceaseless signification. Because people do not stand in front of *Beauty* as if before a picture, but rather *inside* it, actively engaged, the work posits the very act of looking as a social experience.

The 2001 installation *360° expectations* (pl. 150) features a perfectly circular room, thirty-three feet in diameter, that houses a lens salvaged from a lighthouse and fitted with a white halogen bulb. Its gyrating movement projects a loop of ethereal light that undulates on the surrounding walls like a horizon line, affecting the viewer's sense of balance and dismantling traditional definitions of viewing. Working in the interstitial space between film and sculpture, Eliasson's piece invites viewers to participate in

150
Olafur Eliasson
360° expectations, 2001
Installation view at the Zentrum für Kunst und Medientechnologie, Karlsruhe, Germany, 2001. Wood, lighthouse lens, halogen lamp, tripod, and motor. Collection of Martin and Rebecca Eisenberg

an event that overturns everything they might expect of a projected image. The artist notes that because society is conformist and organized in ways that help us avoid surprises, experiencing "the value of something that's unpredictable can also be seen as a critique of society."[8] As in most of his installations, here a mechanical device is used to simulate a natural phenomenon. Yet the effect is oddly unnatural, and is obviously artificially induced. Inspired by the meteorology and terrain of his native Scandinavia, Eliasson's indoor rainbows, artificial sunsets, fabricated geysers, reversed waterfalls, enclosed ice fields, and projected wave patterns do not invoke the wonders of nature. On the contrary, they underscore the ways in which cultural institutions mediate the viewer's perception of seemingly pure processes. By exposing the mechanics of the works and thus laying bare the artifice of his illusions, Eliasson points to the elliptical relationship between reality, perception, and representation.

Such work embodies neither a quest for nature nor a desire to make artifice synonymous with high culture, but rather an attempt to renew the experience of vision by disrupting normative exhibition conventions. The same holds true for his photographic series. Eliasson considers the photographs, begun in the early 1990s during his annual hiking trips to Iceland, to be studies for issues explored in his installations. Taken while walking, sailing, or flying, his pictures of the landscape underscore the importance of time and motion—indelible factors in the protocinematic experience—to the act of looking. Characteristic of the work is a sense of shifting perspective that highlights the artist's bodily relationship to the pictured scenes. For instance, *The aerial river series* (2000; pl. 109) presents a series of views taken far above the water, providing an artificial perspective of a natural landscape that would seem incomprehensibly enormous from the ground. The initial motivation for the pictures came from 1950s military

151
Olafur Eliasson in collaboration with Luc Steels
Look into the box, 2002
Installation view at the Musée d'Art moderne de la Ville de Paris, 2002. Camera, projector, projection foil, and computer with sound. Courtesy the artist; Tanya Bonakdar Gallery, New York; and neugerriemschneider, Berlin

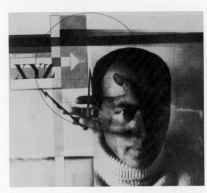

152
El Lissitzky
Self-Portrait, 1924
Gelatin silver print. 3 x 3 3/8 in. (7.6 x 8.6 cm). Museum of Modern Art, New York, Thomas Walther Collection, purchase

shots that were subsequently published as maps for hikers. As the critic Jonathan Napack points out, they "underline how we 'produce' nature in the act of looking, and how misleading is any attempt to 'see' outside of the social context."[9]

Indeed, just as Lissitzky and Moholy-Nagy sought to destabilize perception with compositions shot from disorienting angles, which they believed would help the viewer escape the numbing effect of reliance on routine, Eliasson considers the disruption of our visual habits the sine qua non for individual freedom. During a 2002 collaboration with Luc Steels, a Belgian scientist who studies artificial intelligence and the origins of language, Eliasson conceived *Look into the box* (pl. 151), one of several pieces that seek to articulate the act of seeing. For this installation, the viewer looks into the lens of a camera situated in a box. The camera makes a snapshot of the viewer's eye, which is projected as a still image onto one wall of the gallery. To see one's own disembodied eye raises questions about the paradox of looking at oneself from a second-person perspective. This Brechtian exercise emphasizes both the artist's and the viewer's active, critical roles in the process of perception. Marking a shift from a concern with things seen to the experience of seeing oneself, Eliasson's projection foregrounds its own production process in terms analogous to those dictated by the French filmmaker Jean-Luc Godard, who once described the ultimate movie as a camera filming itself in the mirror.

Look into the box is a self-reflexive experiment that works against the transparency and illusionist power of the cinematic experience. In this sense it nods to Lissitzky's 1924 photomontage self-portrait (pl. 152), which also puts the act of seeing at center stage. Lissitzky has superimposed an exposure of his hand, holding a compass, over a shot of his head that explicitly highlights his eye. Insight is passed through the eye and transmitted to the hand, and through it to the tools of production. (In addition to the compass, Lissitzky has overlaid a number of other elements, including graph paper and the stenciled letters *XYZ*, on the image.) Devised from six different exposures, the picture merges Lissitzky's personae as photographer (eye) and constructor of images (hand) into a single likeness. In an autobiographical typescript from 1928 titled "The Films of El's Life," the artist notes, "My eyes. Lenses and eyepieces, precision instruments and reflex cameras, cinematographs which magnify or hold split seconds. Roentgen and X, Y, Z rays have all combined to place in my forehead 20, 2,000, 200,000 very sharp, polished searching eyes."[10] Lissitzky's self-portrait is both a metaphor for the creative process and an equation of the mechanism of human perception and the perfectible lens of the camera.

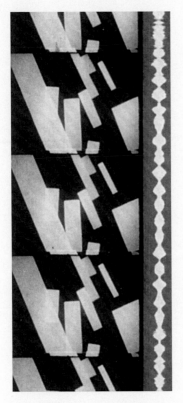

153
Hans Richter
Stills from *Rhythmus 23*, 1923–25
35mm film with sound, 2:20 min. Musée national
d'art moderne, Centre Pompidou, Paris

Continuing this exploration of the human eye as an instrument, Eliasson recently engaged in a series of experiments with afterimages for a potential movie production. The screen for this project is intended to be hemispheric, insuring that the moving image fills the audience's entire retinal field. Half of the film is meant to be projected onto the screen and the other half "projected" by the viewers' eyes. What would such a film look like? According to the artist, who screened a short segment at Berlin's Zeiss Planetarium in 2006, it might begin with the projection of a colored disc—yellow, for instance—which would fade or increase slightly in intensity and then disappear, leaving in its stead a purple afterimage. Next, a green shape would appear on the screen, to be followed by a red afterimage. To complicate the audience's perception of color, the subsequent form would be projected beside the ghostly red shape, resulting in an artificial afterimage. Since looking at any color for an extended period of time produces patterns and modulations in appearance, Eliasson is asking the viewer to preserve and inscribe the effects of earlier perceptions onto new color shapes, generating images that might resemble buildings or landscapes. Like Hans Richter's pioneering abstract films, which codified a visual syntax based on the polar relationships of forms and primary colors and the laws of human perception, Eliasson's film project operates through analogy and association rather than traditional narrative. Richter's *Rhythmus 21* (1921), *Rhythmus 23* (1923–25; pl. 153), and *Rhythmus 25* (1925)—now classics of the cinema—play with reductionist squares, trapezoids, and lines of different colors and sizes that interact in space. These geometric shapes move in and out of screen, creating contrasting light and dark planes as well as negative reversals. By superimposing the planes, Richter composed sequences of evolving patterns that range from very simple to increasingly complex. Devised according to musical scores, his films translate rhythm into cinematic sensation.

Eliasson's interest in perceptual phenomena is also related to Duchamp's abstract optical experiments of the 1920s and 1930s. Duchamp first explored the notion of the eye as a camera in 1920 when he collaborated with Man Ray on the production of a three-dimensional film. Using the anaglyphic process, wherein two images with slightly different viewpoints are superimposed, he synchronized two cameras—the left with red-colored glass and the right with green-colored glass—and trained them on a spiral painted on a rotating demisphere, hoping to combine the resulting images on the viewer's retina. Although the test failed,[11] Duchamp continued to pursue experiments with afterimages and other subjective features of human vision, creating his first optical machine, *Rotary Glass Plates (Precision Optics)*, in 1920. Five years later he produced an improved version, *Rotary Demisphere (Precision Optics)*, in which concentric black circles painted on a white dome convey the effect of depth when the machine is set in motion. This kinetic work inspired Duchamp to make another three-dimensional film in 1926, but this time he did not use the anaglyphic process. Instead he filmed another rotary disc work, *Discs Bearing*

Spirals (1923), to make *Anémic cinéma*. The title, an anagram in both French and English, reveals the methodology of the film: to make an object turn on itself. The film alternates shots of ten rotating spirals with views of nine cardboard discs inscribed with erotic puns set in slight relief. The various discs emphasize the different processes of seeing verbal and optical images: one reads the discs with puns while perceiving the discs with spirals, due to optical illusion, as pulsating forms that render vision both corporeal and manifestly erotic. Duchamp conceived the final version of the rotary discs in 1935, when he produced the *Rotoreliefs* (pl. 154). On each side of a set of six cardboard discs he drew whimsical images—a goldfish in a bowl, the eclipsed sun seen through a tube, a lightbulb—along with a spiral or concentric circles. The latter are the key to Duchamp's production of 3-D effects, which become visible only when the discs revolve on a turntable, and which incited the surrealist writer Michel Leiris to observe that the *Rotoreliefs* are "records to be looked at, not to be heard"—a paraphrase of Duchamp's earlier dictum that "one can look at seeing; one can't hear hearing."[12] Like Eliasson's *Your concentric welcome* (2004) and *Colour space embracer* (2005; pls. 212–13), installations in which suspended, rotating glass discs induce a hypnotic self-awareness of one's physical presence in space, Duchamp's *Rotoreliefs* reclaim the corporeal dimension of vision. But whereas Duchamp's optical devices sought to address vision's relation to desire, Eliasson's simulations of the luminous impact of perceived color are intended to enhance the viewer's sensory faculties and restore to perception a sense of subjective criticality.

154
Marcel Duchamp
Rotoreliefs, 1935
Lithography on cardboard. Each 7⁷/₈ x 7⁷/₈ in.
(20 x 20 cm). Musée national d'art moderne,
Centre Pompidou, Paris

Another protocinematic feature of Eliasson's oeuvre is his use of simple technologies—from glass discs and floor lamps to fans and mirrors—to explore ideas of space and create phenomenal effects. On one level these mechanics invoke the fundamental principle of photography and cinema: light passing through a lens in order to expose or project film. However, such devices also exemplify the artist's interest in more complex filmic techniques, from the representation of passing time to narrative construction. His 1993 installation *Mental* (pl. 24), for example, is an empty room furnished with a mirrored wall and hidden speakers that play the soft sound of the artist's own heartbeat. The room is activated only by the entrance of the viewers and their reflections in the mirror. Encouraged to decipher a set of relationships between the visual and the aural, they become alert to their own internal rhythms and to how the installation changes as they shift in space. As in a dance studio, the mirror becomes an instrument for studying one's movements and pace. Watching themselves look, viewers explore the ways in which they see and, in turn,

155
Olafur Eliasson
I grew up in solitude and silence, 1991
Installation view at Campbells Occasionally,
Copenhagen, 1991. Mirror and candle. 9⁷/₈ x
19⁵/₈ x 19⁵/₈ in. (25.1 x 49.8 x 49.8 cm).
Courtesy the artist; Tanya Bonakdar Gallery,
New York; and neugerriemschneider, Berlin

observe themselves being observed. Every time the viewers change physical position, they not only change their viewpoints but also disrupt and reorder the artwork's narrative structure, provoking new cognitive situations.

Eliasson often creates situations that propel viewers from the gallery space into the realm of the senses through direct confrontation with visual phenomena. In doing so, he not only questions the boundaries between nature and culture, but also explores how we imagine relevant narratives as we become active participants in the work. In *I grew up in solitude and silence* (1991; pl. 155), a lit candle stands on a circular mirror with a twenty-inch diameter. Here one's perception is split between the experiential narrative of watching the candle slowly burn and the projected narrative of anticipating different scenarios about the object. According to the philosopher Henri Bergson, the mind tackles duration as a simultaneous process merging past memory and future projection within a continually unfolding present. Looking at the flickering flame, the viewer thus experiences three overlapping temporalities: memory, actual perception, and projected narrative. The latter is essentially an amplified, fast-forward version of what happens in the present, but it summarizes any number of likely scenarios (the candle gradually becomes shorter as it burns; the wax drips on the mirrored surface; the mirror gets too hot and cracks under the candle's increasing heat; viewers approach the work to look more closely and see their reflections in the mirror). At once absorbing and analytical, the work exists only for the duration of the burning candle, yet it calls up a roster of prior experiences and corporeal states.

Such is also the case with *Green river* (1998; pls. 72–77), an intervention Eliasson has made by adding uranin, a nontoxic substance used by marine biologists to test ocean currents, to rivers in a number of different cities. Upon contact with water, the substance turns a shimmering green hue, provoking alarming associations with environmental disaster. Each river's flow carried the green pigment along its regular currents, creating an ever-changing scene that could seem disorienting, alarming, or poetic, depending on the viewer. As people grappled with the meaning of what they saw, the situation inspired them to reflect on their preconceptions and subjective responses.

The status of vision in Eliasson's experiments may also be discussed in terms of his protocinematic preoccupation with the sun. The mechanics he used to create *The weather project* (2003; pls. 1–2, 15, 196–97) at the Tate Modern, London, are—despite the project's spectacular effect and monumental scale—surprisingly similar to those of his earlier mirror pieces. Using reflective panels and yellow monofrequency lights to evoke an incandescent sun, the work hearkens back to nineteenth-century visual investigations into the relationship between the eye and the sun that eventually led to the development of cinema. Visionary scientists such as Gustav Fechner and Joseph Plateau, fascinated by the persistence of luminous impressions on the retina, performed perilous experiments with afterimages by staring directly into the sun. Plateau went blind later in life, but not before his research into visual phenomena led to his invention of the phenakistiscope, a stroboscopic device consisting of two discs, one with small radial windows and another displaying a sequence of images. When rotated at the correct speed, the discs created the illusion of a moving image, thus anticipating the motion picture.

Lying down in the Turbine Hall, beholders of Eliasson's artificial sun could feel the intensity of the light, watch their mirrored images in the virtual distance of the doubled ceiling, and project their own cinematic imaginings of sunrise or sunset as rarified moments of heightened perception. A sunset is romantic, an extraordinary, gradual experience that lasts from the moment the sun nearly touches the horizon until its afterglow disappears. A sunrise is literally an awakening, a glowing field of light glimpsed on the horizon before the sun reveals its full shape. Both are short-lived moments that allow one to glimpse the sun's fading or increasing brightness without being blinded. Whether rising or setting, eclipsed or in dazzling color, the sun is a motif rehearsed in countless films and has been a source of inspiration for painters and architects throughout the ages. Ancient pyramids were designed as sites to honor the sun god (a pyramid is essentially a building whose architectural form connects the shape of the sun and the earth in an equilateral triangle). The original Roman Pantheon was designed to allow the sun to shine from the dome's oculus through the front door on the day of the summer solstice.

In 1997 Eliasson produced *Your sun machine* (pls. 47–50), a project that reflects his early and unrelenting concern with these precedents. Cutting a circular hole in the ceiling of Marc Foxx Gallery in Los Angeles, he let the light flood in and rotate across the walls and floor during the course of the day. Bergson's concept of duration, or lived time (as distinct from Newtonian objective time, or time divisible into measurable units), is for Eliasson inextricably linked with the beholder's consciousness. It is both intuitive, in the way in which it structures daily life against solar and lunar patterns, and subjective, in that each individual experiences time according to his or her own lifestyle, reference system, social context, and projected narrative. Eliasson's cut transforms the gallery space into a chamber for charting the movement of the solar orb. Yet, as we know, the sun does not move; although it may seem to be rotating around us, it is in fact our own orbit around the sun that makes things appear as they do. In 1851 the French physicist Léon Foucault hung a huge pendulum from the roof of the Panthéon in Paris to demonstrate the rotation of the earth on its axis. Umberto Eco describes Foucault's pendulum as a single point of suspension that has been stood still so that it has no dimension. It cannot move around its own axis, or around the earth, but instead conditions us, as *Your sun machine* does, to perceive the motion of the world.[13]

By exploring ideas related to the moving image and light-time ratio, Eliasson builds on earlier artistic experiments with light and motion, including Gordon

Matta-Clark's anarchitectural projects (works created by carving unexpected, vertiginous apertures of light into abandoned buildings) and James Turrell's skyspaces (large-scale, often architectural installations involving the complex interplay of sky, light, and atmosphere). When Matta-Clark and Turrell envision pieces in remote, provisional, or ramshackle environments, they engage the camera in preserving the work either on film or in photographs. This is the case with any number of Matta-Clark's site-specific interventions in dilapidated buildings, including *Splitting* (Englewood, New Jersey, 1974), *Bingo* (Niagara Falls, New York, 1974), *Conical Intersect* (Paris, 1975), and *Office Baroque* (Antwerp, Belgium, 1977). Sculpting with cuts and fissures, he deconstructed apartments, often on several floors, by opening their dark spaces and facades to light. Describing *Day's End* (1975; pl. 156), a project in which the artist removed part of the roof and floor of a deserted Manhattan steel wharf to create a "sun and water temple," Gerry Hovagimyan, who assisted Matta-Clark with the project, writes: "200 feet to the front, facing out over the river, loomed an oval penetration in the corrugated facade of the structure. . . . A circular removal revealed sky and . . . a jaunty cut-out seemed to mimic the outline of an unfurled sail. Light, air, sky and water. Everything was alive with motion and light."[14] After photographing his works, Matta-Clark arranged the pictures as storyboards or recomposed them into kaleidoscopic collages that take on a sculptural dimension of their own. In this way he re-created the disorienting experience of incised spaces opened to the sky and invaded by sunlight.

156
Gordon Matta-Clark
Day's End (Pier 52), 1975
Color photograph. 16 x 20 in. (40.6 x 50.8 cm).
Courtesy the Estate of Gordon Matta-Clark and
David Zwirner, New York

Mining the zone of the phenomenal, Turrell's Roden Crater project in Arizona's Painted Desert creates a similar experience. Since 1977 the artist has been carving out a natural volcanic crater and turning it into a colossal observatory for viewing celestial phenomena. The son of an aeronautical engineer, and a pilot from the age of sixteen, Turrell engages the sky in his practice. For *Meeting*, his permanent 1986 installation at P.S.1 Contemporary Art Center in New York, Turrell framed a rectangular segment of the firmament that echoes the geometric shape commonly used to represent the sky in two-dimensional theatrical sets, in children's drawings, or on movie screens. In a room lined with wooden benches, a movable roof allows the ceiling to open; weather permitting, visitors can enter the space at dusk and watch the color of the sky change gradually from bright azure to deep midnight blue. Only when a bird or plane crosses overhead is the illusion of this sublime, monochromatic, abstract field interrupted. As emphasized by the work's title, it is a socially engaging space in which viewers play an active role. Like the imagined sunrise or sunset of Eliasson's *The weather project*, Turrell's actual transitory light binds the space of art to the outside world. Both works rupture the traditional self-containment of the museum space.

This conceptual as well as physical opening to the outside world is linked to the idea of art in the expanded field and the consequent dissolution of a transcendent, monadic viewpoint in favor of peripatetic perception. Robert Smithson explored the notion of perception as both itinerant and filmic in his monumental *Spiral Jetty*, orchestrated in 1970 at the Great Salt Lake in Utah (pl. 157). In the first phase of this project, Smithson made a storyboard to illustrate, scene by scene, the process of creating the jetty, just as a movie director visualizes a film's concept, context, and eventual realization. He also recorded the moving and leveling of fifteen hundred feet of black basalt, limestone, and earth using heavy construction machinery. In the next

157
Robert Smithson
Spiral Jetty, 1970
Installation view at the Great Salt Lake, Utah, 1970. Black rock, salt crystals, earth, and red water (algae). 180 x 180 in. (457.2 x 457.2 cm), total length of coil 18,000 in. (45,720 cm), height varies with water level. Dia Center for the Arts, New York

phase, Smithson filmed the completed sculpture from a helicopter, trying to capture the moment when the sun's reflection hit the water at the exact center of the spiral. "From that position," Smithson observed, "the flaming reflection suggested the ion source of a cyclotron that extended into a spiral of collapsed matter. . . . All existence seemed tentative and stagnant. . . . Was I but a shadow in a plastic bubble hovering in a place outside mind and body?"[15] The artist's accounts of filming *Spiral Jetty* consistently reference his extended exposure to the burning sun: "On the slopes of Rozel Point I closed my eyes, and the sun burned crimson through the lids."[16] As in a walking dream, the experience of being close to the sun and distant from the earth suggests a heightened awareness of an imagined state—in Smithson's words, a form of "lucid vertigo."[17] Inverting Plato's philosophical allegory of the cave, Smithson's turn away from the world of the senses toward the bright light above entailed not only illumination, but also revealed disorientation.

Smithson intended to show the *Spiral Jetty* film in a subterranean movie theater near the site. The projection booth was to be made of rough timbers, the screen improvised from a rock wall painted white, and the seats adapted from simple boulders. The cinema cavern, however, was never constructed.[18] Smithson also developed several other ideas for unrealized films, some of which are mentioned in his 1971 article "A Cinematic Atopia." One such concept occurred to him while walking through the long, horizontal tunnels of the Britannia copper mine near Vancouver, British Columbia. Arriving at the end of a tunnel he "looked back at the entrance, where only a pinpoint of light was visible." Smithson imagined a film made in one long take from the interior of the tunnel toward the entrance, ending outside in blinding light.[19]

The act of looking directly into the light, as in the short moments of sunrise and sunset, is similar to turning away from the screen in a movie theater to look into the light of the film projector. Drawing upon this accidental occurrence, Anthony McCall's solid light films of the 1970s exemplify the attempt to materialize light. In *Line Describing a Cone* (1973; pl. 158), McCall articulates the beam of the projector as a three-dimensional volume in space. Over a period of thirty minutes, in a dark room filled with mist, a volumetric form emerges out of immaterial light. As the beam increases in length over time, it gradually develops from a line into a hollow cone ending in a circular projection on the wall. Reversing the conventions of a typical cinema, McCall invites the audience to watch the film by looking directly at the light as it emanates from the projector, and even to follow the light through the exhibition space. Viewers are free to encounter the work from multiple viewpoints—to walk into the conical shape of light, to stand inside of it, or even to lie under it—resulting in an intensely corporeal experience.

McCall's projection, like Eliasson's installations, points to the ways in which viewers negotiate between actual and perceived realities. Fusing the properties of film and sculpture, such work takes an essentially unseeable phenomenon and renders it visible through artificial means. Something similar happens with Eliasson's *No nights in summer, no days in winter* (1994; pls. 32–33), an auratic ring of burning gas that evokes a solar eclipse or the retinal afterimage caused by looking at the sun. The reason a simulated phenomenon can look real is that we tend to naturalize the real world to the point where it can begin to resemble its own representation. Indeed, Eliasson calls his works "phenomena-producers"; they are, he says, "like machines, or stage sets, producing a certain thing in a more or less illusory way." The question, then, is "when do you reveal the illusion?"[20] As high-definition technologies increasingly seek to emulate the illusion that lived experience is seamless, Eliasson's protocinematic approach underscores the fallacy of such illusionism and refocuses attention on the responses of individual viewers. His ongoing exploration of subjectivity, perception, and the fluid boundary between nature and culture reveals the degree to which our shared reality is constructed, thus helping us to reflect more critically on our experience of it.

158
Anthony McCall
Line Describing a Cone, 1973
Installation view at Artists Space, New York, 1974.
16mm film, 30 min. Courtesy the artist. Photo by
Peter Moore

NOTES

1. The term *situational aesthetics* invokes the strategies of the 1960s Situationist International movement, which developed an art of *dérive*, or "drift," in the form of clandestine walks and direct interventions in urban spaces. Acting against the so-called society of the spectacle (the culture of media events, marketing, and commodities), Situationists such as Guy Debord, the group's spokesperson, insisted on the dictates of communal play, establishing vectors, itineraries, and passageways through the city in an effort to redirect travelers away from the prerogatives of real-estate capitalism and toward subversive sights and situations. In the 1970s, artists such as James Turrell, Gordon Matta-Clark, Robert Smithson, and Anthony McCall devised new paradigms for situations that also confounded routine experience, encouraging social interaction among their viewers and within their social milieu.

    The idea that art is a forum for exchange and that social relations can be treated as an artistic medium became increasingly significant in the 1990s. The French curator and critic Nicolas Bourriaud coined the phrase *relational aesthetics* to describe work that makes social interaction an aesthetic prerogative. For more on relational aesthetics and its relevance to Eliasson's art, see Daniel Birnbaum's essay in this volume.

2. Lissitzky spoke of the *Proun* as an "interchange station between painting and architecture." The name is an acronym derived from *Proekt + UNOVIS* ("Architectural design of UNOVIS") or *Proekt Utverzhdenya Novoga* ("Project for the Affirmation of the New"). See Matthew Drutt, "El Lissitzky in Germany, 1922–1925," in *El Lissitzky: Beyond the Abstract Cabinet*, by Margarita Tupitsyn (New Haven, CT: Yale University Press, 1999), 9.

3. Terence A. Senter, "Moholy-Nagy: The Transition Years," in *Albers and Moholy-Nagy: From the Bauhaus to the New World*, ed. Achim Borchardt-Hume (London: Tate Publishing, 2006), 85.

4. El Lissitzky, "The Conquest of Art" (1922), quoted in Peter Nisbet, "Lissitzky and Photography," in *El Lissitzky, 1890–1941: Architect, Painter, Photographer, Typographer* (Eindhoven, Netherlands: Municipal Van Abbemuseum; Madrid: Fundaçion Caja de Pensiones; Paris: Musée d'Art moderne de la Ville de Paris / ARC, 1990), 66.

5. László Moholy-Nagy, "Photography in Creation with Light" (1928), quoted in Walter Benjamin, "News about Flowers," in *Walter Benjamin: Selected Writings*, vol. 2, part 1, ed. Michael W. Jennings, Howard Eiland, and Gary Smith (Cambridge, MA: Harvard University Press, 1999), 156.

6. See László Moholy-Nagy, *The New Vision and Abstract of an Artist*, 4th ed. (New York: Wittenborn, 1947), 230.

7. See Hal Foster, Rosalind Krauss, Yve-Alain Bois, and Benjamin H. D. Buchloh, *Art Since 1900: Modernism, Antimodernism, Postmodernism* (New York: Thames & Hudson), 187. Further evidence is Dziga Vertov's 1929 film *Man with a Movie Camera*, which shows cinema transforming traditional craft into industrial production through the juxtaposition of a series of images: turning spools of thread are likened to the turning reels of a film projector; cleaning the streets is equated to cleaning film; sewing is compared to editing; and the hydroelectric plant providing the energy for the textile industry is linked to the power on which the cameraman and the film industry rely.

8. Olafur Eliasson, quoted in Leslie Camhi, "And the Artist Recreated Nature (or an Illusion of It)," *New York Times*, January 21, 2001.

9. Jonathan Napack, "Olafur Eliasson," in *Vitamin Ph: New Perspectives in Photography* (London: Phaidon, 2006), 84.

10. Quoted in Drutt, "El Lissitzky in Germany," 21.

11. Man Ray left the following description of their venture: "[Duchamp] had conceived an idea for making three-dimensional movies. Miss [Katherine Sophie] Dreier had presented him with a movie camera, and he obtained another cheap one—the idea was to join them with gears and a common axis so that a double, stereoscopic film could be made of a globe with a spiral painted on it. . . . Duchamp decided to develop the film by himself; I helped him. First, we obtained a couple of shallow garbage-can covers for tanks, a round plywood board was cut to fit, then waterproofed with paraffin. To wind the film on these, Duchamp drew radiating lines from the centers and hammered four hundred nails along them. After taking fifty feet of film, we waited for nightfall and in the dark managed to wind the film into one of the trays, the fixing liquid into the other. We immersed the board into the first and timed the development, then transferred it to the fixer tanks. After about twenty minutes we turned on the light. The film looked like a mass of tangled seaweed. It had swelled and was stuck together, most of it not having been acted on by the developer" (quoted in Jean Clair, "Opticeries," *October* 5 [Summer 1978]: 111).

12. See Arturo Schwarz, *The Complete Works of Marcel Duchamp* (New York: Abrams, 1970), 54. Interestingly, Duchamp's quote seems to anticipate Eliasson's adage about "seeing yourself seeing" (see his interview with Jessica Morgan in *Olafur Eliasson: Your Only Real Thing Is Time* [Boston: Institute of Contemporary Art; Ostfildern-Ruit, Germany: Hatje Cantz, 2001], 17, 21).

13. See Umberto Eco, *Foucault's Pendulum*, trans. William Weaver (San Diego: Harcourt Brace Jovanovich, 1989).

14. Gerry Hovagimyan, quoted in Thomas Crow, "Gordon Matta-Clark," in *Gordon Matta-Clark*, ed. Corinne Diserens (London: Phaidon, 2003), 11.

15. Robert Smithson, "The Spiral Jetty" (1972), in *The Writings of Robert Smithson*, ed. Nancy Holt (New York: New York University Press, 1979), 113.

16. Ibid.

17. Ibid., 115.

18. Tragically, Smithson met a premature death in a 1973 plane crash while shooting cinematic documentation of his *Amarillo Ramp* in Texas.

19. See Robert Smithson, "A Cinematic Atopia," *Artforum* 10 (September 1971): 53–55; reprinted in Holt, *Writings of Robert Smithson*, 105–8.

20. Olafur Eliasson, interview with Daniel Birnbaum, in *Olafur Eliasson*, by Madeleine Grynsztejn et al. (London: Phaidon, 2002), 14.

PROJECTS 2002–2006

159
The horizon series, 2002 (EXH.)
Forty framed chromogenic prints. Each 9³/₄ x 42 in. (24.8 x 106.7 cm); 89 x 219 in. (226 x 557.3 cm) overall. Collection of Michael and Jeanne Klein, partial and promised gift to the Menil Collection, Houston

Each picture in this grid shows a different horizon within the Icelandic landscape. The artist uses an exaggerated horizontal format, underscoring the natural phenomenon limiting visual perception.

160–62
Remagine (large version), 2002
Installation views at the Kunstmuseum Wolfsburg, Germany, 2004. Spotlights, wall mounts or tripods, and control unit. Kunstmuseum Bonn, Germany

Twelve spotlights cast rectilinear patterns of light across the length of a gallery wall toward a given vanishing point. A computerized control system turns the lamps on and off at different intervals, shifting the position, size, angle, and contrast of the projections, which overlap in fluctuating patterns on the wall. A smaller version of this piece (EXH.) creates the same effects with seven spotlights.

163–64
Lava floor, 2002
Installation views at the Musée d'Art moderne de la Ville de Paris, 2002. Volcanic rocks. Courtesy the artist; Tanya Bonakdar Gallery, New York; and neugerriemschneider, Berlin

Several tons of igneous Icelandic rocks are arranged on the floor of an exhibition space. Visitors are invited to walk over the rocks, which they feel and hear shifting beneath their feet.

165–66
Quasi brick wall, 2002
Installation views at the Fundación NMAC, Cádiz, Spain, 2002. Clay and stainless-steel mirrors. 63 x 236¹/₄ x 7⁷/₈ in. (160 x 600 x 20 cm). Fundación NMAC

This permanent, site-specific project stands in a remote garden. Mirrors are mounted on a subtly curved wall of geometric clay bricks, reflecting the natural surroundings and changing light conditions.

167–72
360° room for all colours, 2002 (EXH.)
Installation views at the Kunstmuseum Wolfsburg, Germany, 2004. Stainless steel, projection foil, fluorescent lights, wood, and control unit. 126 x 321 x 321 in. (320 x 815.3 x 815.3 cm). Private collection, courtesy Tanya Bonakdar Gallery, New York

Inside a darkened gallery stands an open-topped, circular structure with one entry. A screen lines the interior, covering an intricate electrical system that comprises more than five hundred fluorescent lights. When viewers enter the space they are immersed in a panorama of changing light representing the entire color spectrum. A computerized control unit regulates the color combinations, which change approximately every thirty seconds.

173
Model room, 2003 (EXH.)
Installation view at the Lunds Konsthall, Lund, Sweden, 2005. Chipboard display cabinets and mixed-media models, maquettes, and prototypes. Courtesy the artist; Tanya Bonakdar Gallery, New York; and neugerriemschneider, Berlin

A collaboration with the artist and architect Einar Thorsteinn, this installation presents an abounding array of sculptural models and maquettes, which are arranged on customized shelving units, positioned on tables, and hung from the ceiling and walls. The objects on display include forms based on geodesic domes, kaleidoscopes and other mirrored surfaces, and intricate lattice shapes that demonstrate mathematic principles.

174
Your spiral view, 2002
Installation view at the Fondation Beyeler, Riehen, Switzerland, 2002. Stainless-steel mirrors and steel. 126 x 126 x 315 in. (320 x 320 x 800 cm). Collection of Christian Boros, Berlin

The viewer walks on a raised platform through a torqued tunnel lined with intricately faceted mirrors. As the viewer passes through, light reflects off the fractured geometric planes, and the structure appears to spiral toward the opening on the other side.

175
Flower pavilion, 2003
Installation view at the 5th Shenzhen International Public Art Exhibition, China, 2003. Stainless-steel mirrors and steel. 492¹/₈ x 551¹/₆ x 551¹/₆ in. (1,250 x 1,400 x 1,400 cm). Courtesy the artist

This giant, site-specific steel sculpture was designed for an urban park. Viewers walked under the crystalline, polyhedral structure—which was supported by a steel frame—and gazed up into dozens of kaleidoscopes reflecting the environment.

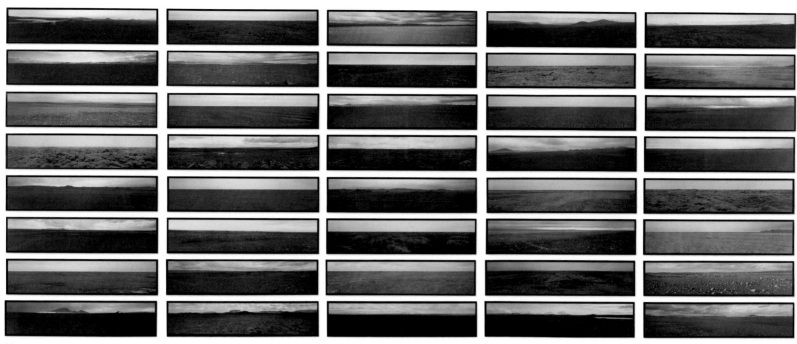

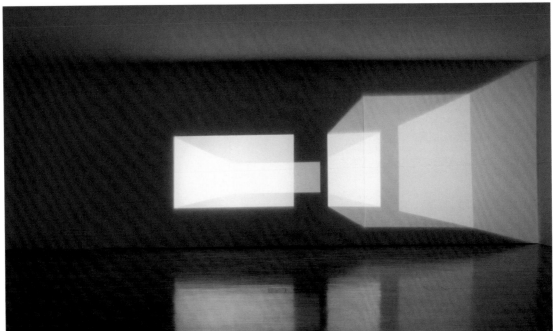

160–62

163

164

165

166

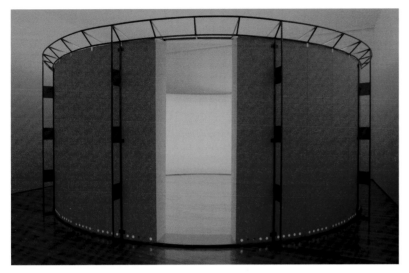

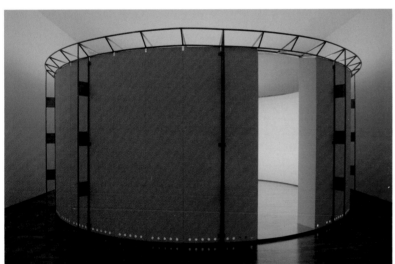

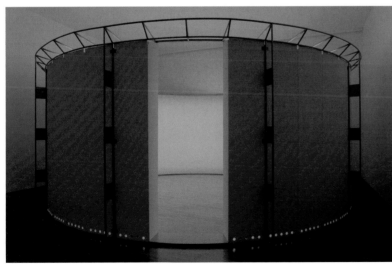
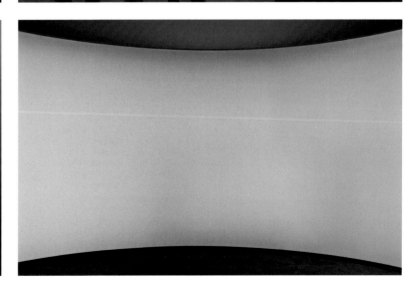

167–72

a

b

c

d

e

f

g

h

176–94
The blind pavilion, 2003
Installation views at the 50th Venice Biennale, Italy, 2003. See overleaf for information on individual artworks

The artist transformed the Danish Pavilion by constructing a long, looping walkway along which visitors encountered a sequence of artworks built into the terraced levels of the architecture. The installation utilized both the interior and exterior spaces, often piercing walls so that viewers could look through to the other side and see fellow spectators. Upon entering the pavilion, visitors had the choice of turning right or left.

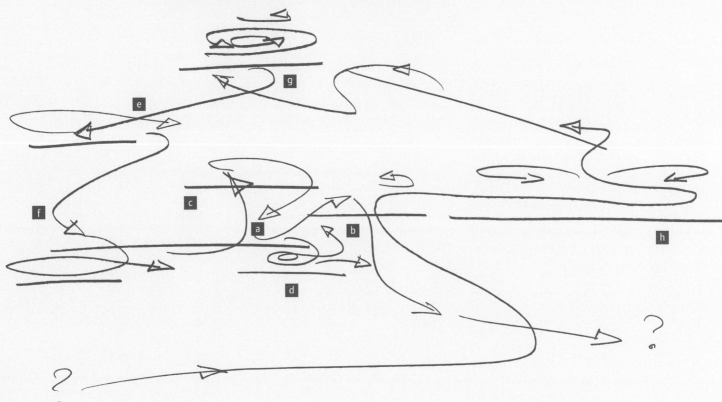

176, 179–80
Soil quasi bricks, 2003 (EXH.)
Fired compressed-soil tiles and wood. Courtesy the artist; Tanya Bonakdar Gallery, New York; and neugerriemschneider, Berlin

The artist covers the walls from floor to ceiling with thousands of compactly fitted tiles, each shaped in the form of a three-dimensional hexagon.

177
Colour spectrum kaleidoscope, 2003
Color-effect filter glass and stainless steel. 29 1/2 x 29 1/2 x 78 1/2 in. (75 x 75 x 200 cm). Collection of David Teiger

A hexagonal kaleidoscope lined with myriad plates of colorful glass looks out a window onto the natural landscape. When viewers in a darkened space peer into the kaleidoscope, they see brilliant, prismatic reflections.

178
Room for one colour, 1997 (EXH.)
Monofrequency lights. Courtesy the artist; Tanya Bonakdar Gallery, New York; and neugerriemschneider, Berlin

Yellow light floods a room. Spectators see purple, yellow's complementary color, as an afterimage when they close their eyes.

179–80
Camera obscura for the sky, 2003
Wood, lens, and plastic. Private collection, courtesy neugerriemschneider, Berlin

The artist inserts a lens into a hole he has cut in the ceiling of a darkened room and places a circular table directly beneath. The lens directs an image of the natural surroundings onto the table's flat surface, which matches the proportions of the lens.

181–82, 189
Triple kaleidoscope, 2003
Stainless-steel mirrors. 94 1/2 x 39 3/8 x 39 3/8 in. (240 x 100 x 100 cm). Private collection, Dublin

Built into a deck, three hexagonal kaleidoscopes join at the base, forming a single unit. The work pierces the flooring and opens onto a room beneath. Viewers outside can peer through each of the three openings to see reflections of the other side. From below one can see exterior reflections as well as other viewers looking through the opposing apertures.

183
The glass house, 2003
Aperture cut into existing facade. 29 1/2 x 38 2/3 in. (75 x 98 cm). Private collection, courtesy neugerriemschneider, Berlin

The artist cuts a trapezoidal window into the wall at eye level in a darkened room. Over the course of the day, natural light casts shadows of the exterior environment inside the space and onto adjacent walls, producing multiple perspectival lines.

184, 188, 190–91
The blind pavilion, 2003
Steel and glass. 98 1/2 x 295 1/4 x 295 1/4 in. (250 x 750 x 750 cm). Private collection

This open-air pavilion is comprised of angular sections of alternating black opaque and transparent clear glass. Viewers enter to discover a smaller, similar structure inside. When spectators walk between the layers of glass, dancing reflections obscure their ability to locate themselves and other visitors within the pavilion's various spaces.

185–87
The antigravity cone, 2003
Strobe light, water, foil, wood, and pump. 31 1/2 x 19 5/8 x 19 5/8 in. (80 x 50 x 50 cm). Collection of David Teiger

A hexagonal cone on a deck covers a fountain built into the flooring. Viewers look through an opening at the top and see gurgling water below; a strobe light makes the liquid appear to defy gravity and remain suspended in air when illuminated.

188, 191
Wooden construction, 2003
Wooden ramps, stairs, and platforms. Courtesy the artist; Tanya Bonakdar Gallery, New York; and neugerriemschneider, Berlin

Viewers cross a series of connected ramps, platforms, and staircases that traverse the exterior levels of a multistory building. The continuous construction features three different types of stairs with varying slopes.

192–94
La situazione antispettiva (The antispective situation), 2003
Stainless-steel mirrors. 196 7/8 x 196 7/8 x 590 2/3 in. (500 x 500 x 1,500 cm). 21st Century Museum of Contemporary Art, Kanazawa, Japan

Visitors climb a short staircase and walk across a platform into a monumental, enclosed crystalline form. Dozens of hexagonal and pentagonal kaleidoscopes of varying size radiate inside the space, creating an infinite array of dazzling geometric reflections within.

178

179

181

182

183

185

186

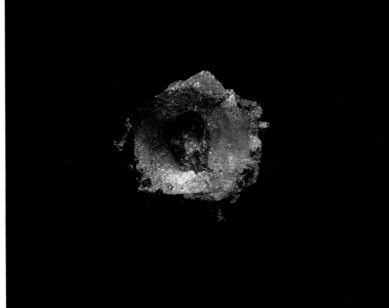

187

188

189

190

191

194

preceding: 193

195
Yellow versus purple, 2003 (EXH.)
Installation view at the Tate Modern, London, 2007. Color-effect filter glass, floodlight, tripod, motor, and wire. Tate, purchased with funds provided by the 2003 Outset Frieze Acquisitions Fund for Tate 2003

A spotlight shines on a colored glass disc that hangs suspended from the ceiling. As the disc slowly rotates, it casts changing patterns on the walls and reflects complementary colors throughout the space. When viewers walk through the piece, the shapes and colors play over the surfaces of their bodies and they become part of the installation.

196–97
The weather project, 2003
Installation views at the Tate Modern, London, 2003. Monofrequency lights, projection foil, haze machine, mirror foil, aluminum, and scaffolding. Courtesy the artist; Tanya Bonakdar Gallery, New York; and neugerriemschneider, Berlin

This site-specific installation for the Unilever Series introduced an artificial climate within the cavernous Turbine Hall. The artist lined the ceiling with mirrors that doubled the height of the space and reflected the viewers below. At the east end of the hall, abutting the ceiling, a semicircular screen covered hundreds of yellow monofrequency bulbs. The screen and its mirrored reflection combined to produce a spherical shape resembling a brilliant sun. Throughout the course of the day, a machine released mist into the space.

198
I only see things when they move, 2004
Installation view at the Aspen Art Museum, Colorado, 2004. Wood, motors, color-effect filter glass, aluminum, wire, control unit, HMI lamp, tripod, metal, and ballast. Courtesy the artist; Tanya Bonakdar Gallery, New York; and neugerriemschneider, Berlin

Colored glass filters are affixed to a lamp placed in the center of a darkened gallery. A motor individually turns the plates, casting a colorful, moving pattern of vertical reflections onto the surrounding walls.

199
The inverted shadow tower, 2004
Installation view at the Kunstmuseum Wolfsburg, Germany, 2004. Stainless steel, aluminum, fluorescent lights, acrylic, and control unit. 236 1/4 x 187 x 187 in. (600 x 475 x 475 cm). Foundation for Contemporary Art Victor Pinchuk, Kiev, Ukraine

Rising nearly twenty feet, the exterior of this metallic tower is made of pointed diamond forms; fluorescent lights inside illuminate the structure. A computer controls the light intensity, which changes at approximately the same speed at which the viewer's eyes adjust. From outside one can see the shifting glow through the structure's square negative spaces.

200–205
Wall eclipse, 2004
Installation views at the Astrup Fearnley Museet for Moderne Kunst, Oslo, 2004. Mirror, HMI lamp, motor, and tripod. Private collection

A mirror, its size proportional to the gallery wall, rotates in the center of a darkened space. A lamp projects a beam of light onto it; as the reflective side turns, it casts a rectilinear shape of light onto the surrounding walls. When it faces away from the lamp, the entire wall behind it goes dark, creating the effect of an eclipse. Alternately, when the mirror faces the lamp, the opposite wall is bathed in light.

206
Frost activity, 2004
Installation view at the Reykjavík Art Museum—Hafnarhús, 2004. Mirror foil, aluminum, dolerite, rhyolite, and basalt. Ellipse Foundation Contemporary Art Center, Cascais, Portugal

The artist lines a ceiling with mirrors, doubling the perceived height of the space, and covers the floor with tiles of Icelandic rock cut to resemble that country's distinctive basalt formations. Visitors see themselves reflected in the ceiling, together with the intricate geometric pattern of the floor tiles, altering their sense of classical perspective and the surrounding architecture.

207–8
Multiple grotto, 2004 (EXH.)
Installation views at the San Francisco Museum of Modern Art, 2006. Stainless-steel mirrors. 180 x 180 x 180 in. (457.2 x 457.2 x 457.2 cm). San Francisco Museum of Modern Art, Accessions Committee Fund purchase

The artist made this hollow crystalline structure to be installed inside an exhibition space. Standing within its core and gazing through its myriad openings, the viewer sees the surrounding environment reflected kaleidoscopically in the radiating panels.

209–11
Your activity horizon, 2004
Installation views at the Reykjavík Art Museum—Hafnarhús, 2004. LED lights, control unit, and steel. Israel Museum, Jerusalem

In a dark room, a thin line of luminescent LED lights are embedded into the walls at eye level, simulating a horizon line. Approximately every minute the light's color changes, rotating through the entire spectrum.

212–13
Colour space embracer, 2005
Installation views at the Hara Museum of Contemporary Art, Tokyo, 2005. Color-effect filter glass, motor, control unit, spotlight, mounting, iris diaphragm, metal, and wire. San Francisco Museum of Modern Art, purchase through a gift of Chara Schreyer and the Accessions Committee Fund

In a darkened space three colored glass rings nestle inside one another, hanging suspended from the ceiling; a motor simultaneously rotates each in a different direction. Light from a nearby lamp shines through them, producing colorful, gleaming arcs that move across the surrounding walls.

214–17
The light setup, 2005
Installation views at the Malmö Konsthall, Sweden, 2005. Fluorescent lights, projection foil, and control unit. Courtesy the artist; Tanya Bonakdar Gallery, New York; and neugerriemschneider, Berlin

In this site-specific environment, the artist installed fluorescent lights behind screens on separate gallery walls. He placed another panel beneath the skylight, partially covering it; half of this overhead light was artificial while the other half was natural. The value of the "white" light changed over time: a control unit adjusted the intensity of the fluorescents, challenging the viewer to distinguish between artificial and natural illumination.

218–19
Inverted Berlin sphere, 2005 (EXH.)
Installation views at Tanya Bonakdar Gallery, New York, 2006. Stainless steel, mirror, wire, bulb, and dimmer. 63 x 63 x 63 in. (160 x 160 x 160 cm). Collection of Martin Z. Margulies

This torqued sphere hangs from the ceiling and contains a lamp within. Light radiates out into a darkened space through the individual reflective components; luminous patterns flood the surfaces of the room.

220–21
Sunset kaleidoscope, 2005 (EXH.)
Installation views at Emi Fontana West of Rome, Jamie Residence, Pasadena, California, 2005. Wood, color-effect filter glass, mirrors, and motor. 18 x 18 x 70 in. (45.7 x 45.7 x 177.8 cm). Collection of John and Phyllis Kleinberg

An elongated wooden box, lined with mirrors, abuts a window looking out on the horizon. When viewers peer into the box, they see the outside environment and a rotating yellow disc infinitely reflected in the kaleidoscope.

222
Your waste of time, 2006
Installation view at neugerriemschneider, Berlin, 2006. Vatnajökull ice, cooling aggregate, Styrofoam, wood, and lacquer. Courtesy the artist; Tanya Bonakdar Gallery, New York; and neugerriemschneider, Berlin

The artist retrieves approximately six tons of ancient ice after pieces have broken off an Icelandic glacier. He transports them to a gallery setting, where a cooling system maintains the physical integrity of the ice.

223–25
Your wave is, 2006
Installation views at the Palazzo Grassi, Venice, Italy, 2006. Light wire, aluminum, steel, and control unit. François Pinault Foundation

For this site-specific commission, the artist devised a three-dimensional net of glowing electrical wire covering the front of the building from the roof to the water, establishing a second facade. Its intricate geometric pattern was inspired by the waves of the Grand Canal, where boat passengers see the illuminated net by night.

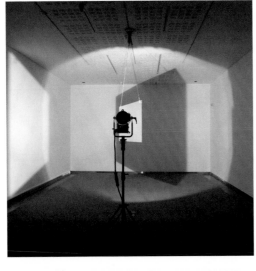

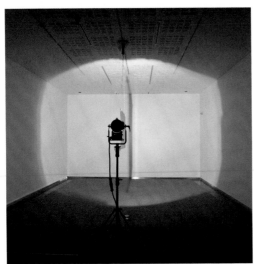

200–205

208

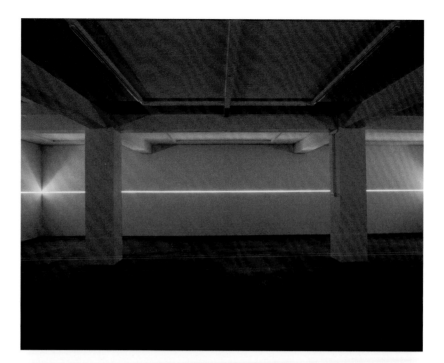

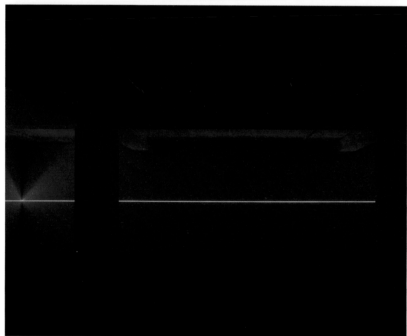

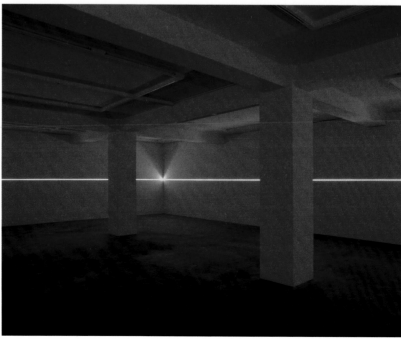

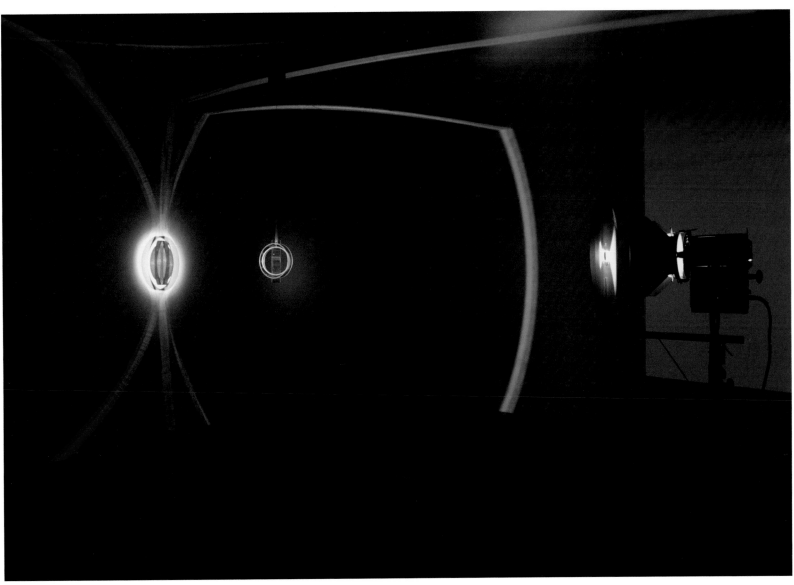

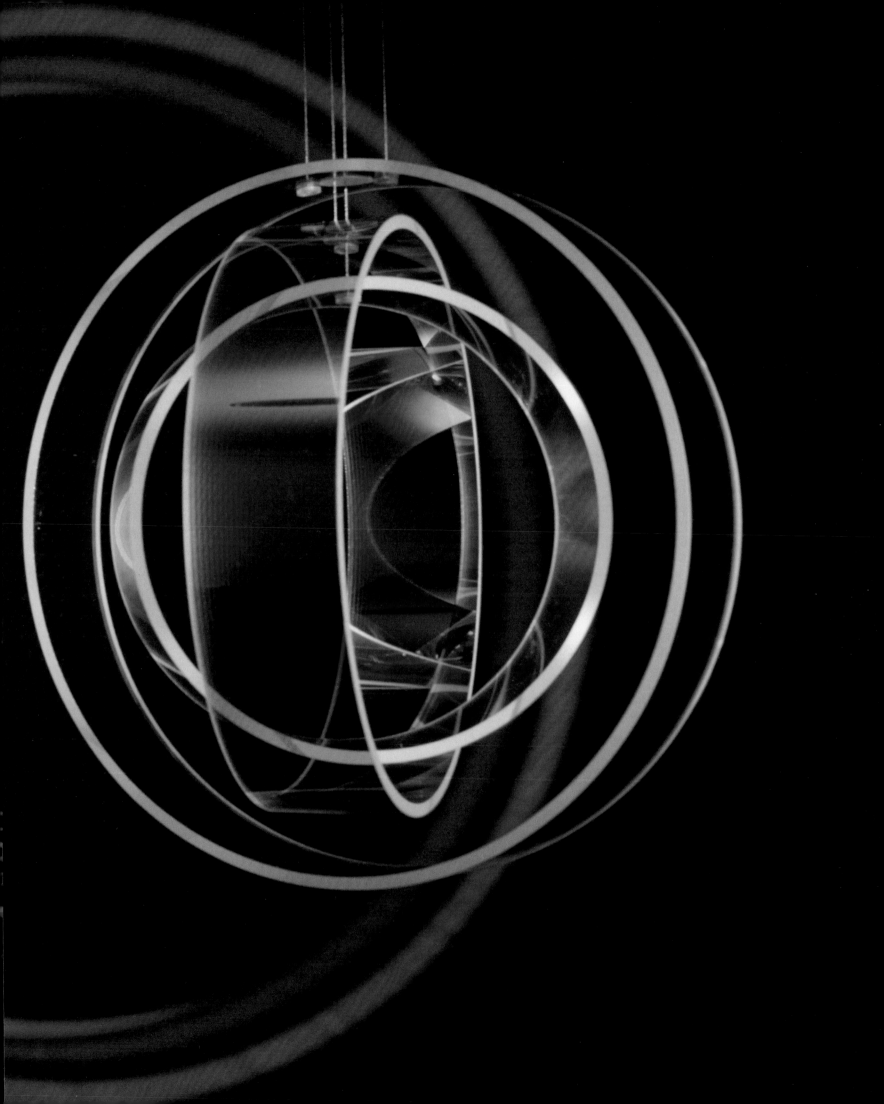

214–17

preceding: 213

218

219

220

221

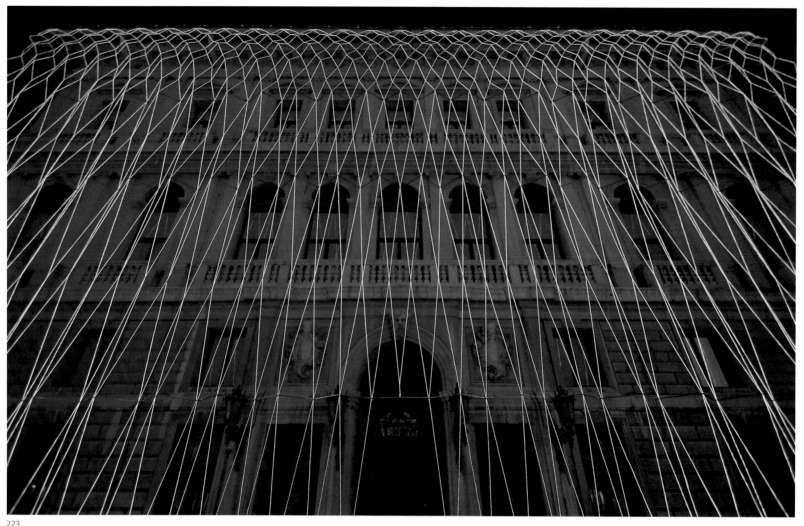

223

224

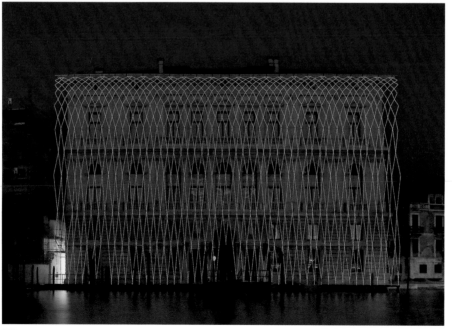

225

preceding: 222

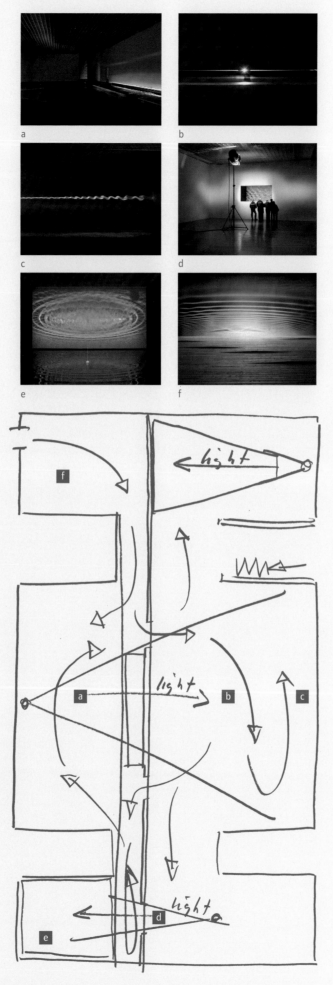

a

b

c

d

e

f

226–33
Notion motion, 2005 (EXH.)
Installation views at the Museum Boijmans Van Beuningen, Rotterdam, Netherlands, 2005. HMI spotlights, tripods, water, projection foil, wood, nylon, and sponge. Museum Boijmans Van Beuningen, on loan from the H+F Mecenaat

The artist constructed a long wall extending the length of three galleries, dividing the rooms in half and placing shallow pools of water in each space. Light cast upon the liquid surfaces by lamps produced different wave patterns in each room. Visitors encountered the water-reflection phenomena on walls, on screens, and through deliberately placed apertures. A narrow walkway along the dividing wall widened into a large wooden floor with selectively raised planks that visitors stepped on to trigger wave patterns. With numerous entry and exit points throughout the space, the viewer's experience was potentially infinite and entirely contingent upon a self-selected route.

226

227

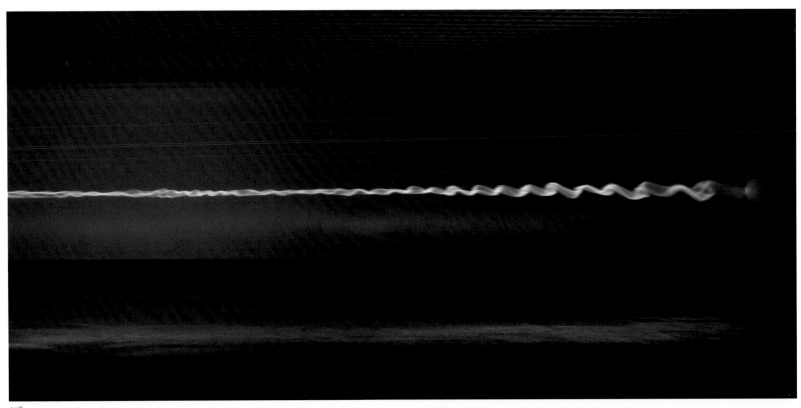

228

229

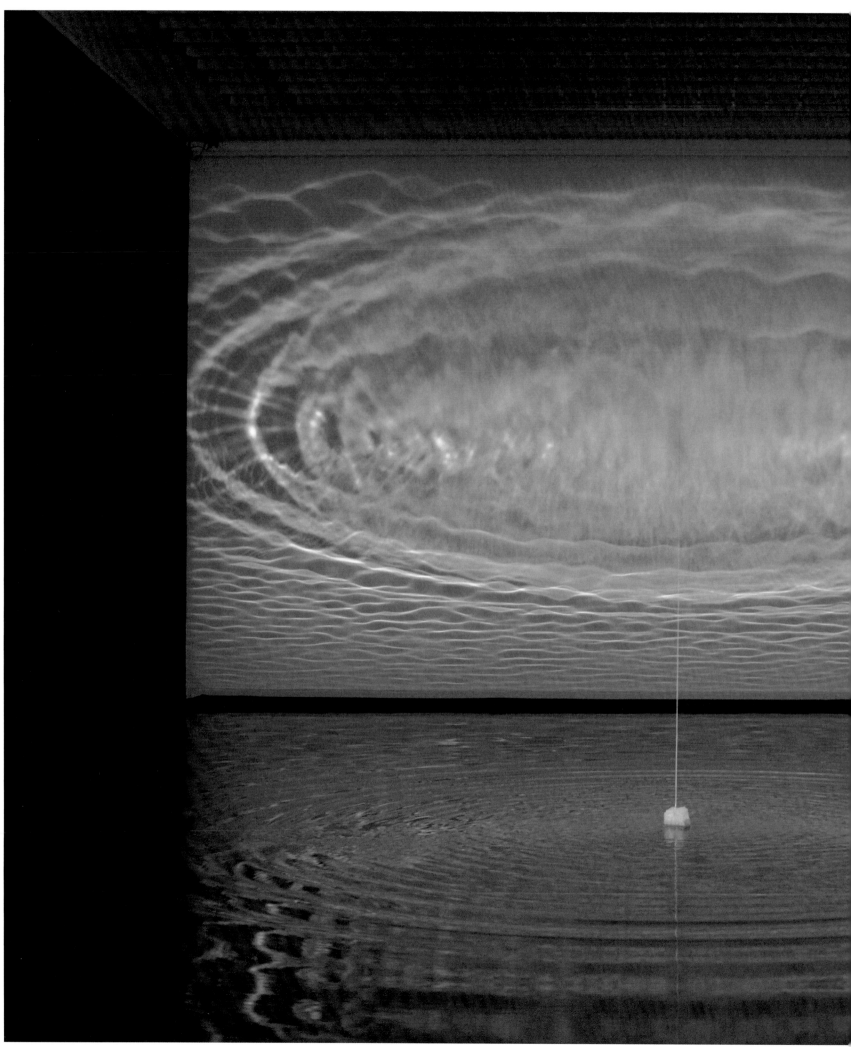

232

overleaf: 233

CATALOGUE OF THE EXHIBITION

This catalogue is arranged chronologically and represents the exhibition's presentation at the San Francisco Museum of Modern Art, which may vary from presentations at other venues. Each project is keyed by number to its location in SFMOMA's fifth-floor galleries. Artwork dimensions are variable unless otherwise noted. This information reflects the Museum's most complete knowledge at time of publication.

1. *Beauty*, 1993 (pls. 5, 31)
   Fresnel lamp, water, nozzles, hose, wood, and pump. Museum of Contemporary Art, Los Angeles, purchased with funds provided by Paul Frankel

2. *Moss wall*, 1994 (pl. 30)
   Wood, moss, and wire. Courtesy the artist; Tanya Bonakdar Gallery, New York; and neugerriemschneider, Berlin

3. *Crystal stone wall series*, 1996 (pl. 40)
   Thirteen framed gelatin silver prints. Each 10 5/8 x 13 in. (27 x 33 cm); 49 5/8 x 59 1/8 in. (126 x 150.2 cm) overall. San Francisco Museum of Modern Art, fractional and promised gift of James and Dana Tananbaum

4. *The waterfall series*, 1996 (pl. 45)
   Fifty framed chromogenic prints. Each 15 x 10 1/4 in. (38 x 26 cm); 81 3/4 x 114 in. (207.6 x 289.6 cm) overall. Collection of Arthur and Carol Goldberg

5. *The island series*, 1997 (pl. 55)
   Fifty-six framed chromogenic prints. Each from 6 3/8 x 16 1/2 in. (16 x 42 cm) to 11 x 16 1/2 in. (28 x 42 cm); 92 1/4 x 141 in. (234.3 x 358.1 cm) overall. Private collection

6. *Room for one colour*, 1997 (pl. 178)
   Monofrequency lights. Courtesy the artist; Tanya Bonakdar Gallery, New York; and neugerriemschneider, Berlin

7. *Ventilator*, 1997 (pl. 71)
   Altered fan with cable. Collections of Peter Norton and Eileen Harris Norton, Santa Monica, California

8. *The inner cave series*, 1998 (pl. 84)
   Thirty-six framed chromogenic prints. Each 14 x 20 1/2 in. (35.5 x 52 cm); 99 3/4 x 140 1/2 in. (253.4 x 356.9 cm) overall. Collection of Ruth and Carl Pite

9. *The aerial river series*, 2000 (pl. 109)
   Forty-two framed chromogenic prints. Each 15 3/4 x 23 5/8 in. (40 x 60 cm); 106 x 182 in. (269.2 x 462.3 cm) overall. San Francisco Museum of Modern Art, gift of Helen and Charles Schwab

10. *The horizon series*, 2002 (pl. 159)
    Forty framed chromogenic prints. Each 9 3/4 x 42 in. (24.8 x 106.7 cm); 89 x 219 in. (226 x 557.3 cm) overall. Collection of Michael and Jeanne Klein, partial and promised gift to the Menil Collection, Houston

11. *Remagine*, 2002 (large version, pls. 160–62)
    Spotlights, wall mounts, and control unit. Collection Fonds National d'Art Contemporain, Ministère de la Culture, Paris

12. *360° room for all colours*, 2002 (pls. 167–72)
    Stainless steel, projection foil, fluorescent lights, wood, and control unit. 126 x 321 x 321 in. (320 x 815.3 x 815.3 cm). Private collection, courtesy Tanya Bonakdar Gallery, New York

13. *Model room*, 2003 (pls. 10–11, 173)
    Chipboard display cabinets and mixed-media models, maquettes, and prototypes. Courtesy the artist; Tanya Bonakdar Gallery, New York; and neugerriemschneider, Berlin

14. *Soil quasi bricks*, 2003 (pls. 176, 179–80)
    Fired compressed-soil tiles and wood. Courtesy the artist; Tanya Bonakdar Gallery, New York; and neugerriemschneider, Berlin

15. *Yellow versus purple*, 2003 (pl. 195)
    Color-effect filter glass, floodlight, tripod, motor, and wire. Tate, purchased with funds provided by the 2003 Outset Frieze Acquisitions Fund for Tate 2003

16. *Multiple grotto*, 2004 (pls. 207–8)
    Stainless steel. 180 x 180 x 180 in. (457.2 x 457.2 x 457.2 cm). San Francisco Museum of Modern Art, Accessions Committee Fund purchase

17. *Inverted Berlin sphere*, 2005 (pls. 218–19)
    Stainless steel, mirror, wire, cable, bulb, and dimmer. 63 x 63 x 63 in. (160 x 160 x 160 cm). Collection of Martin Z. Margulies

18. *Notion motion*, 2005 (pls. 4, 137, 226–33)
    HMI spotlights, tripods, water, projection foil, wood, nylon, and sponge. Museum Boijmans Van Beuningen, Rotterdam, the Netherlands, on loan from the H+F Mecenaat

19. *Sunset kaleidoscope*, 2005 (pls. 220–21)
    Wood, color-effect filter glass, mirrors, and motor. 18 x 18 x 70 in. (45.7 x 45.7 x 177.8 cm). Collection of John and Phyllis Kleinberg

20. *The Domadalur daylight series (south)*, 2006
    Forty-two framed chromogenic prints. Each 11 5/8 x 17 1/8 in. (29.3 x 43.3 cm); 79 1/8 x 131 1/8 in. (200.8 x 331.1 cm) overall. Courtesy the artist; Tanya Bonakdar Gallery, New York; and neugerriemschneider, Berlin

21. *One-way colour tunnel*, 2007 (pl. 145)
    Stainless steel, color-effect acrylic, and acrylic mirrors. 100 3/4 x 70 7/8 x 413 3/8 in. (256 x 180 x 1,050 cm). Courtesy the artist; Tanya Bonakdar Gallery, New York; and neugerriemschneider, Berlin

22. *Space reversal*, 2007
    Mirror foil, aluminum, wood, steel, drywall, and fluorescent lights. Courtesy the artist; Tanya Bonakdar Gallery, New York; and neugerriemschneider, Berlin

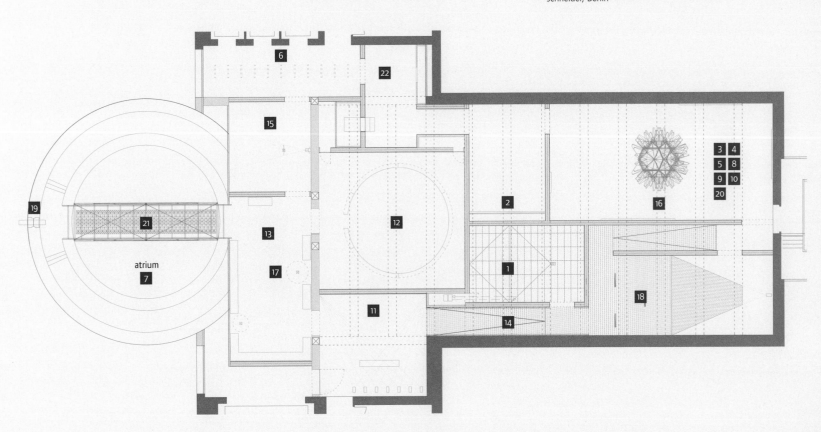

CHRONOLOGY

Compiled by Joshua Shirkey and Lindsey Westbrook.

No title is listed for exhibitions simply called Olafur Eliasson. Entries cite artist's books, catalogues, brochures, and selected reviews whenever possible. For additional books and periodicals, please consult the bibliography on pages 269–71.

Thanks are due to Apsara DiQuinzio, Caroline Eggel, Anna Engberg-Pedersen, Amanda Glesmann, Biljana Joksimović, and Karen Levine for their assistance in gathering and verifying information.

OLAFUR ELIASSON

Born Copenhagen, 1967
Studied at the Royal Danish Academy of Fine Arts, Copenhagen, 1989–95

AWARDS

Kunstpreis der Böttcherstraße in Bremen, Germany, 1997
Edstrandska Foundation Prize, Sweden, 1998
Third Benesse Prize, Japan, 1999
Jyllands-Posten's Art Prize, Denmark, 2004
mfi Preis Kunst am Bau, Germany, 2004
Nykredit's Architecture Prize, Denmark, 2004
Henrik-Steffens-Preis, Alfred Toepfer Stiftung F.V.S., Germany, 2005
Prince Eugen Medal, Sweden, 2005
Danish Crown Prince Couple Award, Denmark, 2006
Frederick Kiesler Prize for Architecture and the Arts, Austria, 2006
Joan Miró Prize, Spain, 2007

SELECTED SOLO EXHIBITIONS, PROJECTS, AND REVIEWS

1992
Expectations, Copenhagen.

1994
Einige erinnern sich, dass sie auf dem Weg waren diese Nacht, Galerie Lukas & Hoffmann, Cologne, October 8–November 5.

Lilja lever (Petrun, Vølven), Galleri Stalke, Copenhagen, December 2, 1994–January 12, 1995.

No nights in summer, no days in winter, Forumgalleriet, Malmö, Sweden.

1995
Olafur Eliasson og Ann Kristin Lislegaard, Galleri Tommy Lund, Odense, Denmark, March 31–April 29.

Olafur Eliasson und Christa Näher, Künstlerhaus Stuttgart, Germany, May 27–June 20.

Eine Beschreibung einer Reflexion, oder aber eine angenehme Übung zu deren Eigenschaften, neugerriemschneider, Berlin, November 4–December 22.
- Metzel, Tabea. Review. Zitty, no. 25 (December 1995): 132.
- Schneider, Christiane. Review. Frieze, no. 26 (January–February 1996): 77–78.

Thoka, Kunstverein in Hamburg, Germany.
- Bonami, Francesco. Review. Flash Art 29, no. 188 (May–June 1996): 105.

1996
Your strange certainty still kept, Tanya Bonakdar Gallery, New York, April 27–May 25.
- Smith, P. C. Review. Art in America 84, no. 12 (December 1996): 92–93.
- Smith, Roberta. "Enter Youth, Quieter and Subtler." New York Times, May 17, 1996.

Tell me about a miraculous invention, Galleri Andreas Brändström, Stockholm, May 4–29. Traveled to Malmö Konstmuseum, Sweden.
- Ericsson, Lars O. "Den nya viktlösheten." Dagens Nyheter, May 12, 1996.

Your foresight endured, Galleria Emi Fontana, Milan, September 24–November 30.

1997
The curious garden, Kunsthalle Basel, Switzerland, January 19–February 23. Traveled to Irish Museum of Modern Art, Dublin. Catalogue by Jonathan Crary and Madeleine Schuppli (copublished with Schwabe & Co., Basel).
- Abutille, Mario C. "Und alles ist reine Subjektivität . . ." Basellandschaftliche Zeitung, January 20, 1997.
- Beil, Ralf. "Der König und die Windmaschine." Neue Zürcher Zeitung, February 7, 1997.
- Christofori, Ralf. "Die natürliche Ordnung der Dinge." Neue Bildende Kunst, no. 2 (April–May 1997): 99–100.
- Daly, Catherine. Review. Sunday Times (Dublin), February 6, 2000.
- Gassert, Siegmar. Review. Dreiland-Zeitung, February 7, 1997.
- "Gelbes Licht und Dornen." Aargauer Zeitung, February 15, 1997.
- "Kunst Olafur Eliasson." Süddeutsche Zeitung, January 1, 1997.
- Reust, Hans Rudolf. Review. Artforum 35, no. 10 (Summer 1997): 146.
- Review. Kunst-Bulletin, nos. 1–2 (January–February 1997): 46.
- Wegelin, Anna. "Wenn weiße Räume lila sind." Wochen Zeitung, January 17, 1997.

Galleri Stalke, Copenhagen, March 11–May 17.

Your sun machine, Marc Foxx Gallery, Los Angeles, April 26–May 31.
- Birnbaum, Daniel. Review. Artforum 36, no. 8 (April 1998): 106–7.

Your windy corner, Galleri Andreas Brändström, Stockholm, May 29–June 28.

1998
Galerie Peter Kilchmann, Zurich, January 24–March 14.
- Eliasson, Olafur, and Barbara Steiner. "Gegen die Zeit gehen." Kunst-Bulletin, nos. 1–2. (January–February 1998): 10–17.

Reykjavík Art Museum—Kjarvalsstadir, March 14–April 13. Artist's book titled Hellisgerði.
- Árnason, Gunnar J. "Olafur Eliasson's Work Is Both Visually Arresting and Intellectually Intriguing." Nu: The Nordic Art Review, no. 1 (January 1999): 84–85.

Fotografier, BildMuseet, Umeå University, Sweden, March 15–April 12. Artist's book titled Landscapes with Yellow Background.

The inventive velocity versus your inverted veto, Bonakdar Jancou Gallery, New York, April 30–June 4.
- Damianovic, Maia. Review. Tema Celeste, nos. 69–70 (July–September 1998): 73.
- Levin, Kim. Review. Village Voice, June 2, 1998, 86.

Tell me about a miraculous invention, Aarhus Kunstmuseum, Denmark, August 29–October 18. Catalogue by Anders Kold et al.

Yet untitled, neugerriemschneider, Berlin, September 8–25.
- Fricke, Harald. "Wand und Boden Chillen in den Bergen." taz, die tageszeitung, September 12, 1998.
- Herbstreuth, Peter. "Ist Konvention der neue Ton?" Der Tagesspiegel, September 19, 1998.

Galerie für Zeitgenössische Kunst, Leipzig, Germany, November 8–December 6. Catalogue / artist's book titled My Now Is Your Surroundings—Process as Object by Olafur Eliasson and Jan Winkelmann (published by Walther König, Cologne, 2001).

New paperworks, Galleri Stalke, Copenhagen, November 27–December 19.

i8 galleri, Reykjavík, December 9, 1998–January 10, 1999.

Raum für eine Farbe, Kunsthalle Bremen, Germany.

1999
Beauty, Marc Foxx Gallery, Los Angeles, January 9–February 6.
- Miles, Christopher. Review. Artforum 37, no. 7 (March 1999): 119.

Riflessi di una certa importanza, Galleria Emi Fontana, Milan, February 11–March 16.

Your circumspection disclosed, Castello di Rivoli, Museo d'Arte Contemporanea, Turin, Italy, March 24–May 23. Catalogue titled Un progetto per il Castello / A Project for the Castle by Marcella Beccaria; catalogue titled Castello di Rivoli: 20 anni d'arte contemporanea by Ida Gianelli (copublished with Skira, Milan, 2005); brochure by Marcella Beccaria.
- Grasskamp, Walter. "Kunst in der Stadt: Eine italienische-deutsche Kunstgeschichte." Frame, no. 7 (March–April 2000): 60–67.

Yet untitled, Kunstverein Wolfsburg, Germany, May 11–June 20.
- "Beim Kunstverein kreist das Licht." Westdeutsche Allgemeine Zeitung, May 11, 1999.
- Karweik, Hans-Adelbert. "Fotoreportage der Veränderung." Wolfsburger Nachrichten, May 14, 1999.
- ——— . "Vor den Augen des Publikums." Wolfsburger Nachrichten, May 11, 1999.

Job Koelewijn / Olafur Eliasson, De Appel, Amsterdam, June 18–August 22.
- Blomberg, Katja. "Bad im wohligen Licht." Frankfurter Allgemeine Zeitung, August 5, 1999.
- Koplos, Janet. Review. Art in America 88, no. 2 (February 2000): 151.

Your position surrounded and your surroundings positioned, Dundee Contemporary Arts, Scotland, September 18–November 7. Catalogue / artist's book titled Olafur Eliasson: Your Position Surrounded and Your Surroundings Positioned by Katrina Brown and Olafur Eliasson.
- Colin, Beatrice. "Chalk One Up for Light Fantastic." Sunday Times (London), September 19, 1999.

Grant, Simon. "Olafur Eliasson: Poetry in Motion." *Tate: The Art Magazine*, no. 19 (Winter 1999): 12.

Mahoney, Elisabeth. "Let's Have a Kickabout." *Scotsman*, July 7, 1999.

——. "Romance of the Sea." *Guardian* (London), September 23, 1999.

——. "Storm Warning." *Scotland on Sunday*, September 12, 1999.

Ross, Peter. "The Main Geysers on the Iceland Scene." *Sunday Herald* (Glasglow), September 12, 1999.

Wiensowski, Ingeborg. "Ach, Europa! Nie wieder Eiffelturm, Akropolis und Big Ben: Kultur-Reisetips von denen, die es besser wissen; Ishellir-Höhle, Island." *Kultur SPIEGEL*, July 1, 1999, 11.

2000

New Work, Aldrich Museum of Contemporary Art, Ridgefield, Connecticut, January 23–April 30. Brochure.

Webb, Sarah. "Containing the Infinite." *Afterimage* 28, no. 1 (July 2000): 15.

The only thing we have in common is that we are different, Center for Contemporary Art, Kitakyushu, Japan, February 21–March 10.

Your blue afterimage exposed, Masataka Hayakawa Gallery, Tokyo, February 24–March 25.

McGee, John. "Icelandic Artist Puts Subjectivity to Work." *Mainichi Daily News*, March 7, 2000.

Your orange afterimage exposed, Gallery Koyanagi, Tokyo, February 24–March 25.

Surroundings surrounded, Neue Galerie am Landesmuseum Joanneum, Graz, Austria, April 1–May 21. Traveled to Zentrum für Kunst und Medientechnologie, Karlsruhe, Germany. Catalogue titled *Olafur Eliasson: Surroundings Surrounded; Essays on Space and Science* edited by Peter Weibel (copublished with MIT Press, Cambridge, Massachusetts, 2001); brochure by Peter Weibel.

Anton, Saul. Book review. *Bookforum* 9, no. 2 (Summer 2002): 41, 47.

Birnbaum, Daniel. "Best of 2001: Top Ten." *Artforum* 40, no. 4 (December 2001): 98–99.

Buhr, Elke. "Diesseits des Regenbogens." *Frankfurter Rundschau*, July 10, 2001.

Engler, Martin. Review. *Kunst-Bulletin*, nos. 7–8 (July–August 2001): 44–45.

Hess, Barbara. "Nase im Wind." *Texte zur Kunst* 10, no. 39 (September 2000): 143–47.

Hoffmann, Gabriele. "Blicke in ein Kaleidoskop." *Stuttgarter Zeitung*, July 10, 2001.

Hofleitner, Johanna. "Nordlicht." *Die Presse: Schaufenster*, March 2000, 39.

Huck, Brigitte. "Schöne synthetische Welt." *Der Standard*, April 11, 2000.

Ione, Amy. Review. *Leonardo* 36, no. 2 (April 2003): 162.

Jothady, Manisha. Review. *Frame*, no. 3 (July–August 2000): 137.

Lübbke, Maren. Review. *Camera Austria*, no. 71 (2000): 61.

Unnützer, Petra. Review. *Kunstforum*, no. 156 (August–October 2001): 422–23.

Vogel, Sabine B. "Fantasie hinterm Tropfenvorhang." *Frankfurter Allgemeine Zeitung*, May 5, 2000.

Wailand, Markus. Review, trans. Helen Slater. *Frieze*, no. 54 (September–October 2000): 127–28.

Wilson, Petra Rigby. Book review. *Parachute*, no. 109 (January–February 2003): 140.

Focus: Olafur Eliasson; Your intuitive surroundings versus your surrounded intuition, Art Institute of Chicago, May 10–August 13. Brochure by James Rondeau.

Artner, Alan. "Playing with Perception." *Chicago Tribune*, June 11, 2000.

Camper, Fred. "Nature Containers." *Chicago Reader*, August 4, 2000.

Hawkins, Margaret. Review. *Chicago Sun-Times*, June 10, 2000.

Zdanovics, Olga. Review. *New Art Examiner* 28, no. 1 (September 2000): 54–55.

Kunstverein Wolfsburg, Germany, May 31–June 11. "Kunstverein: Fotos beleuchten Anfänge." *Westdeutsche Allgemeine Zeitung*, May 31, 2000.

Syndrome 2: Olafur Eliasson and Rivane Neuenschwander, International Artists Studio Program in Sweden, Stockholm, September 1–30.

Your now is my surroundings, Bonakdar Jancou Gallery, New York, October 24–December 2.

Chen, Aric. "Spatial Transcendence." *Dutch*, no. 32 (March–April 2001): 58.

Dailey, Meghan. Review. *Time Out New York*, November 16–23, 2000, 82.

Heartney, Eleanor. Review. *Art in America* 89, no. 2 (February 2001): 135.

Hunt, David. Review. *Flash Art* 34, no. 216 (January–February 2001): 111.

Jones, Kristin M. Review. *Frieze*, no. 59 (May 2001): 96–97.

Levin, Kim. "Turning the Gallery Inside Out: Natural Wonder." *Village Voice*, November 14, 2000, 77.

Review. *The New Yorker*, November 20, 2000, 21.

Richard, Frances. Review. *Artforum* 39, no. 5 (January 2001): 136.

Smith, Roberta. Review. *New York Times*, November 17, 2000.

Der drehende Park, permanent installation, Sammlung Kunstwegen, Nordhorn, Germany. Catalogue titled *Kunstwegen: Das Reisebuch; Kunst, Natur und Geschichte im deutsch-niederländischen Vechtetal* edited by Henning Buck, Martin Köttering, and Roland Nachtigäller (published by Kunstwegen EWIV, Nordhorn, 2002).

The movement meter for Lernacken, permanent installation commissioned by City of Malmö, Sweden. Catalogue / artist's book titled *Olafur Eliasson: Movement Meter for Lernacken* by Caroline Eggel and Olafur Eliasson (2002).

2001

Your only real thing is time, Institute of Contemporary Art, Boston, January 24–April 1. Catalogue titled *Olafur Eliasson: Your Only Real Thing Is Time* edited by Jessica Morgan (copublished with Hatje Cantz, Ostfildern-Ruit, Germany); brochure.

Allen, Jane Ingram. "Putting the Viewer First: Olafur Eliasson." *Sculpture* 20, no. 8 (October 2001): 28–33.

Camhi, Leslie. "And the Artist Recreated Nature (or an Illusion of It)." *New York Times*, January 21, 2001.

Sherman, Mary. Review. *Art New England* 22, no. 2 (February–March 2001): 41.

——. Review. *ARTnews* 100, no. 4 (April 2001): 147.

——. "Special Effects." *Boston Herald*, February 6, 2001.

Silver, Joanne. "Unnatural Wonders." *Boston Herald*, January 26, 2001.

Temin, Christine. "Icelandic Circles Ring the ICA." *Boston Globe*, January 27, 2001.

The mediated motion, Kunsthaus Bregenz, Austria, March 31–May 13. Catalogue titled *Olafur Eliasson: The Mediated Motion* edited by Rudolf Sagmeister and Eckhard Schneider (copublished with Walther König, Cologne); brochure by Olafur Eliasson.

Engler, Martin. "Dschungel an Beton." *Die Zeit*, no. 19 (May 3, 2001): 52.

Loschwitz, Gesa. "Landschaften im Kunsthaus Bregenz." *Garten + Landschaft* 111, no. 5 (May 2001): 7.

Mead, Andrew. "The Great Outdoors." *Architects' Journal* 215, no. 22 (June 6, 2002): 48.

Müller, Dorothee. "Die Natur und ihre Grenzen." *Süddeutsche Zeitung*, May 3, 2001.

Review. *Kunst-Bulletin*, no. 5 (May 2001): 47–48.

Stokholm, Peter. "Den formidlede bevægelse." *Dagbladet Information*, May 7, 2001.

Vogt, Günther. Review. *Lotus International*, no. 122 (November 2004): 98–101.

Windspiegelwand, permanent installation commissioned by Deutsche Gesellschaft für Technische Zusammenarbeit (GTZ), Berlin, opened June 21.

The young land: Fourth Annual ICA Vita Brevis, Institute of Contemporary Art, Boston, August 4–September 30. Catalogue titled *Vita Brevis: History, Landscape, and Art 1998–2003* by Jill Medvedow and Carole Ann Meehan (copublished with Steidl, Göttingen, Germany, 2004).

Silver, Joanne. "Innovative Works of Lava and More Erupt in City." *Boston Herald*, May 18, 2001.

——. "A New Landscape Erupts in Harbor." *Boston Herald*, August 10, 2001.

Temin, Christine. "Curator Meehan Up to the Challenge." *Boston Globe*, August 12, 2001.

——. "An Icelandic Rock Invasion Makes Fan Pier a Work of Art." *Boston Globe*, August 12, 2001.

Projects 73: Olafur Eliasson; Seeing yourself sensing, Museum of Modern Art, New York, September 13, 2001–May 21, 2002. Brochure by Roxana Marcoci et al.

Eakin, Hugh. "Magic Kingdom." *ARTnews* 100, no. 11 (December 2001): 116–17.

Louie, Elaine. "Now You See the Modern's Construction, Now You Don't." *New York Times*, September 6, 2001.

Newhall, Edith. "Discomfiting Panes." *New York*, September 24, 2004, 71.

Ryan, Zoë. "An Out-of-Gallery Experience." *Blueprint*, no. 189 (November 2001): 121.

Die Dinge, die du nicht siehst, die du nicht siehst, neugerriemschneider, Berlin, November 3–December 15.

Berg, Ronald. "Nebel hinter Panzerpappe." *Frankfurter Allgemeine Zeitung*, November 22, 2001.

Daniels, Corinna. "Eine Galerie in Olafur Eliassons Kunstnebel." *Die Welt*, November 23, 2001.

Fricke, Harald. Review. *taz, die tageszeitung*, November 6, 2001.

Sorbello, Marina. Review. *Tema Celeste*, no. 89 (January–February 2002): 88.

Wittneven, Katrin. "Die Konstruktion der Natur." *Der Tagesspiegel*, November 16, 2001.

The structural evolution project, Mala Galerija, Ljubljana, Slovenia, November 22, 2001–January 6, 2002. Artist's book titled *Olafur Eliasson: The Structural Evolution Project*.

Petrešin, Nataša. Interview. *Delo*, January 5, 2002.

I only see when I move, permanent installation commissioned by Metro Arts in Transit for Central West End MetroLink station tunnel, Saint Louis. Catalogue titled *Arts in Transit: 2000–2001* (published by Bi-State Development Agency, Saint Louis, 2001).

Cooper, Ivy. "A Child Shall Lead Them." *Riverfront Times*, May 12, 2004.

2002

Chaque matin je me sens différent, chaque soir je me sens le même, Musée d'Art moderne de la Ville de Paris, March 22–May 12. Catalogue / artist's book titled *Olafur Eliasson: Chaque matin je me sens différent, chaque soir je me sens le même* edited by Angeline Scherf.

Boyer, Charles-Arthur. Review, trans. L. S. Torgoff. *Art Press*, no. 280 (June 2002): 80–82.

Colard, Jean-Max. "Avis de tempête." *Les inrockuptibles*, April 3–9, 2002, 84–85.

Damianovic, Maia. Review. *Tema Celeste*, no. 91 (May–June 2002): 86.

Juillard, Nicolas. "L'oeil trompé d'Olafur Eliasson." *Le Temps*, April 9, 2002.

Laubard, Charlotte. "L'Oeil de Olafur Eliasson." *L'Oeil*, no. 536 (May 2002): 22–23.

Lebovici, Elisabeth. "Laboratoires du regard." *Libération*, April 18, 2002.

McBreen, Ellen. Review. *Art Monthly*, no. 257 (June 2002): 35–37.

Mohal, Anna. Review. *Kunst-Bulletin*, no. 5 (May 2002): 55.

Pinte, Jean-Louis. "Le bon oeil." *Le Figaro*, April 10, 2002.

Troncy, Éric. "Olafur Eliasson: Fait la pluie et le beau temps." *Beaux Arts*, no. 215 (April 2002): 58–63.

i8 Gallery, Reykjavík, May 12–June 22.

Der reflektierende Korridor—Entwurf zum Stoppen des freien Falls, permanent installation, Zentrum für Internationale Lichtkunst Unna, Germany, opened October 11. Catalogue titled *Zentrum für Internationale Lichtkunst Unna: Die Sammlung / Center for International Light Art Unna: The Collection* edited by Martina Sehlke (published by Wienand Verlag & Medien, Cologne, 2004).

Pinetzki, Katrin. "Neonröhren statt Öl und Tusche: Lichtkunst-Museum in Unna." *Hamburger Morgenpost*, November 11, 2003.

Udsigten der aldrig tænker, Galleri Kirke Sonnerup, Kirke Såby, Denmark, and Galleri Stalke, Copenhagen, October 12–November 30.

The cartographic series I + II, Niels Borch Jensen Galerie und Verlag, Berlin, November 28, 2002–January 16, 2003.

Ruthe, Ingeborg. "Nach Island fahren, um hinauszuschauen." *Berliner Zeitung*, February 21, 2001.

Lichtvorhang and *Mooswand* (collaboration with Baumschlager + Eberle), permanent installations commissioned by Münchener Rückversicherungsgesellschaft for Münchener Rück South 1, Munich.

Bergers, Gerard. "Untitled (Office Renovation)." *Frame* (Amsterdam), no. 30 (January–February 2003): 92–103.

Bode, Peter M. "Schönheit durch Recycling." *Art: das Kunstmagazin*, no. 2 (February 2003): 115.

Cohn, David. Review. *Architectural Record* 190, no. 10 (October 2002): 140.

2003

Funcionamiento silencioso, Palacio de Cristal, Parque del Retiro, Madrid, January 30–May 19. Catalogue / artist's book titled *Olafur Eliasson: Funcionamiento silencioso* by Olafur Eliasson et al. (published by Museo Nacional Centro de Arte Reina Sofía, Madrid).

De la Villa, Rocío. "Jardines efímeros." *La Vanguardia*, May 11, 2003.

De Miguel, Marina. "El jardín artificial de Olafur Eliasson." *La Voz de Galicia*, February 4, 2004.

Grijalba, Silvia. "Corazón de Madrid." *El Mundo*, February 10, 2003.

Molina, Ángela. "Pequeñas diabluras." *Babelia*, March 15, 2003.

"Olafur Eliasson mete un jardín utópico en el Palacio de Cristal." *El País*, January 31, 2003.

Stevenheydens, Ive. "Een dubbelzinnige betovering." *De Financieel Economische Tijd*, April 12, 2003.

Sonne statt Regen, Städtische Galerie im Lenbachhaus und Kunstbau München, Munich, March 8–June 15. Catalogue / artist's book titled *Olafur Eliasson: Sonne statt Regen* by Susanne Gaensheimer and Olafur Eliasson (copublished with Hatje Cantz, Ostfildern-Ruit, Germany).

Endter, Heike. "Seelsorger am Gletscher." *taz, die tageszeitung*, April 25, 2003.

Hauffen, Michael. Review. *Kunstforum*, no. 165 (June–July 2003): 334–35.

Hoffmann, Justin. Review. *Kunst-Bulletin*, no. 6 (June 2003): 69–70.

Siedenberg, Sven. "Mehr Luft!" *Süddeutsche Zeitung*, March 7, 2003.

The scent wall, Museum Boijmans Van Beuningen, Rotterdam, Netherlands, May 10–August 31.

Sun reflector, permanent installation commissioned by Statens Konstråd for AlbaNova University Center, Royal Institute of Technology / Stockholm University, opened May 13.

Tanya Bonakdar Gallery, New York, May 26–June 14.

Burton, Johanna. Review. *Artforum* 42, no. 1 (September 2003): 224.

Gronlund, Melissa, Review. *Contemporary*, no. 55 (2003): 73.

Johnson, Ken. Review. *New York Times*, May 23, 2003.

King, Elaine A. Review. *Sculpture* 22, no. 10 (December 2003): 70–71.

Krenz, Marcel. Review. *Flash Art* 36, no. 231 (July–September 2003): 65.

Levin, Kim. Review. *Village Voice*, May 7–13, 2003, 70.

Review. *The New Yorker*, May 26, 2003, 20

Rosenberg, Karen. "Room with a View." *Village Voice*, May 14–20, 2003, 49.

Sundell, Margaret. "Second Nature." *Time Out New York*, May 22–29, 2003, 74.

The blind pavilion, Danish Pavilion, 50th Venice Biennale, Italy, June 15–November 2. Catalogue titled *Dreams and Conflicts: The Dictatorship of the Viewer* by Francesco Bonami; catalogue / artist's book by Olafur Eliasson et al. (published by Danish Contemporary Art Foundation, Copenhagen).

Cabañas, Kaira. Review. *Parachute*, suppl. no. 112 (October–December 2003): 7–8.

Cumming, Laura. "But Where's the Art?" *Guardian* (London), June 22, 2003.

Descombes, Mireille. "Venise, la foire au zapping." *L'Hebdo*, June 19, 2003.

Dunne, Aidan. "Few Signs of Life on Planet Art." *Irish Times*, June 21, 2003.

Gayford, Martin. "Love in a Hot Climate." *Sunday Telegraph* (London), June 15, 2003.

Glover, Michael. "Free Spirits Cross No New Frontiers." *Independent* (London), June 16, 2003.

Hornung, Peter Michael. "Kunstens hovedstad ligger i Venedig." *Politiken*, June 15, 2003.

Hübl, Michael. Review. *Kunstforum*, no. 166 (August–October 2003): 241–43.

Juhl-Nielsen, Thea. "Betragterens diktatur." *Dagbladet Information*, June 21, 2003.

Kalhama, Pilvi. "Tilan diktatuuria Venetsian biennaalissa." *Taide*, no. 4 (2003): 12–15.

Kimmelman, Michael. "Cramming It All In at the Biennale." *New York Times*, June 26, 2003.

LaBelle, Charles. Review. *Frieze*, no. 77 (September 2003): 98–99.

Lavarini, Beatrice. Review. *Das Münster* 56, no. 4 (2003): 291–94.

Levin, Kim, "Power Vacuum." *Village Voice*, July 9–15, 2003, 55.

Lorch, Catrin. Review. *Kunst-Bulletin*, nos. 7–8 (July–August 2003): 22–27.

Mack, Gerhard. "Glücklich nur im Sommerkleid." *Neue Zürcher Zeitung am Sonntag*, June 15, 2003.

Madoff, Steven Henry. Review. *ARTnews* 102, no. 8 (September 2003): 128–29.

Morris, Roderick Conway. "Heat and Promise at the Venice Biennale." *International Herald Tribune*, June 17, 2003.

Müller, Silke. Review. *Art: das Kunstmagazin*, no. 6 (June 2003): 19.

Ramade, Bénédicte. Review. *L'Oeil*, no. 548 (June 2003): 58–59.

Saccoccia, Susan. "The World's Fair of Contemporary Art." *Christian Science Monitor*, June 20, 2003.

Scavenius, Bente. "Store forventninger til dansk kunst i Venedig." *Børsen*, June 13, 2003.

Schwartz, Rune Born. "Her bliver vi farveløse." *Dagbladet Information*, June 16, 2003.

Searle, Adrian. "Stop That Racket." *Guardian* (London), June 17, 2003.

Sommer, Tim, and Dirk Reinartz. "Der große Jahrmarkt." *Art: das Kunstmagazin*, no. 8 (August 2003): 10–29.

Vetrocq, Marcia E. "Venice Biennale: 'Every Idea But One.'" *Art in America* 91, no. 9 (September 2003): 76–87, 136–37.

Vogel, Carol. "Heat Upstages Art at the Venice Biennial." *New York Times*, June 16, 2003.

Ward, Ossian. "The Weather Man." *Art Review* 1, no. 8 (June 2003): 54–59.

Quasi brick wall, permanent installation, Fundación NMAC, Cádiz, Spain, opened July 5. Catalogue titled *Fundación Montenmedio Arte Contemporáneo 2002–2003*.

Portikus im Leinwandhaus: Tobias Rehberger / Olafur Eliasson & Zumtobel Staff, Portikus, Frankfurt, Germany, July 7–August 10. Catalogue titled *Turbulenz: Portikus Projekte 2001–2004* by Jochen Volz (2004).

The weather project, Tate Modern, London, October 16, 2003–March 21, 2004. Catalogue edited by Susan May; brochure by Susan May.

Adam, David. "The Science behind the News." *Guardian*, October 30, 2003.

Adam, Hubertus. "Un artificio atmosférico." *Arquitectura Viva*, no. 93 (November–December 2003): 94–95.

Aspden, Peter. "The Year That Culture Became Popular." *Financial Times*, December 29, 2003.

Barkham, Patrick. "Crowds Roll Up for an Indoor Sun, a Spiritual Experience . . . and Leg Waggling." *Times*, October 21, 2003.

Beatty, Emma. "Rachel Whiteread Is Next, But Where Are the Other Turbine Hall Commissions Now?" *Art Newspaper* 14, no. 157 (April 2005): 22.

Benhamou-Huet, Judith. "Rêves d'Algérie et fantômes modernes." *Les Echos*, October 31, 2003.

Birnbaum, Daniel. "Best of 2003: Top Ten." *Artforum* 42, no. 4 (December 2003): 124–25.

Bødker, Kirsten. "Olafur Eliasson hyldet i London." *Børsen*, October 16, 2003.

——. "Olafur Eliasson leger med vejret på Tate Modern." *Børsen*, October 8, 2003.

Braun, Christoph. "Erfundene Naturstimmungen." *taz, die tageszeitung*, February 19, 2004.

Bredekamp, Horst, and Barbara Maria Stafford. "One Step Beyond." *Tate Etc.*, no. 6 (Spring 2006): 80–89.

Brown, Ismene. "Spinning through Space." *Daily Telegraph*, November 6, 2003.

Burton, Johanna. "The 'Urmaterial' Urge." *Parkett*, suppl. no. 70 (May 2004): 3–7.

Bush, Kate. "Best of 2003: Top Ten." *Artforum* 42, no. 4 (December 2003): 118.

Bussel, Abby. "Mist and Mirrors." *Architectural Lighting* 18, no. 7 (November–December 2003): 10.

Cheetham, Mark A. "Natural Anxieties: Why Go to a Museum to See the Sun?" *Walrus* 4, no. 3 (April 2006): 82–87.

Coates, Nigel. "St. Paul's? I Prefer the Cathedral over the River." *Independent*, November 23, 2003.

Cooke, Rachel. "The Brightest and the Best." *Guardian*, October 19, 2003.

Coomer, Martin. "Reign Predicted." *Time Out London*, September 3–10, 2003.

Corbetta, Caroline. "Viaggiando verso Nord / Travelling North." *Domus*, no. 868 (March 2004): 14.

Cork, Richard. "Promethean Flames." *New Statesman*, December 15, 2003, 102–3.

Costa, José Manuel. "Un gigantesco sol de Olafur Eliasson deslumbra en la Sala de Turbinas de la Tate Modern." *ABC*, October 16, 2003.

Cronin, David. "Bush and Putin Should Join 'Sun-Worshipers.'" *European Voice*, January 22, 2004.

Curtis, Nick. "Sun Sets at the Tate." *Evening Standard*, March 22, 2004.

Daenen, Ward. "Ondertussen in Tate Modern." *De Morgen*, December 20, 2003.

Dale, C. James. "London Draws the Sun Inside." *Globe and Mail* (Toronto), January 14, 2004.

Detheridge, Anna. "Parola d'artista." *Il Sole*, January 4, 2004.

Didock, Barry. "When We Saw the Light." *Sunday Herald* (Glasglow), November 21, 2004.

Diez, Renato. "Olafur Eliasson a Londra: Forme dell'immaginazione." *Arte*, no. 362 (October 2003): 134–41.

Dorment, Richard. "A Terrifying Beauty." *Daily Telegraph*, November 12, 2004.

Durtis, Nick. "Crowds Applaud as Lights Are Switched Off." *Evening Standard*, March 22, 2004.

Eyres, Harry. "Short-Changed by Today's Artists?" *Spectator*, no. 6 (December 2003): 59.

Falconer, Morgan. Review. *Burlington Magazine* 145, no. 1209 (December 2003): 873–75.

——. "A Space Odyssey." *Art Review*, suppl. 3, no. 10 (October–November 2005): 12–15.

Field, Marcus. "Smoke and Mirrors." *Independent*, October 19, 2003.

Freudenheim, Tom L. "The Weather in London." *Curator* 47, no. 2 (April 2004): 149–54.

Gayford, Martin. "They're Great in the Tate: Now Let's Put Big Sculpture in Our Cities." *Daily Telegraph*, December 13, 2003.

Gibbons, Fiachra. "Mellow Yellow Haze Gives Tate Staff Touch of the Sun." *Guardian*, October 24, 2003.

——. "Tate Modern Awakes to Dane's Rising Sun." *Guardian*, October 16, 2003.

Glausiusz, Josie. Review. *Discover* 25, no. 2 (February 2004): 81.

Godfrey, Mark, and Rosie Bennett. "Public Spectacle." *Frieze*, no. 80 (January–February 2004): 56–59.

Goodhart, Hanna. "Ein anziehender Sonnenaufgang." *Solothurner Zeitung*, December 22, 2003.

Greenstreet, Rosanna. "Q&A: Olafur Eliasson." *Guardian*, December 27, 2003.

Gregory, Rob. "Bankside Revisited." *Architectural Review* 215, no. 1288 (June 2004): 82–87.

Guido, Curto. "Il sole sintetico di Eliasson." *La Stampa*, December 20, 2003.

Hardwicke, Adrian. "Secret Diary of an Art Gallery Attendant: They Came in Santa Outfits, with Picnics—Even a Canoe." *Guardian*, March 18, 2004.

Hensher, Philip. "Videos That Don't Move." *Mail on Sunday*, November 9, 2003.

Hernando, Ana. "Atardecer apocalíptico en la Tate." *Cinco Días*, October 18, 2003.

"Het weer binnenshuis." *De Standaard*, October 17, 2003.

Holroyd, Alex. "Under the Weather?" *Morning Star*, November 11, 2003.

Hornung, Peter Michael. "Den iscenesatte kunst." *Politiken*, February 8, 2004.

——. "Her kommer solen." *Politiken*, January 5, 2004.

"Hot Property." *Daily Post* (Liverpool), December 20, 2003.

Hübl, Michael. Review. *Kunstforum*, no. 169 (March–April 2004): 314–15.

Januszczak, Waldemar. "Try Your Hand at Ping Pong, Read Philosophy, Then Bask in the Sun." *Sunday Times*, November 9, 2003.

Johansson, Hanna. "Me ja poliittinen ilmakehä." *Taide*, no. 6 (2003): 30–33.

——. "The Sun, the Owl, the Car, and the Flower: On Art and Criticism." *Framework*, no. 1 (2004): 104–5.

Jones, Jonathan. "Reflected Glory." *Guardian*, October 30, 2003.

——. "Watch This Space." *Guardian*, December 15, 2003.

Kaufer, Stefan. "Leg dich hin und sei still." *Frankfurter Rundschau*, January 5, 2004.

Kent, Sarah. Review. *Time Out London*, November 5–12, 2003, 54.

Kimmelman, Michael. "Illusion and Reality Cozy Up at Tate Modern." *New York Times*, March 18, 2004.

——. "Putting the Spectator at the Center." *International Herald Tribune*, March 16, 2004. Reprinted as "The Sun Sets at Tate Modern." *New York Times*, March 21, 2004.

Lack, Jessica. Preview. *Guardian*, October 11, 2003.

Lavrador, Judicaël. "Soleil de Synthèse." *Beaux Arts*, no. 236 (January 2004): 34–35.

Lebovici, Elisabeth. "Du soleil plein la Tate." *Libération*, November 7, 2003.

Leitch, Luke. "A Tate Sunset." *Evening Standard*, October 15, 2003.

Levene, Louise. "While the Sun Shines, Dance." *Sunday Telegraph*, November 9, 2003.

Liebs, Holger. "Im Westen geht die Sonne auf." *Süddeutsche Zeitung*, October 23, 2003.

Lloyd, Sian. "Meteorology—But Is It Weather?" *Guardian*, October 16, 2003.

Lowenthal, Jonah. Review. *Log*, no. 2 (Spring 2004): 6.

Lubbock, Tom. "The Five Best Shows in London." *Independent*, October 11, 2003.

Mackrell, Judith. "The Joy of Sets." *Guardian* (Manchester), June 6, 2005.

——. Review of Merce Cunningham Dance Company. *Guardian*, November 6, 2003.

Maddocks, Fiona. "The Weather Man." *Evening Standard*, November 20, 2003.

Malmberg, Carl-Johan. "Missa inte Eliassons sol i dis." *Svenska Dagbladet*, December 13, 2003.

Martin, Colin. "Making Haze." *Nature* 426, no. 6963 (November 13, 2003): 123.

May, Susan. "Olafur Eliasson: The Weather Project." *A + U: Architecture and Urbanism*, no. 422 (November 2005): 8–11.

McNamara, T. J. "Special Spaces That Tell Stories." *New Zealand Herald*, February 4, 2004.

McWilliams, Brendan. "A Weather Project, Yes—But Is It Art." *Irish Times*, October 23, 2003.

Meade, Fionn. "You Are Not Here: Why Skylines Feel So Unreal." *Stranger*, July 20–26, 2006, 20.

Meyer, James. "No More Scale: The Experience of Size in Contemporary Sculpture." *Artforum* 42, no. 10 (Summer 2004): 220–28.

Meyer, James, et al. "What Is the Object?" *Frieze* 82 (April 2004): 64–73.

Millar, Bruce. "The Sun King." *Times Magazine*, March 20, 2004.

Millen, John. "Artwork for All Seasons." *South China Morning Post*, March 4, 2004.

Paine, Andrew. "Hallucinogenic Haze Trips Up Visitors at Tate." *Evening Standard*, October 24, 2003.

Parry, Jann. "Skipping the Light Fantastic." *Observer*, November 9, 2003.

Pekarik, Andrew J. "Engineering Answers." *Curator* 47, no. 2 (April 2004): 145–48.

Piccoli, Cloe. "The Weather Man." *Carnet Arte* 1, no. 1 (September–October 2003): 42–52.

Ramade, Bénédicte. "États d'âmes du paysage." *L'Oeil*, no. 573 (October 2005): 78–83.

——. "Exposer, surexposer." *L'Oeil*, no. 565 (January 2005): 16–19.

——. "Questions de temps." *L'Oeil*, no. 555 (February 2004): 40.

Review. *Creative Review*, December 2003, 81.

Reynolds, Nigel. "A Giant Neon Sun Fills Tate Space." *Daily Telegraph*, October 16, 2003.

Rumbelow, Helen. "Outlook Stormy, If He Has His Way." *Times*, October 17, 2003.

Saltz, Jerry. "After Shock." *Village Voice*, November 5, 2003, 86.

Salvadé, Christine. "À la Tate Modern, le soleil artificiel d'un Islandais réconforte les Londoniens." *Le Temps*, January 12, 2004.

Schjeldahl, Peter. "England Swings." *The New Yorker*, March 1, 2004, 94.

Searle, Adrian. "Give Me Sunshine." *Guardian Weekly*, October 30–November 5, 2003.

———. "Happy Birthday, Tate Modern." *Guardian*, May 5, 2005.

———. "Reflecting on Sublime Smoke and Mirrors." *Guardian*, October 16, 2003.

Simons, Paul. "Art Show Puts Weather Anoraks in Their Element." *Times*, October 16, 2003.

Skau, Minna. "Eliasson har lagt London ned." *Politiken*, March 17, 2004.

———. "Vejret indenfor." *Politiken*, October 16, 2003.

Smee, Sebastian. "The Artist Who Paints with the Weather." *Daily Telegraph*, September 30, 2003.

Smith, Dan. "Size Matters." *Art Monthly*, no. 282 (December 2004–January 2005): 1–4.

Smith, Marquard. Interview with Hal Foster. *Journal of Visual Culture* 3, no. 3 (December 2004): 320–35.

"The Sun? We Put It in Storage." *Guardian*, April 6, 2005.

"Verbatim." *Times*, October 17, 2003.

Von Weber, L. "Sonnentanz." *Neue Zürcher Zeitung*, November 14, 2003.

"Weather Obsession." *Illawarra Mercury*, November 8, 2003.

Webster, Stephen. "Weatherwatch." *Guardian*, December 31, 2003.

Werner, James P. "Post-Digital Awareness: An Insight into New Immersion Practices in Installation Art." *Analecta Husserliana*, no. 87 (2005): 169–83.

Wivel, Henrik. "Måder at se på." *Nordisk Tidskrift för Vetenskap, Konst och Industri* 80, no. 4 (2004): 299–308.

Projekt Sammlung (1): The body as brain, Kunsthaus Zug, Switzerland, November 30, 2003–February 2, 2004. Artist's booklet titled *The Body as Brain* by Olafur Eliasson et al.

Light ventilator mobile, World Class Boxing, Miami, Florida, December 2003–February 2004. Brochure by Gean Moreno.

Feinstein, Roni. "Report from Miami: Expanding Horizons." *Art in America* 91, no. 12 (December 2003): 48–59.

Gordon, Margery. "Art Basel Miami Profile: Bulking Up." *Art & Auction* 29, no. 3 (November 2005): 114–18.

Hoban, Phoebe. "7BRs, OcnVu, WrldClass Art." *New York Times*, March 14, 2004.

Delight and other luminous movements, Galleria Emi Fontana, Milan, December 2, 2003–January 31, 2004.

Zanfi, Claudia. "Le architetture meteorologiche di Olafur Eliasson." *Corriere della Sera*, January 17, 2004.

Farbspiegellichtfeld, permanent installation commissioned by Zurich Building Authority, Department of Art and Construction, for Werkhof Zentrum Zürich Nord.

Sphere, permanent installation commissioned by HypoVereinsbank for Fünf Höfe development, Munich.

2004

Frost activity, Reykjavík Art Museum—Hafnarhús, January 17–April 25. Catalogue titled *Olafur Eliasson: Frost Activity* by Gunnar J. Árnasson and Paul Virilio.

Bhatnagar, Priya. Review. *Flash Art* 37, no. 235 (March–April 2004): 116.

Bjørnkjær, Kristen. "En blockbuster krydser sit spor." *Dagbladet Information*, January 21, 2004.

Dean, Corinna. Review. *Contemporary*, no. 62 (2004): 55.

Herbert, Martin. Preview. *Contemporary*, no. 60 (2004): 62–65.

Schiavi, Isabelle. "Chilling Icelandic Art." *NY Arts* 9, nos. 5–6 (May–June 2004): 85.

Game of Life: Elias Hjörleifsson and Olafur Eliasson, Hafnarborg, Hafnarfjördur, Iceland, January 18–March 14.

Ásgeirsson, Bragi. "Leikur lífsins." *Morgunblaðið*, February 3, 2004.

Björnsson, Anna Margrét. "Rising Sun." *Iceland Review* 41 (April 2003): 24–27.

"Fjöldi manns við opnun í Hafnarborg." *Morgunblaðið*, January 19, 2004.

Ingólfsson, Einar Falur. "Óvaent sjónarhorn." *Morgunblaðið*, February 3, 2004.

"Óheftur sköpunarkraftur." *Lesbók Morgunblaðsins*, January 17, 2004.

Colour memory and other informal shadows, Astrup Fearnley Museet for Moderne Kunst, Oslo, January 24–May 2. Catalogue / artist's book titled *Olafur Eliasson: Colour Memory and Other Informal Shadows* by Olafur Eliasson and Paul Virilio; brochure.

Umschreibung, permanent installation, KPMG corporate headquarters, Munich, opened March 24.

Escher, Gudrun. "Auf und ab und rundherum." *Deutsche Bauzeitschrift* 52, no. 8 (August 2004): 64.

Dufttunnel, permanent installation commissioned by Autostadt GmbH for Wolfsburg, Germany, opened April 1. Catalogue / artist's book titled *Olafur Eliasson: Dufttunnel; Ein Projekt für die Autostadt in Wolfsburg/ Scent Tunnel; A Project for the Autostadt in Wolfsburg* by Thomas Worm et al. (published by Hatje Cantz, Ostfildern-Ruit, Germany, 2005).

360° room for all colours, Schirn Kunsthalle Frankfurt, Germany, April 18–25.

Hierholzer, Michael. "Mehr Licht am Main." *Frankfurter Allgemeine Sonntagszeitung*, April 18, 2004.

Hohmann, Silke. "Die inneren 'special effects.'" *Frankfurter Rundschau*, April 20, 2004.

Loichinger, Stephan. "Glanzlos." *Frankfurter Rundschau*, April 20, 2004.

Photographs, Menil Collection, Houston, May 26–September 5. Catalogue titled *Olafur Eliasson: Photographs* by Matthew Drutt.

"Best of Arts & Entertainment: Best Curator." *Houston Press*, September 23, 2004.

Johnson, Patricia C. "Dual Realities." *Houston Chronicle*, July 3, 2004.

Klaasmeyer, Kelly. "Going to Iceland." *Houston Press*, June 10, 2004.

———. "Shining Star." *Houston Press*, May 20, 2004.

Wilson, Michael. Preview. *Artforum* 42, no. 9 (May 2004): 85.

Your lighthouse: Works with light 1991–2004, Kunstmuseum Wolfsburg, Germany, May 28–September 4. Catalogue titled *Olafur Eliasson: Your Lighthouse; Works with Light 1991–2004* edited by Gijs van Tuyl and Holger Broeker (copublished with Hatje Cantz, Ostfildern-Ruit, Germany); brochure.

Ackermann, Tim. "Das Licht in Olafurs Welt." *taz, die tageszeitung*, June 21, 2004.

Bortolotti, Maurizio. "Il modello infinito / An Unfinished Model." *Domus*, no. 886 (November 2005): 113–14.

Briegleb, Till. "Noch mehr Licht." *Süddeutsche Zeitung*, June 22, 2004.

Buchholz, Elke Linda. "Geburtstagsfeier mit optischen Wundern." *Stuttgarter Zeitung*, July 15, 2004.

Büsing, Nicole, and Heiko Klaas. "Licht am Ende des Tunnels." *Nürnberger Nachrichten*, June 26, 2004.

Clewing, Ulrich. "Mit allen Wassern der Suggestion gewaschen." *Frankfurter Rundschau*, June 1, 2004.

Gardner, Belinda Grace. "Moderner Irrgarten aus Licht und Spiegeln." *Welt am Sonntag*, May 30, 2004.

Gärtner, Barbara. "Sehe ich, was du nicht siehst?" *Stuttgarter Nachrichten*, July 8, 2004.

Kuhn, Thomas W. Review. *Kunstforum*, no. 171 (July–August 2004): 323–25.

"Kunst, die Licht ins Museum bringt." *Die Welt*, May 29, 2004.

Maak, Niklas. "Narziß im Wunderleuchten." *Frankfurter Allgemeine Zeitung*, July 30, 2004.

Reinewald, Chris. "Technologisch spel met de natuur." *Het Financieele Dagblad*, August 21, 2004.

Ruthe, Ingeborg. "Der Lichtmacher." *Berliner Zeitung*, June 8, 2004.

Von Goetz, Ulrike. "Hinter seinen Sonnen stecken Glühbirnen." *Welt am Sonntag*, April 11, 2004.

Walde, Gabriela. "Licht bitte!" *Die Welt*, June 28, 2004.

Wittneven, Katrin. "Der Regenbogen hinter dem Regenbogen." *Der Tagesspiegel*, May 30, 2004.

Projekt Sammlung (2): The body as brain, Kunsthaus Zug, Switzerland, June 13–August 8.

"À Zoug, l'art contemporain descend dans la rue." *L'Hebdo*, July 15, 2004.

Von Affetranger, A. "Topographie des Sehens." *Neue Zürcher Zeitung*, June 26, 2004.

"Zug: Eine Bleibe für den Modellraum von Olafur Eliasson." *Kunst-Bulletin*, nos. 7–8 (July–August 2004): 81.

Camera Obscura für die Donau, commissioned by Kunst im Öffentlichen Raum Niederösterreich and Arbeitskreis Wachau for Rollfähre Spitz, Arnsdorf, Germany, June 26, 2004–January 1, 2005. Artist's booklet by Brigitte Huck et al. (published by Niederösterreich Kultur).

I only see things when they move, Aspen Art Museum, Colorado, August 6–October 3.

MacMillan, Kyle. "Art Unchained Graces Aspen." *Denver Post*, August 27, 2004.

Your colour memory, Arcadia University Art Gallery, Glenside, Pennsylvania, September 1, 2004–January 9, 2005. Catalogue titled *Olafur Eliasson: Your Colour Memory* by Jonathan Crary et al (2006).

Fallon, Roberta. "Color Me Rad." *Philadelphia Weekly*, December 8–14, 2004, 42.

McGroarty, Cynthia J. "One Man's Mauve Is Another Man's Purple." *Philadelphia Inquirer*, October 24, 2004.

Rapkin, Mickey. Preview. *Details*, August 2004, 44.

Rice, Robin. "Color Schemes." *Philadelphia City Paper*, December 9–16, 2004, 26.

Sample, Hilary. "Fragile Syntheses." *NY Arts* 10, nos. 1–2 (January–February 2005): 83.

Sozanski, Edward J. "Color Becomes All in Arcadia Installation." *Philadelphia Inquirer*, October 24, 2004.

Minding the world, ARoS Aarhus Kunstmuseum, Denmark, October 8, 2004–January 16, 2005. Catalogue / artist's book titled *Olafur Eliasson: Minding the World* by Olafur Eliasson and Gitte Ørskou; brochure.

Ifversen, Karsten R. S. "Verdenssindet." *Politiken*, October 8, 2004.

Jones, Ronald. Review. *Frieze*, no. 90 (April 2005): 113.

Scavenius, Bente. "Rum i bevægelse." *Børsen*, October 8, 2004.

Thøgersen, Birger. "Kunstneren er hjemme." *Politiken*, May 8, 2004.

Thyssen, Nikolai. "Er der et kunstværk til stede?" *Dagbladet Information*, October 8, 2004.

Verhagen, Marcus. "On Art and Illusion." *Modern Painters* (December 2004–January 2005): 100–103.

Forgetting, Brändström & Stene, Stockholm, December 12, 2004–February 6, 2005.

Ekroth, Power. Review. *Flash Art*, no. 38 (March–April 2005): 49.

Orrghen, Anna. "Kontemplative solkatter går till botten med ljuset." *Svenska Dagbladet*, December 18, 2004.

Poellinger, Clemens. "Eliasson utmanar tid och rum." *Svenska Dagbladet*, December 13, 2004.

Fog doughnut, permanent installation, Tiscali Campus, Sa Illeta, Cagliari, Sardinia, Italy.

2005

Opera house chandeliers, permanent installation commissioned by A. P. Møller and Chastine Mc-Kinney Møller's Foundation for Copenhagen Opera House, opened January 15.

Hornung, Peter Michael. "Kunst i et hus uden historie." *Politiken*, January 16, 2005.

Lorentzsen, Erika. "In Copenhagen, There's Music in the Air." *Washington Post*, March 27, 2005.

Scavenius, Bente. "Fornem kunst spiller op til opera-arkitektur." *Børsen*, September 24, 2004.

Steffensen, Erik. "I Hendes Majestæts hemmelige tjeneste / In Her Majesty's Secret Service." *Arkitektur DK* 49, no. 3 (May 2005): 198–202.

Studium bez końca / The endless study, Fundacja Galerii Foksal, Warsaw, Poland, April 9–May 16. Traveled to Kiesler Stiftung, Vienna. Catalogue titled *Olafur Eliasson: A Laboratory of Mediating Space* by Olafur Eliasson et al. (published by Aedes am Pfefferberg, Berlin, and Öster-reichische Friedrich und Lillian Kiesler-Privatstiftung, Vienna, 2006).

Spiegler, Almuth. "Eliasson: Ich bin ein Mainstream-Künstler." *Die Presse*, July 7, 2006.

Meant to be lived in (today I'm feeling prismatic), organized by Emi Fontana West of Rome. Jamie Residence, Pasadena, California, April 21–May 31.

Chen, Aric. "Mirrors, Prisms and Light Turn a House into 3-D Art." *New York Times*, May 12, 2005.

Duncan, Michael. Review. *Art in America* 93, no. 11 (December 2005): 157.

Graves, Jen. Review. *Flash Art* 38, no. 244 (October 2005): 121.

Harvey, Doug. "Helter Shelter." *LA Weekly*, May 13, 2005, 62.

Knight, Christopher. "Heightened Light Sensitivity." *Los Angeles Times*, April 29, 2005.

Steiner, Shep. "Facing the Music." *Parachute*, no. 120 (October–December 2005): 5.

Welchman, John C. Review. *Domus*, no. 884 (September 2005): 87–88.

Wilson, Larry. "Shining Example of Art." *Pasadena Star-News*, May 15, 2005.

101 Gallery, May 14–July 1.

Wei, Lilly. "Nordic Odyssey." *Art in America* 93, no. 10 (November 2005): 72–78.

Your black horizon, commissioned by Thyssen-Bornemisza Art Contemporary (T-B A21), Vienna, for 51st Venice Biennale, Italy, June 12–November 6. Traveled to Lopud, Croatia. Catalogue; brochure.

Kimmelman, Michael. "A Global Village Whose Bricks Are Art." *New York Times*, June 16, 2005.

Thomas, Emma. Review. *Architects' Journal* 221, no. 26 (July 7–14, 2005): 66–67.

Yellow sunlight, commissioned by Global Campaign for Education for Oxo Tower, London, June 17–19.

Murray, Janet. "Marching Orders." *Guardian* (Manchester), June 7, 2005.

Eyeball stamp, postage stamp commissioned by Post Danmark, issued August 24.

The light setup, Lunds Konsthall, Lund, Sweden, September 10, 2005–January 8, 2006; Malmö Konsthall, Sweden, September 10, 2005–January 22, 2006. Catalogue / artist's book titled *Olafur Eliasson: Your Engagement Has Consequences; On the Relativity of Your Reality* by Olafur Eliasson et al. (published by Lars Müller Publishers, Baden, Switzerland, 2006); brochure by Lars Grambye et al.

Griffin, Tim. Preview. *Artforum* 44, no. 1 (September 2005): 163.

Kern, Kristine. "Lysets poetik." *Politiken*, September 11, 2005.

Marklund, Therese. "Roande ljuslek lurar ögat." *Svenska Dagbladet*, September 17, 2005.

Review. *Architectural Lighting* 19, no. 6 (September–October 2005): 24.

Scavenius, Bente. "Det psykologiske lys." *Børsen*, September 13, 2005.

The colour spectrum series, Niels Borch Jensen Galerie und Verlag, Berlin, September 26–November 12.

Notion motion, Museum Boijmans Van Beuningen, Rotterdam, Netherlands, October 8, 2005–January 8, 2006. Catalogue / artist's book titled *Olafur Eliasson: Your Engagement Has Consequences; On the Relativity of Your Reality* by Olafur Eliasson et al. (published by Lars Müller Publishers, Baden, Switzerland, 2006); brochure by Hanneke de Man.

Berk, Anne. "Kijken met cultuurogen." *Het Financieele Dagblad*, October 22, 2005.

Daenen, Ward. "Labo van licht en water." *De Morgen*, November 24, 2005.

"Museumzaal vol waterreflecties." *De Telegraaf*, October 7, 2005.

Schenke, Menno. "Weldoener steunt Boijmans." *Rotterdams Dagblad*, November 22, 2005.

Schoenberger, Janna. "Magic with Light, Water, and a Sponge (Forget the Smoke and Mirrors)." *NY Arts* 11, nos. 3–4 (March–April 2004): 22–23.

Schoonen, Rob. "De onnavolgbare wereld van Olafur Eliasson." *Eindhovens Dagblad*, October 22, 2005.

Searle, Adrian. "Frieze Art Fair: 'If Contemporary Art Is All a Fraud, Why Do People Keep Looking? Why Do I Keep Going Back to It?'" *Guardian* (London), October 21, 2005.

"Spelen met licht en water." *De Standaard*, November 4, 2005.

Zonnenberg, Nathalie. "Schatgraven in Rotterdam." *Metropolis M*, no. 5 (October–November 2005): 77–78.

Your loss of senses, permanent installation, Louis Vuitton boutique, Paris, opened October 9.

Barr, Vilma. "Crown Jewel." *Display and Design Ideas*, May 1, 2006.

Bonvin, Stéphane. "XXLuxe." *Le Temps*, October 11, 2005.

Cardani, Elena. "Il più grande del mondo / A Cathedral of Luxury." *L'Arca*, no. 211 (February 2006): 89.

Lutyens, Dominic. "Bon Voyage." *Art Review* 4, no. 1 (January–February 2006): 88–93.

Sausset, Damien. "Dans la lumière d'Olafur Eliasson." *Connaissance des arts*, no. 634 (January 2006): 54–59.

Vienne, Véronique. "East Meets West on the Champs-Elysées." *Metropolis* 25, no. 7 (March 2006): 74–80, 117–19.

Your light shadow, Hara Museum of Contemporary Art, Tokyo, November 17, 2005–March 5, 2006. Catalogue / artist's book titled *Olafur Eliasson: Your Engagement Has Consequences; On the Relativity of Your Reality* by Olafur Eliasson et al. (published by Lars Müller Publishers, Baden, Switzerland, 2006).

Hopkins, Elisabeth. Review. *International Herald Tribune*, January 21, 2006.

Liddell, C. B. "Elemental Expressions." *Japan Times*, December 22, 2005.

Satterthwaite, Julian. "The Natural World of Olafur Eliasson." *Yomiuri Shimbun*, March 17, 2005.

Schor, Gabriele. "Diesseits des Regenbogens." *Neue Zürcher Zeitung*, November 25, 2005.

Projekt Sammlung (3): The body as brain, Kunsthaus Zug, Switzerland, November 27, 2005–March 19, 2006.

"Im Fluss." *Neue Zürcher Zeitung*, January 28, 2006.

Mathonnet, Philippe. "Une ligne d'eau troublante." *Le Temps*, December 20, 2005.

Spinelli, Claudia. "Alles frisch." *Weltwoche*, December 8, 2005, 81.

2006

Omgivelser, ANDERSEN_S Contemporary, Copenhagen, January 27–March 18.

Hornung, Peter Michael. Review. *Politiken*, February 19, 2006.

Your waste of time, neugerriemschneider, Berlin, March 24–April 22.

Clewing, Ulrich. Review. *Der Tagesspiegel*, March 25, 2006.

Pace, Alessandra. Review. *Tema Celeste*, no. 116 (July–August 2006): 76.

Ruthe, Ingeborg. "Islandeis." *Berliner Zeitung*, March 30, 2006.

Sonna, Birgit. "Aus dem Lot gebracht; Die 'Gletscherdämmerung' in der Alten Residenzpost." *Süddeutsche Zeitung*, October 18, 2006.

Vadonis, Safia. Review. *Berliner Morgenpost*, April 2, 2006.

Your engagement sequence, Tanya Bonakdar Gallery, New York, April 28–May 27.

Diehl, Carol. Review. *Art in America* 94, no. 11 (December 2006): 155–56.

Grosz, David. "Rejecting Modernism's Pieties." *New York Sun*, May 11, 2006.

Kimmelman, Michael. Review. *New York Times*, May 12, 2006.

Lacayo, Richard. "Here Comes the Sun." *Time*, September 4, 2006, 46.

LeMieux Rubal, Bruno. Review. *Lapiz* 25, no. 224 (2006): 86.

Light lab (test I–XII), Portikus, Frankfurt, Germany, May 5, 2006–Spring 2008.

Birnbaum, Daniel. "Air Portikus." *Domus*, no. 893 (June 2006): 77–81.

Huther, Christian. Review. *Kunstforum*, no. 181 (July–September 2006): 346–48.

Schmitz, Rudolf. "Und immer, immer wieder geht die Sonne auf." *Süddeutsche Zeitung*, May 8, 2006.

Remagine, Kunstmuseum Bonn, Germany, May 13–June 18. Catalogue titled *Olafur Eliasson: Remagine; Large Version* by Volker Adolphs.

Projekt Sammlung (4): The body as brain—the water tower project, Kunsthaus Zug, Switzerland, May 20–October 29.

Your constants are changing, Gallery Koyanagi, Tokyo, May 31–July 8.

Eubank, Donald. Review. *Japan Times*, June 29, 2006.

Goto, Shigeo. Interview. *Esquire* (Japan) 20, no. 9 (September 2006): 212.

Caminos de naturaleza, Fundación Telefónica, Madrid, June 2–August 27. Catalogue / artist's book titled *Olafur Eliasson: Caminos de naturaleza / Paths of Nature* by Olafur Eliasson et al. (copublished with La Fabrica Editorial, Madrid).

Garcia, Carolina. Review. *Arte y Parte*, no. 63 (June–July 2006): 104.

Martín, Alberto. "Experimentar la Naturaleza." *El País*, June 24, 2006.

Sooke, Alastair. "Joyless, Creepy—and Sublime: Nature, in All Its variety." *Daily Telegraph* (London), June 6, 2006.

A laboratory of mediating space, Aedes am Pfefferberg, Berlin, June 2–July 20. Catalogue titled *Olafur Eliasson: A Laboratory of Mediating Space* by Olafur Eliasson et al. (copublished with Österreichische Friedrich und Lillian Kiesler-Privatstiftung, Vienna, 2006).

Meixner, Christiane. "Ein Däne in Berlin." *Berliner Morgenpost*, June 6, 2006.

Ruthe, Ingeborg. "Ruhm ist ein Missverständnis." *Berliner Zeitung*, July 8, 2006.

Your uncertainty of colour matching experiment (collaboration with Boris Oicherman), Ikon Gallery, Birmingham, England, July 25–September 17.

Adams, Tim. "Tangled Up in Blues and Yellows." *Observer* (London), July 30, 2006.

Chamberlain, Julie. "Brighter End of the Color Spectrum." *Coventry Evening Telegraph*, August 18, 2006.

Clark, Robert. Preview. *Guardian* (London), July 22, 2006.

Davies, Serena. "A Spot of Light Entertainment." *Daily Telegraph* (London), August 29, 2006.

Durrant, Nancy. "Making Rainbows." *Times* (London), July 25, 2006.

Grimley, Terry. "A Change in the Weather from Olafur." *Birmingham Post*, August 21, 2006.

Hickling, Alfred. Review. *Guardian* (London), August 3, 2006.

Hubbard, Sue. "Tinted Love." *Independent* (London), August 14, 2006.

Spinney, Laura. "How the Light Takes You." *New Scientist* 191, no. 2561 (July 22, 2006): 52.

Sonne statt Regen, Städtische Galerie im Lenbachhaus und Kunstbau, Munich, August 18–October 22.

Göricke, Jutta. "Konstruktionen von Sonne und Regen." *Süddeutsche Zeitung*, August 18, 2006.

Sonna, Birgit. "Der Wettermacher aus Island." *Neue Zürcher Zeitung*, April 26, 2006.

Eye see you, Louis Vuitton boutiques worldwide, November 9, 2006–January 7, 2007.

Baerd, Elodie. "Le luxe joue la carte artistique." *Le Figaro*, December 13, 2006.

Blake, Robin. "The Model of a Modern Artist." *Financial Times*, November 6, 2006.

Bødker, Kirsten. "Olafur Eliassons øje i New York." *Børsen*, November 28, 2006.

Browne, Alix. "An I for an Eye." *New York Times Magazine*, November 5, 2006, 66–67.

Catton, Pia. "A New Take on Window Shopping." *New York Sun*, November 10, 2006.

Conner, Justin. Interview. *Interview*, December 2006–January 2007, 60–62.

Karimzadeh, Marc. "Vuitton's Artistic Expression." *Women's Wear Daily*, November 9, 2006, 3.

Nielsen, Dorothe. "En verdenskunstner som filantrop." *Børsen*, October 19, 2006.

"El ojo que te ve." *El País*, December 26, 2006.

Rubin, Sylvia. "Vuitton Has 'It' Bag, 'It' Party Too." *San Francisco Chronicle*, December 10, 2006.

Socha, Miles. "Why Are Art and Fashion Merging Faster Than Ever? M-O-N-E-Y." *Women's Wear Daily*, November 20, 2006, 48.

Yablonsky, Linda. "Gigantes de la lámpara." *La Vanguardia*, December 31, 2006.

The glacierhouse effect versus the greenhouse effect, permanent installation, Klein Residence, Santa Fe.

2007

Lavaland: Olafur Eliasson & Jóhannes S. Kjarval, Kunstforeningen GL Strand, Copenhagen, February 10–April 29. Catalogue by Anne Kielgast et al.

Works on paper and other flat objects, PKM Gallery, Seoul, March 15–April 13.

Your tempo: Olafur Eliasson, San Francisco Museum of Modern Art, September 8, 2007–January 13, 2008.

Projekt Sammlung (5): The body as brain—the shadow studies, Kunsthaus Zug, Switzerland, November 18, 2007–February 2008.

Serpentine Gallery Pavilion 2007 (collaboration with Kjetil Thorsen), London.

Akbar, Arifa. "Serpentine's Summer Pavilion Gets a Makeover with Teeth." *Independent*, April 26, 2007.

Wright, Karen. "Olafur Eliasson's Berlin Studio Concocts Giant Spinning Top." *Bloomberg News*, April 30, 2007.

Your mobile expectations, BMW H₂R Project. Catalogue / artist's book (published by Lars Müller Publishers, Baden, Switzerland).

Andersen, Kit. "Hvorfor er biler så kedelige?" *M/S Berlingske Tidende*, November 12, 2006.

Buck, Louisa. "Olafur Eliasson to Make Car for BMW." *Art Newspaper* 14, no. 161 (September 2005): 12.

Peick, Morten. "Eine Art Car oder Identität und Differenz." *Die Weltwoche*, September 28, 2006.

2008

Foyer installation, commissioned by Directorate of Public Construction and Property (Statsbygg) for Opera House, Oslo, projected opening spring 2008.

Thøgersen, Birger. "Dansk kunst til norsk opera." *Politiken*, March 1, 2005.

2009

Icelandic National Concert and Conference Center (collaboration with Henning Larsen Architects), commissioned by Portus Group for Reykjavík, projected opening 2009. Catalogue / artist's book.

"Ice Age." *Contract*, November 1, 2006.

Sokol, David. "Hennings Larsens Tegnestue Building Concert Center on Fishery Site." *Architectural Record* 194, no. 1 (January 2006): 41.

Sørensen, Anette. "Det islandske lys." *Danske Ark Byg*, no. 44 (July 2006): 6–8.

SELECTED GROUP EXHIBITIONS, PROJECTS, AND REVIEWS

1992

Group Exhibition, Overgaden—Institut for Samtidskunst, Copenhagen, January 10–February 2.

Paradise EUROPE, Stalke Out of Space / BIZART, Copenhagen, July 3–27.

Summer Exhibition, Demonstrationslokalet for Kunst, Copenhagen, July 17–August 15. Catalogue.

1993

17:00 CET, Stalke Out of Space / Nørregade 7C, Copenhagen, May 29–June 20.

Black Box—Kunst under jorden, GLOBE Kuratorgruppe, Copenhagen, July 3–August 29.

Opening Show, Galleri Nicolai Wallner, Copenhagen, opened October 14.

Overdrive, 10 Young Nordic Artists, Project Room, Copenhagen, November 6–December 19.

1994

Europa '94: Junge europäische Kunst in München, MOC Messehallen, Munich, September 9–28. Catalogue edited by Christian Gögger et al.

1995

Kunst & Ökologie, Mecklenburgisches Künstlerhaus Schloss Plüschow, Germany, June 4–July 2. Traveled to Kunstverein Schloss Plön, Austria. Catalogue titled *Das Sisyphos-Syndrom: Hommage für Joseph Beuys* edited by Jürgen Schweinebraden.

Campo 95, organized by Fondazione Sandretto Re Rebaudengo. 46th Venice Biennale, Italy, June 7–July 30. Traveled to Sant'Antonino di Susa, Turin; Malmö Konstmuseum, Sweden. Catalogue by Francisco Bonami (published by Allemandi Editore, Turin).

Status, Galleri Stalke, Copenhagen, August 11–September 1.

(Landschaft) mit dem Blick der 90er Jahre, Mittelrhein-Museum, Koblenz, Germany, October 12–December 10. Traveled to Museum Schloss Burgk an der Saale, Germany; Haus am Waldsee, Berlin. Catalogue edited by Kathrin Becker and Klara Wallner.

Status 2, Galleri Stalke, Copenhagen, December 1–20.

Alles was modern ist, Galerie Bärbel Grässlin, Frankfurt, Germany, December 16, 1995–January 20, 1996.

1996

Provins-Legende, Museet for Samtidskunst, Roskilde, Denmark, February 10–April 28. Catalogue.

Prospect 96: Photographie in der Gegenwartskunst, Frankfurter Kunstverein and Schirn Kunsthalle Frankfurt, Germany, March 9–May 12. Catalogue edited by Peter Weiermair.

Glow, New Langton Arts, San Francisco, May 15–July 6.
> Rapko, John. Review. *Artweek* 27, no. 7 (July 1996): 20–21.

Il luogo e la memoria: La fotografia di un'esperienza, Ex-Copertificio Sonnino Besozzo, Varese, Italy, May 18–June 30. Traveled to Castello di Spezzano Fiorana Modenese, Modena, Italy. Catalogue by Filippo Maggia (copublished with Charta, Milan).

Náttúrusýn í íslenskri myndlist, Reykjavík Art Museum—Kjarvalsstadir and Reykjavík Arts Festival, June–August. Catalogue.

Declining and becoming, Manifesta 1, Kunsthal Rotterdam, Netherlands, June 9–August 19. Catalogue.

Nach Weimar, Kunstsammlungen zu Weimar, Germany, June 23–July 28. Catalogue.

Summer Show, Tanya Bonakdar Gallery, New York, July 9–September 7.

Remote Connection: Media in the Era of Displacement, Neue Galerie am Landesmuseum Joanneum, Graz, Austria, September 21–November 3; Wäino Aaltonen Museum of Art, Turku, Finland, November 29, 1996–January 12, 1997. Traveled to Art Focus, Tel Aviv, Israel. Catalogue edited by Amnon Barzel.

Tolv, Schaper Sundberg Galleri, Stockholm, October 5–November 10.

Skulpturparken ved Vestvolden—Hvidovre, 1996, Hvidovre, Denmark, opened October 11.

Skriget. Borealis 8, ARKEN Museum for Moderne Kunst, Ishøj, Denmark, November 16, 1996–January 2, 1997. Catalogue.

1997

Schauplatz Museumsquartier. Zur Transformation eines Ortes, Kunsthalle Wien, Vienna, January 24–March 31. Brochure.

(alikeness), Centre for Contemporary Photography, Fitzroy, Australia, March 7–April 6. Brochure by Katya Sander and Rune Gade.

Young Danish Art, Stalke Out of Space / Ringsted Gallery, Copenhagen, March 22–April 5.

Studija Islandija, Šiuolaikinio meno centras, Vilnius, Lithuania, June 6–July 6. Catalogue edited by Aurelijus Vijūnas.

Truce: Echoes of Art in an Age of Endless Conclusions, SITE Santa Fe, July 18–October 12. Catalogue.
> Mitchell, Charles Dee. "Report from Santa Fe: New Narratives." *Art in America* 85, no. 11 (November 1997): 42–47.
> Pulkka, Wesley. "Artists Tackle Global Issues." *Albuquerque Journal*, July 20, 1997.

Kunstpreis der Böttcherstraße in Bremen zu Gast im Bonner Kunstverein, Bonner Kunstverein, Bonn, Germany, September 23–October 30. Catalogue.

Été 97, Centre Genevois de Gravure Contemporaine, Geneva, September 28–December 20.

Louisiana Udstillingen: Ny Kunst fra Danmark og Skåne, Louisiana Museum for Moderne Kunst, Humlebæk, Denmark, October 3, 1997–February 8, 1998. Catalogue.
> Melo, Alexandre, Review. *Artforum* 36, no. 7 (March 1998): 111–12.
> Myers, Terry R. Review. *Art/Text*, no. 60 (February–April 1998): 78–79.

On Life, Beauty, Translations, and Other Difficulties, 5th Istanbul Biennial, October 5–November 9. Catalogue.

Trade Routes: History and Geography, 2nd Johannesburg Biennale, South Africa, October 12–December 12. Catalogue; artist's book titled *Erosion*.
> Becker, Carol. Review. *Art Journal* 57, no. 2 (Summer 1998): 86–100.

Heaven: Public View, Private View, P.S.1 Contemporary Art Center, Long Island City, New York, October 29, 1997–February 1, 1998.

1998

10 Years Anniversary Exhibition, Galleri Stalke, Copenhagen, January 9–31. Catalogue titled *Stalke 1987–1997*.

Sightings: New Photographic Art, Institute of Contemporary Arts, London, January 10–March 15. Catalogue.
> Wahjudi, Claudia. Review. *Kunstforum*, no. 141 (July–September 1998): 431–33.

Undergrund, Galerie Asbæk, Copenhagen, January 16–February 15.

Nuit blanche, scènes nordiques: Les années 90, Musée d'Art moderne de la Ville de Paris, February 7–May 10. Traveled to Reykjavík Art Museum; Bergen Kunstmuseum, Norway; Porin Taidemuseo, Pori, Netherlands; Göteborgs Konstmuseum, Göteborg, Sweden. Catalogue by Laurence Bossé and Hans Ulrich Obrist.
> Birnbaum, Daniel. "Northern Plight." *Art Press*, no. 232 (February 1998): 34–39.
> Hannula, Mika. "Paris Inferno (Disco 2001)." *Siksi* 13, no. 2 (Summer 1998): 66–71.

Interferencias, Sala de Exposiciones del Canal de Isabel II, Madrid, April 3–May 24. Catalogue edited by Octavio Zaya.
> Reindl, Uta M. Review. *Kunstforum*, no. 141 (July–September 1998): 434–35.

Seamless, De Appel, Amsterdam, April 3–June 1. Catalogue.

Transatlántico: Diseminación, Cruce y Desterritorialización, Centro Atlántico de Arte Moderno, Las Palmas de Gran Canaria, Spain, April 15–June 14. Catalogue.

StadtLandschaften, Galerie Sabine Kunst, Munich, April 28–May 30.

Brytningstider: En bok om vår föränderliga värld, Norrköpings Konstmuseum, Norrköping, Sweden, May 16–October 11. Catalogue.

Do All Oceans Have Walls?, Gesellschaft für Aktuelle Kunst, Bremen, Germany, May 17–July 26. Catalogue by Horst Griese and Eva Schmidt.
> "Gefällige Kunst im Techno-Park." *taz, die tageszeitung*, August 17, 2001.
> Puvogel, Renate. Review. *Kunstforum*, no. 142 (October–December 1998): 385–87.

Mai 98: Positionen zeitgenössischer Kunst seit den 60er Jahren, Kunsthalle Köln, Cologne, May 21–July 19. Catalogue edited by Brigitte Oetker and Christiane Schneider.

Pakkhus, Momentum: Nordisk festival for samtidskunst, Moss, Norway, May 23–June 21. Catalogue.

La ville, le jardin, la mémoire, Villa Medici, Académie de France à Rome, May 29–August 30. Catalogue; brochure.

Something Is Rotten in the State of Denmark, Kunsthalle Fridericianum, Kassel, Germany, July 11–September 13. Catalogue.

The Erotic Sublime, Galerie Thaddaeus Ropac, Salzburg, Austria, July 27–August 29.

The Generation of the 90s—17 Artists, Stalke Out of Space, Copenhagen / Amtsgården, Roskilde, Denmark, September 5–October 27.

Warming, The Project, Harlem, New York, September 10–October 10.

Every Day, 11th Biennale of Sydney, September 18–November 8. Catalogue.

Edstrandska Stiftelsens Konstnärsstipendiater 1998, Rooseum Center for Contemporary Art, Malmö, Sweden, September 19–December 13. Catalogue.

Berlin/Berlin, 1st Berlin Biennial, September 28, 1998–January 3, 1999. Catalogue.
> Newson, Sean. "Playing the Galleries." *Sunday Times* (London), November 1, 1998.
> Phillips, Christopher. "Art for an Unfinished City." *Art in America* 87, no. 1 (January 1999): 62–69.
> Wulffen, Thomas. Review. *Kunstforum*, no. 142 (October–December 1998): 364–67.

Cool Places: 7-oji Baltijos šalių meno trienalė, Šiuolaikinio meno centras, Vilnius, Lithuania, October 2–November 1. Catalogue by Kestutis Kuizinas and Jonas Valatkevicius.

Roteiros. Roteiros. Roteiros. Roteiros. Roteiros. Roteiros. Roteiros., 24th Bienal de São Paulo, October 3–December 13. Catalogue by Paulo Herkenhoff and Adriano Pedrosa; artist's book titled *Users* by Olafur Eliasson et al.
> Fortes, Márcia. Review. *Frieze*, no. 44 (January–February 1999): 87–88.
> Haye, Christian. "Om Olafur Eliasson." *Paletten*, no. 233 (April 1998): 24–25.

Rozjazd, Centrum Sztuki Współczesnej Zamek Ujazdowski, Warsaw, Poland, October 10–November 29. Catalogue.

New Photography 14, Museum of Modern Art, New York, October 15, 1998–January 12, 1999.
> Arning, Bill. "Camera Shy." *Time Out New York*, November 19–26, 1998, 63.
> Doyle, Stephen. "Surfing the New Wave." *Creative Review* 18, no. 12 (December 1998): 65.
> Glueck, Grace. Review. *New York Times*, October 30, 1998.

Sharawadgi, Felsenvilla, Baden, Germany. October 18–December 20. Catalogue; brochure by Christian Meyer.
> Weh, Vitus H. Review. *Kunstforum*, no. 143 (January–February 1999): 410–11.

Auf der Spur: Kunst der 90er Jahre im Spiegel von Schweizer Sammlungen, Kunsthalle Zürich, October 31–December 27. Brochure by Bernhard Bürgi.

Fast Forward/Archives, Kunstverein in Hamburg, Germany, November 20, 1998–January 17, 1999.

Dad's art, neugerriemschneider, Berlin, November 21–December 19.

Light x Eight: The Hanukkah Project, Jewish Museum, New York, December 13, 1998–January 31, 1999.
> Johnson, Ken. "Turning a Museum into a Vast Menorah." *New York Times*, January 1, 1999.

1999

Konstruktionszeichnungen, Kunst-Werke Institute for Contemporary Art, Berlin, January–May.

Photography from the Martin Z. Margulies Collection, Art Museum at Florida International University, Miami, January 8–February 13. Catalogue by Dahlia Morgan and Bill Maguire.
> Turner, Elisa. "Photos Capture People Estranged from Their Surroundings." *Miami Herald*, January 10, 1999.

Photography: An Expanded View, Recent Acquisitions, Solomon R. Guggenheim Museum, New York, February 22–May 16.

Landscape: Outside the Frame, MIT List Visual Arts Center, Cambridge, Massachusetts, April 23–June 27. Catalogue.
> McQuaid, Cate. "Exploring the Nexus of Art, Science, and History." *Boston Globe*, June 8, 1999.
> Sherman, Mary. "'Landscape' Creates the Great Indoors." *Boston Herald*, May 9, 1999.

Focused, Galerie Tanit, Munich, April 29–June 26.

Malmö Konstmuseum besöker Wanås, 1999, Stiftelsen Wanås Utställningar, Knislinge, Sweden, May 23–September 12. Catalogue.

Z2000: Positionen junger Kunst und Kultur, Akademie der Künste, Berlin, May 23, 1999–January 1, 2001. Catalogue by Christian Kneisel and Michael Duwe.

To the People of the City of the Euro, Frankfurter Kunstverein, Frankfurt, Germany, May 28–July 11.
> Danicke, Sandra. "Der Raum und seine Ordnung." *Frankfurter Rundschau*, May 31, 1999.
> Hohmann, Silke. "Transparenz als Prinzip." *Journal Frankfurt*, no. 13 (June 11–24, 1999): 38.
> Huther, Christian. Review. *Kunstforum*, no. 147 (September–November 1999): 417–18.

Saman taivaan alla, Nykytaiteen museo Kiasma, Helsinki, June 1–August 31. Catalogue edited by Jari-Pekka Vanhala.

Panorama 2000: Kunst in Utrecht te zien vanaf de Domtoren, Centraal Museum, Utrecht, Netherlands, June 5–October 3. Catalogue.
> Decter, Joshua. Review. *Flash Art* 33, no. 210 (January–February 2000): 112.
> Larsen, Lars Bang. Review. *Art/Text*, no. 67 (November 1999–January 2000): 95–96.

Schöpfung, Karmelitenkirche, Promenadeplatz, Munich, and Heilig-Geist-Kirche, Landshut, Germany, June 9–July 4; Diözesanmuseum Freising, Germany, June 9–October 10. Catalogue edited by Petra Giloy Hirtz and Peter B. Steiner.
> Herwig, Oliver. "Lilith und die Kröten." *Süddeutsche Zeitung*, May 8, 1999.

d'APERTutto, 48th Venice Biennale, Italy, June 13–November 17. Catalogue edited by Harald Szeeman and Cecilia Liveriero Lavelli; artist's book titled *Sospensione*.

Sogni/Dreams, Fondazione Sandretto Re Rebaudengo, Turin, Italy, June 13–November 17. Catalogue edited by Francesco Bonami and Hans Ulrich Obrist (published by Castelvecchi Editore, Rome).

Paisajes, Galería Heinrich Ehrhardt, Madrid, June 17–July 22. Catalogue.

Overflow, Marianne Boesky Gallery, New York; D'Amelio-Terras, New York; and Anton Kern Gallery, New York, June 30–July 30.

Sommerens mørke og lyse nætter, Aarhus Kunstbygning, Denmark, July 31–August 22. Catalogue.

Drawings, Bonakdar Jancou Gallery, New York, September 9–October 16.

Can you hear me?, 2nd ARS BALTICA Triennial of Photographic Art, Stadtgalerie Kiel, Germany, November 3–December 12. Traveled to Kunsthalle Rostock, Germany; Šiuolaikinio meno centras, Vilnius, Lithuania; Kunsthaus Dresden, Germany; Bergen Kunsthall / Bergens Kunstforening, Bergen, Norway; Galleria Otso, Espoo, Finland. Catalogue.
> Rönnau, Jens. Review. *Kunstforum*, no. 149 (January–March 2000): 345–47.

Carnegie International 1999/2000, Carnegie Museum of Art, Pittsburgh, November 6, 1999–March 26, 2000. Catalogue by Madeleine Grynsztejn et al.
> Arning, Bill. "Carnegie Dilly." *Time Out New York*, November 25–December 2, 1999.
> Brenson, Michael. "Fact and Fiction." *Artforum* 38, no. 1 (September 1999): 67–70.
> Carrier, David. Review. *Burlington Magazine* 142, no. 1163 (February 2000): 128–29.
> Dannatt, Adrian. "The Old Masters of Tomorrow," *Art Newspaper* 10, no. 98 (December 1999): 16.

> Jackson, Charles. "Carnegie International Celebrates Artifice, Not Art." *Pittsburgh Post-Gazette*, January 30, 2000.
> King, Elaine E. Review. *Sculpture* 19, no. 4 (May 2000): 75–77.
> Leffingwell, Edward. "Carnegie Ramble." *Art in America* 88, no. 3 (March 2000): 86–93, 142.
> Siegel, Katy. Review. *Artforum* 38, no. 5 (January 2000): 105–6.
> Sorkin, Jenni. Review. *Art Monthly*, no. 232 (December 1999–January 2000): 28–30.
> Thomas, Mary. "Immersed in Art." *Pittsburgh Post-Gazette*, November 6, 1999.

Children of Berlin: Cultural Developments 1989–1999, P.S.1 Contemporary Art Center, Long Island City, New York, November 7, 1999–January 2, 2000.
> Chin, Daryl. "Berlin Metropolis." *Performing Arts Journal* 22, no. 2 (May 2000): 132–37.
> Cotter, Holland. "Update on Berlin Since the Wall." *New York Times*, November 12, 1999.

Blown Away, 6th International Caribbean Biennial, Saint Kitts, West Indies, November 10–17. Catalogue.

German Open 1999: Gegenwartskunst in Deutschland, Kunstmuseum Wolfsburg, Germany, November 13, 1999–March 26, 2000. Catalogue by Andrea Brodbeck and Veit Görner.

. . . incommensurabilis . . ., Galerija Škuc, Ljubljana, Slovenia, December 16, 1999–January 30, 2000. Catalogue titled *Škuc Gallery Annual Catalogue 1999/2000*.

2000

Organising Freedom: nordisk 90-tals konst, Moderna Museet, Stockholm, February 12–April 9. Traveled to Charlottenborg Udstillingsbygning, Copenhagen. Catalogue edited by David Elliott.

Photogravüre, Niels Borch Jensen Galerie und Verlag, Berlin, February 18–April 15.

Over the Edges: De hoeken van Gent, Stedelijk Museum voor Actuele Kunst, Ghent, Belgium, April 1–June 30. Catalogue by Jan Hoet and Giacinto di Pietrantonio.
> Archer, Michael. Review. *Art Monthly*, no. 236 (May 2000): 33–35.

The Greenhouse Effect, Serpentine Gallery, London, April 4–May 21. Catalogue by Ralph Rugoff and Lisa G. Corrin.
> Searle, Adrian. "Stuck in the Woods." *Guardian*, April 4, 2000.
> Staple, Polly. Review. *Art Monthly*, no. 236 (May 2000): 38–40.

ForwArt, Mont des Arts, Brussels, April 5–May 14. Catalogue.

The Fascination of Gardens, Internationale Gartenschau, Graz, Austria, April 13–October 15.

Erste Arbeiten bei Kilchmann, Galerie Peter Kilchmann, Zurich, May 24–June 8.

Wanås 2000, Stiftelsen Wanås Utställningar, Knislinge, Sweden, May 28–October 22. Catalogue.
> Volk, Gregory. "The Wanås Foundation: Patronage and Partnership." *Sculpture* 20, no. 1 (December 2000–January 2001): 30–35.

Summer Group Exhibition, Paula Cooper Gallery, New York, June 9–July 21.

Naust, Øygarden, Tjeldstø, Norway, June 18–July 30. Catalogue.

Wonderland, Saint Louis Art Museum, July 1–September 24. Catalogue edited by Rochelle Steiner.
  Daniel, Jeff. Review. *Saint Louis Post-Dispatch*, July 2, 2000.
  Hughes, Jeffrey, Review. *New Art Examiner* 28, no. 3 (November 2000): 58–59.
  Schroeder, Ivy. Review. *Riverfront Times*, July 26–August 2, 2000.

Bleibe, Akademie der Künste, Berlin, July 15–August 20.

Benesse Prize Winners Exhibition, Naoshima Contemporary Art Museum, Japan, July 20–September 28. Brochure.

Raumkörper: Netze und andere Gebilde, Kunsthalle Basel, Switzerland, August 26–November 12. Catalogue by Peter Pakesch.

Times Are Changing: Auf dem Wege! Aus dem 20. Jahrhundert! Eine Auswahl von Werken der Kunsthalle Bremen 1950–2000, Kunsthalle Bremen, Germany, September 1–October 29. Catalogue.

On paper, Galleri Stalke, Copenhagen, September 17–October 23.

Vision og virkelighed: Forestillinger om det 20. århundrede, Louisiana Museum for Moderne Kunst, Humlebæk, Denmark, September 21, 2000–January 14, 2001. Catalogue by Kjeld Kjeldsen.

Preis der Nationalgalerie für junge Kunst, Nationalgalerie im Hamburger Bahnhof, Museum für Gegenwart, Berlin, September 29, 2000–January 6, 2001. Brochure.
  Hübl, Michael. "Ruhmeshalle oder Künstlerfalle?" *Kunstforum*, no. 153 (January–March 2001): 306–9.
  Lapp, Alex. "The Turner Preis?" *Art Monthly*, no. 242 (December 2000–January 2001): 12–15.

2001

Freestyle: Werke aus der Sammlung Boros, Museum Morsbroich Leverkusen, Germany, February 4–April 1. Catalogue by Gerhard Finckh and Susanne Küpper.

New Acquisitions from the Dakis Joannou Collection, Deste Foundation Centre for Contemporary Art, Athens, Greece, February 9–May 23.

All-Terrain: An Exploration of Landscape and Place, Contemporary Art Center of Virginia, Virginia Beach, February 22–April 29. Brochure.

Opening, La Colección Jumex, Ecatepec de Morelos, Mexico, March 3–December 16.

+ VRAI QUE NATURE, Musée d'art contemporain, Bordeaux, France, May 15–September 31.

Neue Welt, Frankfurter Kunstverein, Frankfurt, Germany, June 1–September 23. Catalogue edited by Nicolaus Schafhausen (copublished with Lukas & Sternberg, New York).

En el cielo, 49th Venice Biennale, Italy, June 6–10.

Black Box: Der Schwarzraum in der Kunst, Kunstmuseum Bern, Switzerland, June 15–September 9. Catalogue by Ralf Beil.

New Work, Tanya Bonakdar Gallery, New York, July 9–August 17.

En pleine terre: Eine Wanderung zwischen Landschaft und Kunst, Spiral Jetty und Potsdamer Schrebergärten, Museum für Gegenwartskunst der Öffentlichen Kunstsammlung Basel und der Emanuel Hoffmann-Stiftung, Switzerland, August 16–November 18. Brochure.

10 Years with Stalke Out of Space, Galleri Stalke, Copenhagen, August 17–September 14.

Palomino, Galerie für Zeitgenössische Kunst, Leipzig, Germany, August 26–November 4.

Mega Wave: Towards a New Synthesis, Yokohama 2001: International Triennale of Contemporary Art, Japan, September 2–November 11. Catalogue.

Everything Can Be Different, organized by Independent Curators International, New York. Jean Paul Slusser Gallery, Ann Arbor, September 11–November 5. Traveled to the Art Museum of the University of Memphis; California Center for the Arts, Escondido, California. Catalogue and brochure by Maria Lind.
  Hall, David. "Head Games." *Memphis Flyer*, March 15–22, 2002.
  Zdanovics, Olga. Review. *Art Papers* 26, no. 2 (March–April 2002): 46–47.

Aubette: Het verlangen naar een (andere) plaats, Museum Dhondt-Dhaenens, Deurle, Belgium, October 7–December 9. Catalogue by Edith Doove.

Confronting Nature: Icelandic Art of the 20th Century, Corcoran Gallery of Art, Washington, D.C., October 13–November 26. Catalogue edited by Ólafur Kvaran and Karla Kristjánsdóttir (published by National Gallery of Iceland, Reykjavík).

Form Follows Fiction/Forma e finzione nell'arte de oggi, Castello di Rivoli, Museo d'Arte Contemporanea, Turin, Italy, October 17, 2001–January 27, 2002. Catalogue by Jeffrey Deitch.

The Waste Land: Wüste und Eis. Ödlandschaften in der Fotografie, Atelier Augarten, Österreichische Galerie Belvedere, Vienna, October 24, 2001–February 24, 2002. Catalogue by Thomas Trummer.
  Metzger, Rainer. Review. *Kunstforum*, no. 158 (January–March 2002): 359–63.

2002

No Return: Positionen aus der Sammlung Haubrok, Städtisches Museum Abteiberg, Mönchengladbach, Germany, January 27–April 28. Catalogue.
  Krausch, Christian. Review. *Kunstforum*, no. 159 (April–May 2002): 341–43.

Thin Skin: The Fickle Nature of Bubbles, Spheres, and Inflatable Structures, organized by Independent Curators International, New York. AXA Gallery, New York, January 29–April 13. Traveled to Scottsdale Museum of Contemporary Art, Arizona; Gemeentemuseum Helmond, Netherlands; International Museum of Art and Science, McAllen, Texas; Chicago Cultural Center; Ulrich Museum of Art, Wichita, Kansas; Bedford Gallery, Walnut Creek, California; Boise Art Museum, Idaho. Catalogue by Barbara Clausen and Carin Kuoni.
  Camhi, Leslie. "Blow Up." *Village Voice*, February 13–20, 2002, 65.

Johnson, Ken. Review. *New York Times*, March 29, 2002.
Schnoor, Chris. "Think Thin." *Boise Weekly*, April 13–20, 2004, 16.
Susser, Deborah. "The Space Between." *Phoenix New Times*, August 15, 2002.

The Theory of Leisure, La Colección Jumex, Ecatepec de Morelos, Mexico, January 31–August 31.

Beyond Paradise: Nordic Artists Travel East, organized by Moderna Museet, Stockholm; Museet for samtidskunst, Oslo; Danish Contemporary Art Foundation, Copenhagen; Finnish Fund for Art Exchange, Helsinki; and Svenska Institutet, Stockholm. Tadu Contemporary Art Gallery and additional venues, Bangkok, Thailand, February 16–March 29. Traveled to National Art Gallery and additional venues, Kuala Lumpur, Malaysia; Fine Art Museum and Jin Wen Art Center, Shanghai. Catalogues in multiple languages.

Acquiring Taste, Real Art Ways, Hartford, Connecticut, February 23–June 30. Catalogue by Steven Holmes.

Diamanti. Arte Storia Scienza, Scuderie del Quirinale, Rome, March 1–June 30. Catalogue (published by De Luca Editori d'Arte, Rome).

Tomorrow's Fish & Chips, Autocenter, Berlin, March 1–3.

Ars lucis et umbrae: Licht- und Schattenobjekte aus der Neuen Galerie Graz, Wiener Kunstauktionen, Palais Kinsky, Vienna, March 11–May 24. Brochure.

From the Observatory, Paula Cooper Gallery, New York, March 16–April 20.

Claude Monet . . . bis zum digitalen Impressionismus, Fondation Beyeler, Riehen, Switzerland, March 28–August 18. Catalogue.

Opening Exhibition, Galleri Kirke Sonnerup, Kirke Såby, Denmark, April 20–June 1.

From the cool light, Niels Borch Jensen Galerie und Verlag, Berlin, May 3–June 7.

Group exhibition, Overgaden—Institut for Samtidskunst, Copenhagen, May 25–June 23.

The Object Sculpture, Henry Moore Institute, Leeds, England, June 1–September 1. Catalogue edited by Penelope Curtis.
  Lubbock, Tom. Review. *Independent* (London), June 4, 2002.
  Morton, Tom. Review. *Frieze*, no. 69 (September 2002): 103.
  Withers, Rachel. Review. *Artforum* 41, no. 4 (December 2002): 149.

Moving Pictures: Contemporary Photography and Video from the Guggenheim Museum Collection, Solomon R. Guggenheim Museum, New York, June 28, 2002–January 12, 2003. Traveled to Guggenheim Bilbao, Spain. Catalogue.
  Camhi, Leslie. "Cleaning the Mirror." *Village Voice*, September 4–11, 2002, 60.

Regarding Landscape, Museum of Contemporary Canadian Art, Toronto; Art Gallery of York University, Toronto; and Koffler Gallery, Toronto, July 12–August 25. Traveled to Liane and Danny Taran Gallery, Montreal; Saidye Bronfman Centre for the Arts, Montreal. Catalogue.
  Milroy, Sarah. "Mapping the New Landscape." *Globe and Mail* (Toronto), May 18, 2002.

Narrando espacios, tiempos, historias, 27th Bienal de Arte de Pontevedra, Spain, July 14–September 15. Catalogue.

Dialoghi europei d'arte, Castel dell'Ovo / Castel Nuovo, Naples, Italy, July 16–September 7. Catalogue edited by Anna Casotti.

Frequencies [radar], Radar: Electronic Integration, Kulturbro Biennal 2002, Malmö, Sweden, and Copenhagen, September 26–29. Catalogue.

Mirror Mirror, MASS MoCA, North Adams, October 5, 2002–January 6, 2003.
> Boyce, Roger. "Neither Here nor There." *Art New England* 24, no. 2 (February–March 2003): 16–17, 74.

el aire es azul—the air is blue, Casa Luis Barragán, Mexico City, November 2, 2002–March 15, 2003. Catalogue.

Oluf Høst. I dialog med nutiden, Aarhus Kunstmuseum, Denmark, November 9, 2002–February 2, 2003. Catalogue by Anna Krogh.

Topos—Atopos—Anatopos, Center for Contemporary Non-Objective Art, Brussels, November 23, 2002–January 26, 2003.

ars photographica: Fotografie und Künstlerbücher, Neues Museum Weserburg Bremen, Germany, December 1, 2002–March 9, 2003. Catalogue.

Rent-a-Bench, various street locations, Los Angeles, December 1, 2002–January 31, 2003. Traveled to Trapholt Kunstmuseum, Kolding, Denmark. Catalogue.

2003

Air, James Cohan Gallery, New York, January 10–February 15.

Imperfect Innocence: The Debra and Dennis Scholl Collection, Contemporary Museum, Baltimore, January 11–March 11. Traveled to Palm Beach Institute of Contemporary Art, Florida. Catalogue.
> Giuliano, Mike. "Photographers Enlarge on Bechers' Earlier Works." *Baltimore Sun*, January 11, 2003.

Revisitar Canarias, Galería Elba Benítez, Madrid, February 14–March 29. Traveled to Sala La Regenta, Las Palmas de Gran Canaria, Spain; Sala La Granja, Santa Cruz de Tenerife, Spain. Catalogue titled *Lanzarote Series: Olafur Eliasson* by Fernando Gómez Aguilera and Olafur Eliasson (published by ACTAR, Barcelona).

ARKENs Samling 2003, ARKEN Museum for Moderne Kunst, Ishøj, Denmark, March 8–September 14.

Edén. Arte contemporáneo en el Antiguo Colegio de San Ildefonso, Antiguo Colegio de San Ildefonso, Mexico City, March 15–July 13. Traveled to Banco de la República, Bogotá, Colombia. Catalogue (published by La Colección Jumex, Mexico City).

The Straight or Crooked Way, Royal College of Art, London, March 15–April 6. Catalogue.

Matrimoni imperfetti, Galleria Emi Fontana, Milan, April 9–May 17.

See History 2003: Eine Sammlung wird ausgestellt, April 12–May 1, Kunsthalle zu Kiel, Germany. Catalogue by Dirk Luckow et al.

Island i Danmark, Galleri Kirke Sonnerup, Kirke Såby, Denmark, April 26–June 6.

Looking In—Looking Out, Kunstmuseum Basel, Switzerland, April 26–June 29. Brochure.

Bonheur et simulacres, Manif d'art 2, Quebec, May 1–31. Catalogue.

An International Legacy: Selections from the Carnegie Museum of Art, organized by American Federation of the Arts, New York, and Carnegie Museum of Art, Pittsburgh. Oklahoma City Museum of Art, May 16–August 10. Traveled to Nevada Museum of Art, Reno; Mobile Museum of Art, Alabama; Columbus Museum of Art, Ohio. Catalogue edited by Sheryl Conkelton.

Utopia Station, 50th Venice Biennale, Italy, June 15–November 2. Traveled to Mostra d'Oltremare, Naples, Italy; Haus der Kunst, Munich; Kunst + Projekte, Sindelfingen, Germany; World Social Forum, Porto Alegre, Brazil. Catalogue edited by Francesco Bonami and Maria Luisa Frisa.
> Ramade, Bénédicte. "Rendez-vous manqué." *L'Oeil*, no. 550 (September 2003): 14.
> Wulffen, Thomas. Review. *Kunstforum*, no. 166 (August–October 2003): 201.

Frankenstein, Tanya Bonakdar Gallery, New York, June 26–August 22.

De bortbjudna: Malmö Art Museum is visiting Rooseum, Rooseum Center for Contemporary Art, Malmö, Sweden, June 27–September 7.

Spread in Prato, Dryphoto Arte Contemporanea, Prato, Italy, June 28–July 24. Catalogue.

Svjetlina/Brightness, Dubrovnik Galerija Umjetnička, Croatia, July 9–September 6. Catalogue edited by Max Wigram.
> Von Hase, Bettina. "A Dynamo in the Dynasty." *Art Review* 1, no. 11 (2003): 88–93.

In Full View, Andrea Rosen Gallery, New York, July 15–September 13.

Los lugares de lo real: Imágenes de una colección, Villa Iris, Santander, Spain, July 16–September 7. Catalogue by Mónica Álvarez Careaga (published by Fundación Marcelino Botín, Santander).

Hands Up, Baby, Hands Up, Oldenburger Kunstverein, Oldenburg, Germany, September 6–October 26. Brochure.

U-Topos, 2nd Tirana Biennial, Albania, September 12–October 25. Catalogue.
> Morgan, Jessica. "Tirana." *Tate: Arts and Culture* 3, no. 8 (November–December 2003): 60–66.

Warped Space, Wattis Institute for Contemporary Arts, California College of the Arts, San Francisco, September 17–November 15. Catalogue by Ralph Rugoff.

No Art = No City! Stadtutopien in der zeitgenössischen Kunst, Städtische Galerie, Bremen, Germany, September 20–October 26. Catalogue by Florian Matzner.

Support: Die Neue Galerie als Sammlung, Neue Galerie am Landesmuseum Joanneum, Graz, Austria, September 21, 2003–January 18, 2004, and May 14–August 29, 2004. Brochure.

Sitings: Installation Art 1969–2002, Museum of Contemporary Art, Los Angeles, October 12, 2003–June 7, 2004.

Miles, Christopher. "The Language of Installation." *Artweek* 34, no. 10 (December 2003–January 2004): 12–13.

Kunst mod Fordomme, Statens Museum for Kunst, Copenhagen, October 24–November 2.

Einbildung: Das Wahrnehmen in der Kunst, Steirischer Herbst, Graz, Austria, October 25, 2003–January 18, 2004. Catalogue by Peter Pakesch.
> Theiss, Nora. Review. *Flash Art* 37, no. 234 (January–February 2004): 58.

Fra objektiv til objekt, Den Frie, Copenhagen, November 6–23. Catalogue by Anna Krogh.

A Nova Geometria, Galeria Fortes Vilaça, São Paulo, November 28, 2003–January 17, 2004.

The Fifth System: Public Art in the Age of Post-Planning, 5th Shenzhen International Public Art Exhibition, China, December 12, 2003–December 11, 2005. Catalogue (published by He Xiangning Art Museum, Shenzhen).

Montagna: Arte, scienza, mito. Da Dürer a Warhol, Museo di Arte Moderna e Contemporanea di Trento e Rovereto, Italy, December 19, 2003–April 18, 2004. Catalogue by Gabriella Belli et al. (copublished with Skira, Milan).

2004

realityREAL: Arbeiten auf Papier, Galerie Gebr. Lehmann, Dresden, Germany, January 20–February 21.

Colección de fotografía contemporánea de Telefónica, Fundación Telefónica, Madrid, January 28–March 14. Traveled to Museo de Arte Contemporánea de Vigo, Spain. Catalogue.

The Amazing & the Immutable, University of South Florida Contemporary Art Museum, Tampa, February 2–March 13. Catalogue.
> Milani, Joanne. "A Reality Show of a Different Kind." *Tampa Tribune*, February 22, 2004.

Double Exposure, Brigitte March Galerie, Stuttgart, Germany, February 6–28. Catalogue (published by Edition Schellmann, Munich).

Fortælling, myte og drøm, Statens Museum for Kunst, Copenhagen, February 7–October 17. Brochure by Søren Jønsson Granat.

Landscape? 2, Towner Art Gallery, Eastbourne, England, February 7–March 28.
> Kennedy, Maev. "Branching Out." *Guardian* (London), March 9, 2004.
> Ward, Ossian. Review. *Observer* (London), March 21, 2004.

Werke aus der Sammlung Boros, Zentrum für Kunst und Medientechnologie, Karlsruhe, Germany, February 7–May 9. Catalogue by Florian Illies and Silke Immenga.

La relatividad del tiempo y los distintos sistemas de referencia, Oficina para Proyectos de Arte A.C., Guadalajara, Mexico, February 20–April 9.

La Colmena, La Colección Jumex, Ecatepec de Morelos, Mexico, March 18–October 30.

Nouvelles Collections, Centre PasquArt, Biel/Bienne, Switzerland, April 4–May 30.

Atomkrieg, Kunsthaus Dresden, Germany, May 19–July 11. Catalogue by Antje Majewski and Ingo Niermann.

Why Not Live for Art?, Tokyo Opera City Art Gallery, May 26–July 11. Brochure.

Everything Is Connected, he, he, he, Astrup Fearnley Museet for Moderne Kunst, Oslo, May 29–August 15. Brochure.

Reflecting the Mirror, Marian Goodman Gallery, New York, June 14–August 27.

Monument to Now, Deste Foundation Centre for Contemporary Art, Athens, Greece, June 22, 2004– March 6, 2005. Catalogue by Jeffrey Deitch et al.

Paisaje y Memoria, Centro Atlántico de Arte Moderno, Las Palmas de Gran Canaria, Spain, June 30–August 22. Catalogue by Alicia Chillida.

Recherche—entdeckt! Bildarchiv der Unsichtbarkeiten, 6th Esslingen International Foto-Triennale, Germany, July 18–October 3. Catalogue edited by Andreas Baur and Ludwig Seyfarth (published by Revolver, Archiv für aktuelle Kunst, Frankfurt, Germany).

ein-leuchten, Museum der Moderne Salzburg, Austria, July 25–October 31. Catalogue.

Artists' Favourites: Act II, Institute of Contemporary Arts, London, July 30–September 5. Catalogue.

In Focus: Themes in Photography, Albright-Knox Art Gallery, Buffalo, September 24, 2004–January 30, 2005.

Los usos de la imagen: Fotografía, film y video en La Colección Jumex, Espacio Fundación Telefónica, Museo de Arte Latinoamericano de Buenos Aires, September 29– November 17. Catalogue by Carlos Basualdo.

Parallele 64—Art Contemporain Islandais, Espace d'art contemporain Gustave Fayet, Sérignan, France, October 2–December 24. Brochure.

Encounters in the 21st Century: Polyphony—Emerging Resonances, 21st Century Museum of Contemporary Art, Kanazawa, Japan, October 8, 2004–March 21, 2005. Catalogue by Yutaka Mino et al.

Bewegliche Teile: Formen des Kinetischen, Steirischer Herbst, Graz, Austria, October 9, 2004–January 16, 2005. Traveled to Museum Tinguely, Basel, Switzerland. Catalogue by Peter Pakesch and Guido Magnaguagno.

Invisibile, Palazzo delle Papesse Centro Arte Contemporanea, Siena, Italy, October 9, 2004–January 9, 2005. Catalogue by Lorenzo Fusi.

Stadtlicht—Lichtkunst, Stiftung Wilhelm Lehmbruck Museum, Duisburg, Germany, October 17, 2004–January 30, 2005. Catalogue (published by Wienand Publishing Company, Cologne).

WOW: The Work of the Work, Henry Art Gallery and Western Bridge, Seattle, November 6, 2004–February 6, 2005. Catalogue by Elizabeth A. Brown.

Mehr Licht: Targetti Light Art Collection at MAK, Österreichisches Museum für angewandte Kunst, Vienna, November 24, 2004–January 16, 2005.

Modus Operandi, Thyssen-Bornemisza Art Contemporary (T-B A21), Vienna, November 24, 2004–April 30, 2005. Brochure.

Parkett Editionen, Kunsthaus Zürich, November 26, 2004– February 13, 2005. Catalogue edited by Mirjam Varadinis.

dep, art, ment—the multiple shop of Stockholm, Galleri Charlotte Lund, Stockholm, December 2–22.

The Nature Machine: Contemporary Art, Nature, and Technology, Queensland Art Gallery, South Brisbane, Australia, December 4, 2004–February 13, 2005.
   Hart, Cath. "Teach Your Children Well." *Australian*, January 20, 2005.
   Sorenson, Rosemary. "Up to His Armpits in Lego Heaven." *Queensland Courier Mail*, January 15, 2005.

2005

Atlantic & Bukarest, Kunstmuseum Basel, Switzerland, January 29–April 10. Brochure.

Desenhos: A–Z, Colecção Madeira Corporate Services, Porta 33, Ilha da Madeira, Portugal, February 16–April 30. Catalogue by Adriano Pedrosa.

Wolkenbilder: von John Constable bis Gerhard Richter, Aargauer Kunsthaus, Aarau, Switzerland, February 27– May 8. Catalogue.

Dialog Skulptur, Kunstforum Seligenstadt, Germany, February 28–April 24. Traveled to Kunstverein Ludwigshafen, Germany; Museum Kulturspeicher, Würzburg, Germany. Catalogue.

19 Rainstorms, Western Bridge, Seattle, March 10–May 14.

Making Things Public: Atmosphären der Demokratie, Zentrum für Kunst und Medientechnologie, Karlsruhe, Germany, March 20–October 3. Catalogue edited by Bruno Latour and Peter Weibel.

Emergencias, Museo de Arte Contemporáneo de Castilla y Léon, Spain, April 1–August 21. Catalogue.

Raum.Prolog, Akademie der Künste, Berlin, April 3– June 4. Catalogue.

Send min ven i skole, Københavns Bymuseum, Copenhagen, April 26–May 10.

Das verlorene Paradies: Die Landschaft in der zeit-gnössischen Photographie, Stiftung Opelvillen, Rüsselsheim, Germany, April 27–July 3. Brochure by Beate Kemfert.

The Opening, ANDERSEN_S Contemporary, Copenhagen, April 29–June 25.

En/Of, Museum Kurhaus Kleve, Germany, May 12– June 26. Catalogue.

Our Surroundings, Dundee Contemporary Arts, Scotland, May 14–July 17. Brochure.
   Chapman, Peter. Review. *Independent* (London), May 28, 2005.
   Gale, Iain. Review. *Scotland on Sunday*, May 29, 2005.
   Harris, Gillian. "All the Elements of Great Art." *Sunday Times* (London), May 15, 2005.
   Miller, Phil. "Artist Who Created a New Sun Returns to Dundee to Fashion a Man-Made Waterfall." *Glasgow Herald*, May 6, 2005.

Material time / Work time / Life time, Reykjavík Arts Festival, May 14–June 5. Catalogue by Jessica Morgan and Björn Roth.

D'Arcy, David. "Roth and Other Riches." *Modern Painters*, July–August 2005, 43–44.

Out There: Landscape in the New Millennium, Museum of Contemporary Art, Cleveland, May 20–August 28. Brochure.

River Styx, Western Bridge, Seattle, May 28–September 24.

Samtida Skulptur i Norden 1980–2005, Stiftelsen Wanås Utställningar, Knislinge, Sweden, May 29–October 23. Catalogue edited by Marika Wachtmeister.

Die Ordnung der Natur, Museum Moderner Kunst Stiftung Wörlen, Passau, Germany, June 4–July 31. Catalogue.

First Acquisitions: Selezione di opere dalla Fondazione per l'Arte Contemporanea Victor Pinchuk, Kiev, Palazzo Papadopoli, Venice, Italy, June 8–July 10.

Remagine: Oeuvres du Fonds National d'Art Contemporain, Musée d'Art Contemporain, Lyon, France, June 17–July 31. Brochure by Hervé Percebois.

Rauminszenierungen 2006, Garten_Landschaft OstWestfalenLippe, Bielefeld, Germany, June 19– October 15.

DANISH—framing the future of design, Dansk Design Center, Copenhagen, June 22–December 30.

Here Comes the Sun, Magasin 3 Stockholm Konsthall, August 27–December 4. Catalogue by Daniel Birnbaum et al.

In the Middle of the Night, Kunsthalle Bielefeld, Germany, August 28–November 6. Catalogue.

Einstein Spaces: Neun Kunstprojekte in Berlin, Potsdam und Caputh, Einsteinjahr 2005, Berlin, September 6– October 30. Catalogue edited by Yvonne Leonard.

Controlled, Contained, and Configured, Tanya Bonakdar Gallery, New York, September 10–October 1.

Sweet Taboos: Temptations, 3rd Tirana Biennial, Albania, September 10–November 10. Catalogue; artist's book titled *The Negotiation Project* by Olafur Eliasson and Anri Sala.

Expérience de la durée, 8th Biennale d'art contemporain de Lyon, France, September 14–December 31. Catalogue.
   Adams, Brooks. "Report from Lyon: Time after Time." *Art in America* 94, no. 2 (February 2006): 56–61, 63.
   Dagen, Philippe. "À Lyon, les installations font sensa-tion." *Le Monde*, September 15, 2005.

Arte all'Arte 10: Arte Architettura Paesaggio, Associazione Arte Continua, San Gimignano, Italy, September 30, 2005– July 31, 2006. Catalogue.
   Birnbaum, Daniel. "Dawn 'til Dusk." *Artforum* 44, no. 1 (September 2005): 264.
   "Conversazione tra Francesca von Habsburg, David Adjaye, Olafur Eliasson, Daniel Birnbaum." *Domus*, no. 884 (September 2005): 90–93.
   Finessi, Beppe. "Olafur Eliasson and Tobias Rehberger: Oltre i bunker." *Abitare*, no. 458 (February 2006): 95–98.
   Gingeras, Alison M. "Stealing the Show." *Artforum* 44, no. 1 (September 2005): 265–68.

Wittgenstein in New York. Stadt und Architektur in der neueren Kunst auf Papier, Kupferstichkabinett, Berlin, September 30, 2005–January 8, 2006. Traveled to Stadthaus Ulm, Germany. Catalogue.

Ecstasy: In and About Altered States, Museum of Contemporary Art, Los Angeles, October 9, 2005–February 20, 2006. Catalogue edited by Paul Schimmel.
    Bedford, Christopher. Review. *Burlington Magazine* 148 (February 2006): 149–50.
    Kimmelman, Michael. "A Mind-Bending Head Trip (All Legal)." *New York Times*, November 4, 2005.
    Knight, Christopher. "Take a Mind Excursion." *Los Angeles Times*, October 11, 2005.
    Lequeux, Emmanuelle. Review. *Beaux Arts* 259 (January 2006): 137.
    Muchnic, Suzanne. "Mind-Bending Visions." *Los Angeles Times*, October 2, 2005.

Lichtkunst aus Kunstlicht, Zentrum für Kunst und Medientechnologie, Karlsruhe, Germany, November 19, 2005–August 6, 2006. Catalogue edited by Peter Weibel and Gregor Jansen (2006).

Made for this World: Contemporary Art and the Places We Build, Queensland Art Gallery, South Brisbane, Australia, November 26, 2005–February 19, 2006.

Beyond Delirious, Cisneros Fontanals Art Foundation, Miami, Florida, November 30, 2005–February 3, 2006. Catalogue.

36 x 27 x 10, White Cube Berlin / Volkspalast, Palast der Republik, Berlin, December 23–31.
    Tilmann, Christina. "Die letzte Lampe." *Der Tagesspiegel*, December 21, 2005.

2006
Group Exhibition, Galleri MGM, Oslo, February 11–March 26.

Skaalanihe—skulptuur avatud mänguväljal, Kumu Kunstimuuseum, Estonia, February 18–May 21. Catalogue edited by Anna Mustonen.

Peace Tower, Whitney Museum of American Art, New York, February 23–May 23.

Bjerge i dansk kunst: fra Willumsen til Parfyme, Herning Kunstmuseum, Denmark, March 3–June 5. Catalogue.

The Garden Party, Deitch Projects, New York, March 9–May 20.
    Johnson, Ken. Review. *New York Times*, April 21, 2006.

Der erste Blick. Die Sammlung GAG, Neues Museum Weimar, Germany, March 19–July 16. Catalogue edited by Ernst-Gerhard Güse and Ulrike Bestgen.

Premio Biella per l'Incisione 2006, Museo del Territorio Biellese, Biella, Italy, March 19–June 4. Catalogue (published by Skira, Milan).

Museum im Fluss, Kunsthaus Zug, Switzerland, April 2–July 23.

Nature Attitudes, Thyssen-Bornemisza Art Contemporary (T-B A21), Vienna, April 5–September 9. Brochure.

Kapitel VII: Bühne des Lebens—Rhetorik des Gefühls, Städtische Galerie im Lenbachhaus und Kunstbau, Munich, April 8–July 9. Catalogue by Juliane Rebentisch.

Constructing New Berlin, Phoenix Art Museum, April 9–September 24. Traveled to Bass Museum of Art, Miami, Florida. Catalogue by Brady Roberts et al.

"Where are we going?": Opere scelte dalla collezione François Pinault, Palazzo Grassi, Venice, Italy, April 29–October 1. Brochure.
    Dorment, Richard. "Triumph of a Tycoon." *Daily Telegraph* (London), May 2, 2006.

Ikke alt er synlig, Astrup Fearnley Museet for Moderne Kunst, Oslo, May 6–August 27.

Blind Date Seligenstadt, Prälatur der ehemaligen Benediktinerabtei and Galerie Kunstforum im Alten Haus, Seligenstadt, Germany, May 14–July 2. Traveled to Museum Moderner Kunst Stiftung Wörlen, Passau, Germany, as *Blind Date Passau*. Catalogue.

Molnen mellan oss, Moderna Museet, Stockholm, May 20–September 17.

Landscape: Recent Acquisitions, Museum of Modern Art, New York, May 26–September 4.
    Baker, R. C. Review. *Village Voice*, August 30–September 5, 2006, 54.

The Expanded Eye, Kunsthaus Zürich, June 16–September 3. Catalogue.

Anstoß Berlin—Kunst macht Welt, Haus am Waldsee, Berlin, June 22–September 17. Catalogue by Katja Blomberg and Sabine Bartelsheim.

Shifting Terrain: Contemporary Landscape Photography, Wadsworth Atheneum Museum of Art, Hartford, Connecticut, July 15–November 5.

Surprise, Surprise, Institute of Contemporary Arts, London, August 2–September 10. Catalogue.
    Graham-Dixon, Andrew. "Beyond Formaldehyde Art." *London Sunday Telegraph*, July 30, 2006.

Der Blaue Reiter im 21. Jahrhundert, Städtische Galerie im Lenbachhaus und Kunstbau, Munich, opened September 15.

Into Black, Western Bridge, Seattle, September 16–December 16.
    Graves, Jen. Review. *The Stranger*, October 5–11, 2006, 31.

New Space, Pinchuk Art Centre, Kiev, Ukraine, September 16–December 16. Catalogue.
    Babij, Larissa. "New on Kyiv's cultural scene." *Ukrainian Weekly*, November 19–26, 2006, 13–14.

FASTER! BIGGER! BETTER!, Zentrum für Kunst und Medientechnologie, Karlsruhe, Germany, September 24, 2006–January 7, 2007. Catalogue.

Intensive Science, La Maison Rouge, Paris, October 6–7. Catalogue edited by Remi van Trijp.

Eye on Europe: Prints, Books, & Multiples/1960 to Now, Museum of Modern Art, New York, October 15, 2006–January 1, 2007. Catalogue.

Gletscherdämmerung, ERES-Stiftung, Munich, October 18–22. Brochure.

Fantastisk politikk. Kunst i turbulente tider, Museet for samtidskunst, Oslo, October 20, 2006–February 25, 2007. Catalogue (published by Nasjonalmuseet for kunst, arkitektur og design, Oslo).

Nr. 14 Light Play, Z33, Hasselt, Belgium, October 29, 2006–January 21, 2007. Brochure.

2007
Falling Water, Reykjavík Art Museum—Kjarvalsstadir, February 10–April 29.

Refract, Reflect, Project: Light Works from the Collection, Hirshhorn Museum and Sculpture Garden, Washington, D.C., February 15–April 8.

Traum und Trauma. Werke aus der Sammlung Dakis Joannou, Athen, Kunsthalle Wien, Vienna, June 29–September 30; Museum Moderner Kunst Stiftung Ludwig, Vienna, June 29–October 28.

Guggenheim Collection: 1940s to Now; New York–Venice–Bilbao–Berlin, National Gallery of Victoria, Melbourne, Australia, June 30–October 7.

2move—Migrante Video, Zuiderzeemuseum Enkhuizen, Netherlands, September 21, 2007–January 6, 2008.

SELECTED BIBLIOGRAPHY

The following represents a selection of books and periodicals that discuss Olafur Eliasson and his work. Entries are arranged chronologically by year published. For additional exhibition-related publications and reviews, please consult the chronology on pages 256–68.

Thanks are due to Apsara DiQuinzio, Caroline Eggel, Anna Engberg-Pedersen, Amanda Glesmann, Karen Levine, and Joshua Shirkey for their assistance in gathering and verifying information.

ARTIST'S BOOKS, CATALOGUES, AND MONOGRAPHS

Crary, Jonathan, and Madeleine Schuppli. *Olafur Eliasson: The Curious Garden.* Basel, Switzerland: Kunsthalle Basel / Schwabe & Co., 1997.

Eliasson, Olafur. *Erosion: A Project for the 2nd Johannesburg Biennale 1997.* Berlin: Olafur Eliasson, 1997.

———. *Hellisgerði.* Reykjavík: Reykjavík Art Museum—Kjarvalsstadir, 1998.

———. *Landscapes with Yellow Background.* Umeå, Sweden: BildMuseet, 1998.

Eliasson, Olafur, et al. *Users.* Berlin: Olafur Eliasson, 1998.

Brown, Katrina, and Olafur Eliasson. *Olafur Eliasson: Your Position Surrounded and Your Surroundings Positioned.* Dundee, Scotland: Dundee Contemporary Arts, 1999.

Eliasson, Olafur. *Sospensione.* Berlin: Olafur Eliasson, 1999.

Eliasson, Olafur, and Jan Winkelmann. *My Now Is Your Surroundings—Process as Object.* Cologne: Walther König, 2001.

Hjörleifsson, Elias. *What Is This?* Berlin: Olafur Eliasson, 2001.

Morgan, Jessica, ed. *Olafur Eliasson: Your Only Real Thing Is Time.* Boston: Institute of Contemporary Art; Ostfildern-Ruit, Germany: Hatje Cantz, 2001.

Olafur Eliasson: The Structural Evolution Project. Ljubljana, Slovenia: Mala Galerija, 2001.

Olafur Eliasson: Your Difference & Repetition. Kitakyushu, Japan: Center for Contemporary Art, 2001.

Sagmeister, Rudolf, and Eckhard Schneider, eds. *Olafur Eliasson: The Mediated Motion.* Bregenz, Austria: Kunsthaus Bregenz; Cologne: Walther König, 2001.

Weibel, Peter, ed. *Olafur Eliasson: Surroundings Surrounded; Essays on Space and Science.* Graz, Austria: Neue Galerie am Landesmuseum Joanneum; Cambridge, MA: MIT Press, 2001.

Eliasson, Olafur, and Caroline Eggel. *Olafur Eliasson: Movement Meter for Lernacken.* Berlin: Olafur Eliasson, 2002.

Grynsztejn, Madeleine, et al. *Olafur Eliasson.* London: Phaidon, 2002.

Scherf, Angeline, ed. *Olafur Eliasson: Chaque matin je me sens différent, chaque soir je me sens le même.* Paris: Musée d'Art moderne de la Ville de Paris, 2002.

Thorsteinn, Einar, and Olafur Eliasson. *To the Habitants of Space in General and the Spatial Inhabitants in Particular.* Vienna: BAWAG Foundation, 2002.

Eliasson, Olafur, et al. *The Body as Brain.* Zug, Switzerland: Kunsthaus Zug, 2003.

———. *Olafur Eliasson: Funcionamiento silencioso.* Madrid: Museo Nacional Centro de Arte Reina Sofía, 2003.

Gaensheimer, Susanne, and Olafur Eliasson. *Olafur Eliasson: Sonne statt Regen.* Munich: Städtische Galerie im Lenbachhaus und Kunstbau; Ostfildern-Ruit, Germany: Hatje Cantz, 2003.

Gómez Aguilera, Fernando, and Olafur Eliasson. *Lanzarote Series: Olafur Eliasson. Revisitar Canarias / The Canary Islands Revisited.* Barcelona: ACTAR, 2003.

May, Susan, ed. *Olafur Eliasson: The Weather Project.* London: Tate Publishing, 2003.

Olafur Eliasson: The Blind Pavilion; 50th Venice Biennale 2003, Danish Pavilion. Copenhagen: Danish Contemporary Art Foundation, 2003.

Árnasson, Gunnar J., and Paul Virilio. *Olafur Eliasson: Frost Activity.* Reykjavík: Reykjavík Art Museum—Hafnarhús, 2004.

Drutt, Matthew. *Olafur Eliasson: Photographs.* Houston: Menil Collection, 2004.

Eliasson, Olafur, and Gitte Ørskou. *Olafur Eliasson: Minding the World.* Aarhus, Denmark: ARoS Aarhus Kunstmuseum, 2004.

Eliasson, Olafur, and Paul Virilio. *Olafur Eliasson: Colour Memory and Other Informal Shadows.* Oslo: Astrup Fearnley Museet for Moderne Kunst, 2004.

Engberg-Pedersen, Anna, and Karsten Wind Meyhoff. *At se sig selv sanse. Samtaler med Olafur Eliasson.* Copenhagen: Informations Forlag, 2004.

Huck, Brigitte, et al. *Olafur Eliasson: Camera obscura für die Donau.* Berlin: Niederösterreich Kultur, 2004.

Van Tuyl, Gijs, and Holger Broeker, eds. *Olafur Eliasson: Your Lighthouse; Works with Light 1991–2004.* Wolfsburg, Germany: Kunstmuseum Wolfsburg; Ostfildern-Ruit, Germany: Hatje Cantz, 2004.

Eliasson, Olafur, and Doreen Massey. *Lesbók Morgunblaðsins: Jökluserían.* Special issue, *Morgunblaðið,* May 12, 2005.

Eliasson, Olafur, and Anri Sala. *The Negotiation Project.* Berlin: Olafur Eliasson, 2005.

Worm, Thomas, et al. *Olafur Eliasson: Dufttunnel; Ein Projekt für die Autostadt in Wolfsburg / Scent Tunnel; A Project for the Autostadt in Wolfsburg.* Ostfildern-Ruit, Germany: Hatje Cantz, 2005.

Adolphs, Volker. *Olafur Eliasson: Remagine; Large Version.* Bonn: Kunstmuseum Bonn, 2006.

Crary, Jonathan, et al. *Olafur Eliasson: Your Colour Memory.* Glenside, PA: Arcadia University Art Gallery, 2006.

Eliasson, Olafur. *Your House.* New York: Library Council of the Museum of Modern Art, 2006.

Eliasson, Olafur, et al. *The Icelandic National Concert and Conference Centre.* Berlin: Olafur Eliasson, 2006.

———. *Olafur Eliasson: Caminos de naturaleza / Paths of Nature.* Madrid: Fundación Telefónica / La Fabrica Editorial, 2006.

———. *Olafur Eliasson: A Laboratory of Mediating Space.* Berlin: Aedes am Pfefferberg; Vienna: Österreichische Friedrich und Lillian Kiesler-Privatstiftung, 2006.

———. *Olafur Eliasson: Your Engagement Has Consequences; On the Relativity of Your Reality.* Baden, Switzerland: Lars Müller Publishers, 2006.

Eliasson, Olafur, and Hans Ulrich Obrist. *The Goose Lake Trail (Southern Route): A Road Conversation between Olafur Eliasson and Hans Ulrich Obrist.* Eidar, Iceland: Eidar Art Center; Cologne: Walther König, 2006.

Kielgast, Anne, et al. *Lavaland: Olafur Eliasson & Jóhannes S. Kjarval.* Copenhagen: Kunstforeningen GL Strand, 2007.

BOOKS

Bonami, Francesco, ed. *Echoes: Contemporary Art at the Age of Endless Conclusions.* New York: Monacelli, 1996.

Marcoci, Roxana, Diana Murphy, and Eve Sinaiko, eds. *New Art.* New York: Harry N. Abrams, 1997.

Vingt mille lieues / lieux sur l'esker: 3ᵉ symposium en arts visuels de l'Abitibi-Témiscamingue. Amos, Quebec: Centre d'exposition d'Amos, 1998.

Birnbaum, Daniel, and John Peter Nilsson, eds. *Like Virginity, Once Lost: Five Views on Nordic Art Now.* Malmö, Sweden: Propexus, 1999.

Matzner, Florian, and Barbara Engelbach. *Skulptur Biennale 1999 im Münsterland.* Dülmen, Germany: Laumann, 1999.

Kapfinger, Otto. *Martin Rauch: Rammed Earth / Terra Cruda, Lehm und Architektur.* Basel, Switzerland: Birkhäuser, 2001.

Archer, Michael. *Art Since 1960.* London: Thames & Hudson, 2002.

Schulz-Dornburg, Julia. *Arte y Arquitectura: nuevas afinidades / Arte e Arquitetura: novas afinidades.* Translated by Elena Llorens Pujol and Mônica Trinidade Schramm. Barcelona: Gustava Gili, 2002.

Estep, Jan, and Britt Salvesen, eds. *Subjective Realities: Works from the Refco Collection of Contemporary Photography.* New York: Refco Group, 2003.

Obrist, Hans Ulrich. *Hans Ulrich Obrist: Interviews, Volume I.* Edited by Thomas Boutoux. Florence: Fondazione Pitti Immagine Discovery, 2003.

Omlin, Sibylle, and Karin Frei Bernasconi, eds. *Hybride Zonen: Kunst und Architecture in Basel und Zürich / Hybrid Zones: Art and Architecture in Basel and Zurich.* Basel, Switzerland: Birkhäuser, 2003.

Rosenthal, Mark. *Understanding Installation Art: From Duchamp to Holzer.* Munich: Prestel, 2003.

Bott, Gian Casper. *Kunstmuseum Basel.* Geneva: Fondation BNP, 2004.

D'Amécourt, Jacqueline de Ponton. *Limelette: Contemporary Photographs, Group Lhoist Collection/ Photographies Contemporains, Collection de Group Lhoist.* Translated by Carmen Rocia Fernandez Burriel et al. Limelette, Belgium: Group Lhoist, 2004.

Jodidio, Philip. *Architecture Now! 3.* Cologne: Taschen, 2004.

Obrist, Hans Ulrich, ed. *Do It.* New York: e-flux, 2004.

Barzel, Amnon, ed. *Light Art: Targetti Light Art Collection.* Milan: Skira, 2005.

Bonami, Francesco, ed. *Works from Collezione Sandretto Re Rebaudengo.* Milan: Skira, 2005.

Dean, Tacita, and Jeremy Millar. *Place.* New York: Thames & Hudson, 2005.

Hannula, Mika, et al. *Artistic Research: Theories, Methods, and Practices.* Helsinki: Academy of Fine Arts, 2005.

Hoffmann, Jens, and Joan Jonas. *Perform.* New York: Thames & Hudson, 2005.

Jodidio, Philip. *Architecture: Art.* Munich: Prestel, 2005.

PressPLAY: Contemporary Artists in Conversation. London: Phaidon, 2005.

Yáñez, Isabel, ed. *MUSAC: Museo de Arte Contemporáneo de Castilla y León, Colección vol. 1.* León, Spain: MUSAC, 2005.

Aitken, Doug. *Broken Screen: 26 Conversations with Doug Aitken; Expanding the Image, Breaking the Narrative.* Edited by Noel Daniel. New York: D.A.P., 2006.

Cheetham, Mark A. *Abstract Art against Autonomy: Infection, Resistance, and Cure Since the 60s.* Cambridge: Cambridge University Press, 2006.

Dernie, David. *Exhibition Design.* Amsterdam: BIS, 2006.

Huyghe, Pierre. *One Year Celebration.* Paris: One Star Press, 2006.

Obrist, Hans Ulrich. . . . *dontstopdontstopdontstop-dontstop.* New York: Sternberg, 2006.

ESSAYS AND ARTICLES

Karcher, Eva. "Olafur Eliasson: Natur wird wieder Erlebnis." *Art: das Kunstmagazin,* no. 5 (May 1995): 62.

Bonami, Francesco. "Psychological Atmospheres." *Siksi* 12, no. 3 (Fall 1997): 49–55.

———. "Olafur Eliasson." In *Cream: Contemporary Art in Culture; 10 Curators, 10 Writers, 100 Artists.* London: Phaidon, 1998.

Cameron, Dan. "The New Melting Pot." *Flash Art* 31, no. 202 (October 1998): 90–92.

Haye, Christian. "The Iceman Cometh." *Frieze,* no. 40 (May 1998): 62–65.

———. "Om Olafur Eliasson." *Paletten* 59, no. 4 (April 1998): 24–25.

Lind, Maria. "Raumnachbildung und Erfahrungsräume: Einige Überlegungen zur Ortsbezogenheit in der Gegenwartskunst / Spatial Facsimiles and Ambient Spaces: Some Reflections on Site Specificity in Contemporary Art." Translated by Jan Teeland. *Parkett,* no. 54 (December 1998–January 1999): 186–94.

Volk, Gregory. "Olafur Eliasson: Fire and Iceland." *ARTNews* 97, no. 4 (April 1998): 200.

Winkelmann, Jan. "Olafur Eliasson." Translated by Jeremy Gaines. *Art/Text,* no. 60 (February–April 1998): 44–49.

Dziewor, Yilmaz. "Olafur Eliasson." In *Art at the Turn of the Millennium,* edited by Uta Grosenick and Burkhard Riemschneider, 142–44. Cologne: Taschen, 1999.

Hannula, Mika. "Berliner Romanze." *Neue Bildende Kunst,* no. 7 (December 1999): 46–51.

Johansson, Hanna. "Maailma veden sylissä." *Taide,* no. 3 (1999): 36–38.

Winkelmann, Jan. "Olafur Eliasson: Op het ijs bij 37° C." *Metropolis M* 20, no. 1 (February–March 1999): 42–45.

Kunz, Sabine. "Olafur Eliasson: Installationen aus Luft und Licht." *Art: das Kunstmagazin,* no. 3 (March 2000): 62–67.

Müller, Katrin Bettina. "Gegen die Wand segeln." *taz, die tageszeitung,* September 26, 2000.

Sandqvist, Gertrud. "Olafur Eliasson." *Afterall,* no. 2 (2000): 107–10.

Spiegl, Andreas. "Olafur Eliasson: Non-Trueness as the Nature of Theatre." *Afterall,* no. 2 (2000): 99–102.

Steiner, Shep. "It Must Be the Weather." *Afterall,* no. 2 (2000): 74–81.

Bers, Miriam. "Berlin, from Neo Pop to Crossculture." *Tema Celeste,* no. 83 (January–February 2001): 70–75.

Bretton-Meyer, Henriette. "Mellem flygtighed og perma-nens. En analyse af Olafur Eliassons værkbegreb." MA thesis, University of Copenhagen, 2001.

Eliasson, Olafur. "Die einzige Sache, die wir gemeinsam haben, ist, dass wir verschieden sind / The Only Thing We Have in Common Is That We Are Different." In *Public Art: Kunst im öffentlichen Raum,* edited by Florian Matzner, translated by Caroline Eggel, 442–47. Ostfildern-Ruit, Germany: Hatje Cantz, 2001.

———. "457 Words on Color." In *Bridge the Gap?,* edited by Akiko Miyake and Hans Ulrich Obrist, 76–77. Kitakyushu, Japan: Center for Contemporary Art, 2001.

Giller, Sarah. "The Plumbing Aesthetic: Sinks, Tubs, Pipes, and Drains in the Work of Rachel Whiteread, Olafur Eliasson, and Robert Gober." MA thesis, School of the Art Institute of Chicago, 2001.

Sternberger, Lee Glover. "Remembering, Breaking, Sensing: Construction, Identity, and the Works of Matta-Clark, Whiteread, and Eliasson." MA thesis, University of Virginia, 2001.

Birnbaum, Daniel. "Where Is Painting Now?" *Tate: International Arts and Culture,* no. 1 (September–October 2002): 60–63.

Blom, Ina. "Beyond the Ambient / Jenseits des Atmosphärischen." Translated by Bram Opstelten. *Parkett,* no. 64 (May 2002): 20–31.

Corrigan, Susan. "The Beauty of Nature Is Always Beyond Our Control." *i-D,* no. 218 (March 2002): 226–35.

Dziewor, Yilmaz. "Olafur Eliasson." In *Art Now: 137 Artists at the Rise of the New Millennium/137 Künstler zu Beginn des 21. Jahrhunderts/137 artistes au commencement du 21ème siècle,* edited by Uta Grosenick and Burkhard Riemschneider. Cologne: Taschen, 2002.

Morgan, Jessica. "Gartensozialismus." Translated by Bram Opstelten. *Parkett,* no. 64 (May 2002): 32–47.

Ólafsdóttir, Auður. "Þar sem vit verður til: Myndlistarverk Ólafs Elíassonar." *Skírnir,* no. 176 (Fall 2002): 465–71.

Østerby, Annette. "Ethnographic Mapping: Olafur Eliasson." *Arken Bulletin,* January 2, 2002, 22–25.

Rondeau, James. "The Mobility of the Real: Olafur Eliasson Is Now." In *The Hugo Boss Prize 2002,* by Susan Cross et al., 37–50. New York: Solomon R. Guggenheim Foundation, 2002.

Schoen, Anne. "Über Olafur Eliasson." *Künstler: Kritisches Lexikon der Gegenwartskunst* 11, no. 58 (2002): 1–8.

Sonna, Birgit. "Die simulierte Landschaft: 'Land Arch' als hybride Kunst im öffentlichen Raum." In *"Bedeutung in den Bildern": Festschrift für Jörg Traeger zum 60. Geburtstag,* edited by Karl Möseneder and Gosbert Schüssler, 399–411. Regensburg, Germany: Schnell + Steiner, 2002.

Bortolotti, Maurizio. "Il diaframma estetico." *Domus,* no. 859 (May 2003) 8–10.

Buchhart, Dieter. "Wie in der Pop Art klaue ich direkt Naturphänomene und wissenschaftliche Darstellungen: Ein Gespräch mit Dieter Buchhart." *Kunstforum,* no. 167 (November–December 2003): 190–207.

Cathcart, Brian. "Captain Spectacular." *Tate: Arts and Culture,* no. 7 (September–October 2003): 58–64.

Eliasson, Olafur. "Museums Are Radical." *Jahresring: Jahrbuch für moderne Kunst,* no. 50 (2003): 180–85.

———. "Tre tekster: Det, der før hed mellemrummet." *Kritik: Tidsskrift for litteratur, forskning, undervisning* 36, no. 164 (2003): 1–7.

Fricke, Harald. "Sublime Constructions." *Modern Painters* (Winter 2003): 92–95.

"Light Perceptions." *Sleek,* no. 8 (Autumn 2003): 70.

Lo, Melissa, and Valentina Sansone. "Sculpture Forever." *Flash Art* 36, no. 231 (July–September 2003): 100–107.

"Olafur Eliasson." *V Magazine,* September–October 2003, n.p.

Román, Juan Carlos. "Olafur Eliasson: El artista que espera a que la naturaleza realice la obra de arte." *Arte y Parte,* no. 43 (February–March 2003): 58–65.

Rosenberg, Angela. "Olafur Eliasson: Beyond Nordic Romanticism." *Flash Art* 36, no. 230 (May–June 2003): 110–13.

Velez, Marcel Andino. "Bóg w elektrowni." *Przekrój*, November 9, 2003, 64–71.

Wilson-Goldie, Kaelen. "Artist Dossier: Olafur Eliasson." *Art & Auction* 25, no. 4 (April 2003): 108–9.

Aitken, Doug. "Broken Screen: A Project for *Artforum*." *Artforum* 43, no. 3 (November 2004): 191–201.

Braun, Christoph. "Erfundene Naturstimmungen." *taz, die tageszeitung*, February 19, 2004.

Colin, Anne. "Olafur Eliasson: Vers une nouvelle réalité / The Nature of Nature as Artifice." Translated by C. Penwarden. *Art Press*, no. 304 (September 2004): 34–39.

Criqui, Jean-Pierre. "Time Vibe Studies." *Les cahiers du Musée national d'art moderne*, no. 90 (Winter 2004–5): 3–19.

Diehl, Carol. "Northern Lights." *Art in America* 92, no. 9 (October 2004): 108–15.

Gilbert, Chris. Interview. *Bomb*, no. 88 (Summer 2004): 22–29.

Higgins, Charlotte. "Lost in Colour." *Guardian* (London), May 1, 2004.

Kimmelman, Michael. "From Real to Illusion, an Artistic Bridge." *International Herald Tribune*, March 11, 2004.

"La città della partecipazione / Participation City." *Domus*, no. 868 (March 2004): 110–16.

Mack, Gerhard. "Der Nebelwerfer." *Art: das Kunstmagazin*, no. 6 (June 2004): 42–47.

McNatt, Glenn. "Inside a Flower, Gazing at Stars." *Baltimore Sun*, October 10, 2004.

"Power 100: #29, Olafur Eliasson." *Art Review* 2, no. 8 (November 2004): 73.

Stilling, Oliver. "I virkeligheden hvem som helst." *Euroman* 128 (October 2004): 92–96.

––––––. "Samfundsforskeren." *Dagbladet Information*, October 1, 2004.

Thyssen, Nikolai. "Revolutionen kommer ikke i form af en lænestol." *Dagbladet Information*, October 29, 2004.

Ursprung, Philip. "Blur, Monolith, Blob, Box: Atmospheres of Archisculpture." In *ArchiSculpture: Dialogues between Architecture and Sculpture from the Eighteenth Century to the Present Day*, edited by Markus Brüderlin, 42–47. Ostfildern-Ruit, Germany: Hatje Cantz, 2004.

Von Goetz, Ulrike. "Hinter seinen Sonnen stecken Glühbirnen." *Welt am Sonntag*, April 11, 2004.

Von Radziewsky, Elke. "Natur aus der Steckdose." *Architektur&Wohnen*, no. 2 (April–May 2004): 198–204.

Birnbaum, Daniel. "Grüner Fluß ohne Wiederkehr." *Frankfurter Allgemeine Sonntagszeitung*, December 18, 2005.

Bishop, Claire, et al. "Remote Possibilities: A Roundtable Discussion on Land Art's Changing Terrain." *Artforum* 43, no. 10 (Summer 2005): 288–95, 366.

Cheetham, Mark. "Matting the Monochrome: Malevich, Klein, and Now." *Art Journal* 64, no. 4 (Winter 2005): 94–109.

David, Thomas. "'Die meisten Dinge sind sehr viel relativer, als wir denken . . .'" *Du* 761, no. 10 (November 2005): 81–83.

Foster, Hal. "Six Paragraphs on Dan Flavin." *Artforum* 43, no. 6 (February 2005): 160–61.

Frey, James. "The Ten Artists Every Man Should Know." *Best Life*, September 2005, 97–105.

Griffin, Tim. "In Conversation: Daniel Buren and Olafur Eliasson." *Artforum* 43, no. 9 (May 2005): 208–14.

Harris, Henriette. "An Absolute Fan of Design." *Designmatters*, no. 10 (2005): 60–62.

Hofstätter, Amrei. "Olafur Eliasson: Las cosas que ves pero no las ves / The Things That You See But You Don't See." *Belio*, no. 17 (April 15, 2005): 21–26, 107–8.

Jalving, Camilla. "Værk som handling. Performativitet som kunsthistorisk metode og tema i samtidskunsten." PhD diss., University of Copenhagen, 2005.

Jensen, Marianne Krogh, and Olafur Eliasson. "Dekolonisering af Utopia." In *Samtidsarkitekten: "The Compatible X*," 68–71. Copenhagen: Multivers, 2005.

Knippel, Lars Ole. "En stjerne på kunstens himmel." *Morgenavisen Jyllands-Posten*, January 14, 2005.

Liebs, Holger. "Elfen im Stroboskop." *Süddeutsche Zeitung*, December 5, 2005.

Poirier, Matthieu. "Dynamogénie: Olafur Eliasson; Systèmes polysensoriels." *Techniques et architecture*, no. 481 (2005): 112–16.

Romeo, Filippo. "Ieri e oggi." *Case da Abitare*, no. 84 (January–February 2005): 12–13.

Schoof, Jakob. "Seeing Yourself Seeing: Olafur Eliasson." *Daylight & Architecture*, no. 1 (Autumn 2005): 26–31.

Thøgersen, Birger. "Kunstnerens værksted." *Politiken*, July 13, 2005.

Ursprung, Philip. "Hat die Kunst heute ausgespielt?" *Tages Anzeiger*, July 13, 2005.

––––––. "Im Smog der Globalisierung: Olafur Eliasson's *The weather project*." In *Werke im Wandel? Zeitgenössische Kunst zwischen Werk und Wirkung*, edited by Lars Blunck, 107–22. Munich: Silke Schreiber, 2005.

Wagner, Anne M. "Being There: Art and the Politics of Place." *Artforum* 43, no. 10 (Summer 2005): 265–69.

Baker, Kenneth. "SFMOMA's New Acquisitions on View— One from the Inside." *San Francisco Chronicle*, January 10, 2006.

Bartels, Daghild. "Ich habe keine Angst vor Schönheit." *Handelsblatt*, July 28, 2006.

Brener, Julie. "Lost in Place." *ARTNews* 105, no. 10 (November 2006): 160–61.

Casciani, Stefano. "Scritto sull'acqua / Written on Water." *Domus*, suppl. no. 897 (November 2006): 12–21.

Cuevas-Wolf, Cristina. "Nature, Technique, and Perception: Twentieth-Century Afterimages and Modes of Scientific Representation." *Visual Resources* 22, no. 2 (June 2006): 157–70.

De Cecco, Emanuela. "Olafur Eliasson." *Contemporary*, no. 87 (2006): 38–41.

Frenzel, Sebastian. "Das Kollektiv fährt mit." *taz, die tageszeitung*, January 16, 2006.

Harms, Ingeborg. "Die Wirklichkeit ist nicht wirklich." *Frankfurter Allgemeine Zeitung*, October 8, 2006.

Heiser, Jörg. "Motor aus, Tiefkühlung an, Tiefkühlung aus; Der Künstler als Auftragsarbeiter." *Süddeutsche Zeitung*, July 1, 2006.

Hofmeister, Sandra. "The Yellow Sun; the Mist, and the Perceiving Subject." *Topos*, no. 54 (March 2006): 62–66. Also published as "Ich befasse mich in erster Linie mit dem Menschen." *Baumeister* 103, no. 3 (March 2006): 76–77.

Ichihara Kentaro. Interview. *Bijutsu Techō* 58, no. 876 (February 2006): 123–30.

Mittringer, Markus. "Kiesler, Eliasson und die Folgen." *Der Standard*, June 8, 2006.

Napack, Jonathan. "Olafur Eliasson." In *Vitamin Ph: New Perspectives in Photography*, 84–87. London: Phaidon, 2006.

Rauterberg, Hanno. "Heiß auf Matisse." *Die Zeit*, April 20, 2006.

Schouwenberg, Louise. "A Change of Climate." *Frame*, no. 49 (March–April 2006): 68–77.

Sørensen, Rasmus Bo. "Det har ingen konsekvenser at lave samtidskunst i Danmark." *Dagbladet Information*, June 7, 2006.

Vienne, Véronique. "Optical Magic." *Metropolis* 25, no. 9 (May 2006): 128–35.

Zarin, Cynthia. "Seeing Things: The Art of Olafur Eliasson." *The New Yorker*, November 13, 2006, 76–83.

Eliasson, Olafur. "Editoriali visivi #3 / Visual Columns #3." *Domus*, no. 902 (April 2007): 158–59.

Kennedy, Randy. "Blood Stain Reds and Skeptical Grays." *New York Times*, March 28, 2007.

Spiegler, Marc. "In the Studio: Olafur Eliasson." *Art & Auction* 30, no. 10 (June 2007): 70–76.

Ulmer, Brigitte. "Die Kunstmagie." *Bilanz*, January 19, 2007.

Weschler, Lawrence. "Fevered Imagination: Artistic Responses to Global Warning." *The Nation* 284, no. 18 (May 7, 2007): 36–40.

INDEX

The initials "OE" identify the artist, Olafur Eliasson; his writings are identified by "(Eliasson)." All artwork titles given without an artist's name are by Eliasson. Catalogue plate numbers, which appear in square brackets, are provided with the titles of specific artworks and with the names of venues where artworks were installed. "(EXH.)" denotes works in the SFMOMA presentation.

PHOTO CREDITS

Unless otherwise indicated below, all artworks © Olafur Eliasson and reproduced by permission of the artist.

Cover: Fredrik Nilsen.

Plates: 1, 31, 36–40, 45, 71, 130, 137, 142, 159–62, 167, 169, 171, 173, 199, 212–17, 222, 226–29, 231–33: Jens Ziehe; 2–3, 6, 56–70, 72–78, 81, 107–8, 127, 155, 168, 180, 187–89, 191–93: Olafur Eliasson; 4, 230: Hans Wilschut; 5: Kinya Hanada; 7: James Goggin / Practise; 8, 195: © Tate, London 2007; 9: © Trustees of the British Museum; 10: Terje Östling; 11, 206, 209–11: Ari Magg; 12: courtesy Research Library, Getty Research Institute, Los Angeles (85-B1661); 15: www.alexrobinsonphotography.co.uk; 16: Al Mozell, courtesy PaceWildenstein, New York, © Robert Irwin / Artists Rights Society (ARS), New York; 17–18: Malcolm Lubliner, © 2007 Robert Irwin / Artists Rights Society (ARS), New York; 19: courtesy Lions Gate Entertainment / Photofest, © Lions Gate Entertainment; 20: Karen A. Levine; 21: © Robert Irwin / Artists Rights Society (ARS), New York, digital image © The Museum of Modern Art / Licensed by SCALA / Art Resource, New York; 22: Pablo Mason, courtesy Museum of Contemporary Art, San Diego, © Robert Irwin / Artists Rights Society (ARS), New York; 23: Thibault Jeanson, courtesy Dia Art Foundation, New York, © Robert Irwin / Artists Rights Society (ARS), New York; 27: Per Bak Jensen; 29: Mads Gamdrup and Pia Agge; 30: Koinegg; 32–33: Flemming Brusgaard; 34–35: Marcus Keibel; 41: Victor Dahmen; 43–44: Pedro Motta, Belo Horizonte; 51–52, 54, 79: Andrea Stappert; 53: Christian Vogt, © Kunsthalle Basel, Switzerland, 1997; 55, 84, 100–102: Oren Slor; 82–83: Einar Falur Ingolfsson; 86–87: Christopher Baker; 95: Anders Norrsel; 96–97: Franz Wamhof; 98: Colin Ruscoe, courtesy Dundee Contemporary Arts; 99: photography © The Art Institute of Chicago; 103: Oren Slor, courtesy Tanya Bonakdar Gallery, New York; 104–6: Noshe; 109: courtesy San Francisco Museum of Modern Art; 110, 113, 118, 121: Markus Tretter, © 2001 Kunsthaus Bregenz; 111–12, 114–17, 119–20: Olafur Eliasson, © 2001 Kunsthaus Bregenz; 122–23: Cameraphoto Arte, Venezia / T-B A21; 124: © 2007 Artists Rights Society (ARS), New York / VG Bild-Kunst, Bonn; 125: Ben Blackwell, courtesy San Francisco Museum of Modern Art, © Rirkrit Tiravanija; 126: courtesy Gavin Brown's enterprise; 128: Wolfgang Günzel; 129: courtesy Akademie der Künste Archiv, Berlin; 131: Fridrik Orn; 135: Dan Graham, courtesy Dia Center for the Arts, New York; 136: courtesy Diller Scofidio + Renfro; 138: Bildarchiv Preussischer Kulturbesitz / Art Resource, New York; 139–41: courtesy Museum Boijmans Van Beuningen, Rotterdam, Netherlands; 143: Aaron Igler; 144: Ole Hein Pedersen; 146, 149: courtesy Estate of László Moholy-Nagy, © 2007 Artists Rights Society (ARS), New York / VG Bild-Kunst, Bonn; 147, 207–8: Ben Blackwell, courtesy San Francisco Museum of Modern Art; 148: © Collège de France; 150: Franz Wamhof; 151: Marc Domage; 152: © 2007 Artists Rights Society (ARS), New York / VG Bild-Kunst, Bonn, digital image © The Museum of Modern Art / Licensed by SCALA / Art Resource, New York; 153: © Hans Richter Nachlass, courtesy Musée national d'art moderne, Centre Pompidou, Paris; 154: CNAC / MNAM / Dist. Réunion des Musées Nationaux, © Artists Rights Society (ARS), New York / ADAGP, Paris / Succession Marcel Duchamp; 156: courtesy Estate of Gordon Matta-Clark

and David Zwirner, New York, © 2007 Estate of Gordon Matta-Clark / Artists Rights Society (ARS), New York; 157: Gianfranco Gorgoni, courtesy James Cohan Gallery, New York, art © Estate of Robert Smithson / Licensed by VAGA, New York; 158: photo by Peter Moore © Estate of Peter Moore / VAGA, New York; 163–64: Bertrand Huet; 165–66: Gaetane Hermans, courtesy NMAC Foundation, Cádiz, Spain; 172, 200–205: Fin Serck Hanssen; 178–79, 181–86, 190, 194: Giorgio Boato; 196: Andrew Dunkley & Marcus Leith; 218–19: Christopher Burke Studio, courtesy Tanya Bonakdar Gallery, New York; 220–21: Fredrik Nilsen; 223–25: © Santi Caleca.

Other: p. 85, a–b: Christian Vogt, © Kunsthalle Basel, Switzerland, 1997; p. 85, c–d: Andrea Stappert; p. 121, a–b: Olafur Eliasson, © 2001 Kunsthaus Bregenz; p. 121, c: Markus Tretter, © 2001 Kunsthaus Bregenz; p. 207, a–b, d: Olafur Eliasson; p. 207, c, e–h: Giorgio Boato; p. 245, a–c, e, f: Jens Ziehe; p. 245, d: Hans Wilschut. Maps on pp. 85, 121, 207, 245 by Olafur Eliasson.

This catalogue is published by the San Francisco Museum of Modern Art in association with Thames & Hudson, New York and London, on the occasion of the exhibition *Take your time: Olafur Eliasson*, organized by Madeleine Grynsztejn for the San Francisco Museum of Modern Art.

Exhibition Schedule
San Francisco Museum of Modern Art
September 8, 2007–February 24, 2008

The Museum of Modern Art, New York, and P.S.1 Contemporary Art Center
April 13–June 30, 2008

Dallas Museum of Art
November 9, 2008–March 15, 2009

Take your time: Olafur Eliasson is organized by the San Francisco Museum of Modern Art. Lead support is provided by Helen and Charles Schwab and the Mimi and Peter Haas Fund. Generous support is provided by the Bernard Osher Foundation, the Barbro Osher Pro Suecia Foundation, and Collectors Forum. Additional support is provided by Patricia and William Wilson III, the Andy Warhol Foundation for the Visual Arts, the National Endowment for the Arts, and the American-Scandinavian Foundation. Support for education programs has been provided by Helen Hilton Raiser in honor of Madeleine Grynsztejn.

Director of Publications: Chad Coerver
Managing Editor: Karen A. Levine
Designer: Jennifer Sonderby
Design Production: Jody Hanson
Print Production: James Williams
Indexer: Susan DeRenne Coerr
Publications Assistants: Amanda Glesmann and Suzanne Stein

First published in 2007 in hardcover in the United States of America by Thames & Hudson Inc., 500 Fifth Avenue, New York, New York 10110
thamesandhudsonusa.com

First published in the United Kingdom in 2007 by Thames & Hudson Ltd, 181A High Holborn, London WC1V 7QX
thamesandhudson.com

Library of Congress Catalog Card Number: 2006940142

British Library Cataloguing-in-Publication Data
A catalogue record for this book is available from the British Library

ISBN 978-0-500-09340-5

On the cover:
Olafur Eliasson
Sunset kaleidoscope, 2005
Installation view at Emi Fontana West of Rome, Jamie Residence, Pasadena, California, 2005. Wood, color-effect filter glass, mirrors, and motor. 18 x 18 x 70 in. (45.7 x 45.7 x 177.8 cm). Collection of John and Phyllis Kleinberg

Photo credits appear on page 275

Printed and bound in Germany by Cantz